TEACHERS COLLEGE STUDIES IN EDUCATION
Selected Titles

PROGRESSIVES AND URBAN SCHOOL REFORM
  Sol Cohen

FORUM AND FOCUS FOR THE JUNIOR COLLEGE MOVEMENT
  Michael Brick

THE LEADER IN THE GROUP
  Alfred H. Gorman

FRINGE BENEFITS FOR PUBLIC SCHOOL PERSONNEL
  Jack H. Kleinmann

SOCIAL INTEGRATION IN URBAN COMMUNITIES
  Robert B. Knapp

THE EMERGING EVENING COLLEGE
  Ernest E. McMahon

EDUCATION AND SOCIAL INTEGRATION
  William O. Stanley

GUIDANCE: AN INTEGRATING PROCESS IN HIGHER EDUCATION
  May A. Brunson

COLONEL FRANCIS W. PARKER: THE CHILDREN'S CRUSADER
  Jack K. Campbell

A SYSTEM FOR ANALYZING LESSONS
  John Herbert

PROGRESSIVE EDUCATION: FROM ARCADY TO ACADEME
  Patricia Albjerg Graham

Progressive Education: From Arcady to Academe

A HISTORY OF THE PROGRESSIVE EDUCATION ASSOCIATION 1919–1955

᳇

Patricia Albjerg Graham

᳇

TEACHERS COLLEGE PRESS
Teachers College, Columbia University
New York, 1967

To my parents:

Victor L. and Marguerite Hall Albjerg

Preface

≫≪

The progressive education movement, which substantially altered the pedagogical practices and philosophy of American schools during the first half of this century, has been one of persistently doubtful paternity. Historians have traced its ancestry to Rousseau, a few even to Plato. Some, more modest in their search, have looked to Froebel and Pestalozzi. Others have seemed inclined to limit their selection to two American educators, Francis W. Parker and John Dewey.

The problem of paternity is complicated by disagreements about the duration and extent of the progressive education movement in America. A view widely held during the period of most intense criticism of the movement, in the late 1940s and the 1950s, limited it primarily to the period of the Progressive Education Association, which was founded in 1919 and dissolved in 1955. A more recent interpretation is that of Lawrence A. Cremin in his comprehensive history of the movement, *The Transformation of the School.* In that work, the period under consideration is 1876 to 1955, although Professor Cremin notes the differences in emphasis of the movement in the earlier period, 1876 to 1917, and in the later, 1917 to 1955.

≫≪

The focus of this study is upon the Progressive Education Association itself, and one of the central issues is the extent to which it embodied the progressive education movement. The degree to which the Association maintained or diverged from a tradition of educational reform, established twenty or more years prior to its organization, is an interesting though subsidiary question and is examined particularly in Chapters I and VIII. The essential task here has been to provide a picture of the Association as it functioned, showing its pedagogical assumptions, its social and political commitments, and its research activities. It is, like many historical chronicles, a story of rise and fall.

⫶⫶

A number of persons have assisted in the project at various junctures, although the author is, of course, solely responsible for the content. Those persons who generously consented to interviews are cited in the bibliographic essay and in the notes. Among those who gave particular assistance in discussing and clarifying the author's views of the Progressive Education Association and in reading the manuscript in various versions were Professors Joseph G. Brennan, R. Freeman Butts, Kenneth D. Freeman, Geraldine Joncich, Frederick Kershner, Gordon C. Lee, Jonathan C. Messerli, and Dwight Miner. Professor Lawrence A. Cremin, whose own research on the progressive education movement provided the impetus for this study, assisted immeasurably with both criticism and encouragement. The greatest debt, however, is to the author's family: her parents, whose example in the fields of both history and education established a standard at which to aim; her daughter, Meg, whose persistently diverting behavior prevented excessive concern with research; and her husband, Loren R. Graham, whose enthusiasm for the study sometimes exceeded the author's.

June, 1967   *P. A. G.*

Contents

PREFACE   vii

CHAPTER I   Discontinuities in Progressivism   1
Pre-World War I Educational Reforms, 2
Educational Reforms after the First World War, 8

CHAPTER II   The Years of Quest   17
*The Founding of the Progressive Education
    Association, 17*
The Search for a Name, 20
The Search for Members, 22
The Search for Funds, 24
The Search for a Program, 26
Conventions, 32
The New Education Fellowship, 35

CHAPTER III   From Local to National Recognition   39
Evidences of Domestic Tranquility, 40
Problems of the Association: 1924–1930, 45

CHAPTER IV   Ideological Uncertainties   60
Interest in Social Reconstruction, 63
Reconstruction as Curriculum Reform, 75
The Attempt at Synthesis, 79

CHAPTER V   Progressivism in Flower   85
Spreading the Word, 85
Research in the Thirties, 89
Political Interests of the Association, 94
Affiliation with the New Education Fellowship, 97
Money and Membership, 99

CHAPTER VI   Confusions of Purpose   102
                Failure of the 1941 Statement, 105
                Dissension in the War Years, 108
                Attempt at Resurgence, 115
                Final Decline: 1949–1955, 121

CHAPTER VII   Final Projects   128
                The Social Frontier and Frontiers of
                  Democracy, 128
                Closing Activities of the Commissions and
                  the Eight-Year Study, 133
                Commission on the Secondary School Curriculum, 135
                Commission on Human Relations, 138
                Finances: End of the Funds, 139
                Closing Down, 142

CHAPTER VIII   End of an Era   145
                Progressivism, Old and New, 148
                Opposition to the Traditional Curriculum, 149
                Indifference to Crucial Problems, 151
                Isolation of the Leaders, 154
                The Disagreement over Philosophy, 158
                The Problem of Application, 160
                Social Class Bias, 161
                Competition from Other Educational
                  Organizations, 163
                Conclusion: The Legacy of the Association, 163

APPENDIX A   Officers of the PEA   166

APPENDIX B   Commissions and Committees
                  of the PEA   168

BIBLIOGRAPHICAL ESSAY   172

INDEX   187

Progressive Education:

From Arcady to Academe

CHAPTER I

Discontinuities in Progressivism

❧

Presidential candidate Warren Harding's campaign slogan calling upon the nation to return to "normalcy" received an overwhelming endorsement from the electorate in 1920. But neither American educators nor the public was interested in getting back to traditional educational practices. The First World War had interrupted the reforms that were beginning to permeate the American educational system, and with the restoration of peace it became clear that educational leaders were committed to experiment—not tradition. Reverence for classical studies and respect for "mental discipline" had begun to fade away as early as the turn of the century. Scientific education, child study, and learning by doing were well on the way in before the American Expeditionary Force sailed for Europe. When the Progressive Education Association was established in 1919, its founders were already committed to carrying forward reforms along the lines of these new pedagogical ideas.

Although postwar educational innovations differed in certain important respects from those of the prewar period, both had their source in the shifting currents of pedagogical change of the late nineteenth century. The indifference and even disdain for tradition shown by a surprising number of educators in the early 1900s was a function of their response to formidable problems that beset them. Old methods and solutions simply were not adequate to solve the dilemmas they faced, particularly in the urban areas bursting with heavy population increase. Not only were more children attending school, but they were staying there for longer periods of time, thanks in large part to the recently passed and even more recently enforced state compulsory education laws. Many of these children were immigrants, and for them the school

1

provided their introduction to American and (very often) to city life. To add to pedagogical troubles, native Americans were moving off the farms and taking jobs in the cities, and their children too were jamming the schools. Faced with this variegated and often tumultuous overcrowding, schoolmen were unsure of what to teach and even of how to teach. The classical curriculum and traditional methods proved inadequate for youngsters whose most pressing demands in many cases were for English instruction and in all cases for the skills essential for survival in a newly industrialized society.

Pre-World War I Educational Reforms

Inevitably the schools responded to these pressures, although neither so rapidly nor so extensively as many of their critics wished. In the first years after 1900 the chief thrust of the reforms was in the schools serving lower class families, for the immediate effects of urbanization and industrial growth upset that stratum of society most noticeably. Within it jobs changed, and with jobs, modes of living. The schools made their most immediate and fundamental adjustments to accommodate the children of the thousands attracted to the cities by the jobs.[1]

Probably the most radical change in the early twentieth-century American schools was the wide-scale introduction of vocational and technical courses.[2] For the majority of youngsters enrolled in these courses, learning a trade was an economic necessity; a classical education was a luxury. There followed the rapid development throughout

[1] An analysis of the two most comprehensive contemporary surveys of educational reform in the United States prior to World War I reveals vividly the preponderance of experiments with the lower socioeconomic classes. See Scott Nearing, *The New Education* (New York, 1915) and John and Evelyn Dewey, *Schools of To-Morrow* (New York, 1915). See also the yearbooks published by the National Society for the Study of Education between 1905 and 1915.

[2] The developing vocational educational programs prior to the passage in 1917 of the Smith-Hughes Act, which authorized federal funds to support high school vocational courses, is described in Charles A. Bennett, *History of Manual and Industrial Education, 1870 to 1917* (Peoria, Illinois, 1937). Chapter IX, "The Early Development of Pedagogically Organized Shopwork Instruction in the United States of America" and Chapter XIII, "The Vocational Education Movement," are of particular interest. A contemporary account of programs is found in *Industrial Education: Typical Experiments Described and Interpreted,* 11th NSSE Yearbook, Part I (Bloomington, Illinois, 1912).

the nation of vocational and trade schools, usually for youngsters who had already completed elementary school. Although the majority of the programs were for boys only, some cities provided training for girls in homemaking or in some salable skill.[3] Technical education became the twentieth-century American analogue of eighteenth- and nineteenth-century apprenticeships.

Beyond strictly vocational courses, the prewar schools broadened their offerings in urban and rural slum areas to include medical examinations, instruction in hygiene, and free lunch programs.[4] Vacation schools and all-day neighborhood schools provided supervised activities for children whose parents could not give them much attention. Evening study hours in the schools helped children living in rooms too crowded for homework. Rural schools emphasized self-help agricultural projects.[5] School-sponsored "Corn Clubs" sprang up in many areas, and methods of increasing the yield of a plot, making preserves from a variety of home-grown crops, designing and sewing clothes for the family became part of the school curriculum.

The Gary, Indiana, schools perhaps best exemplified the range of the new reforms.[6] Widely known to American educators in the pre-

---

[3] See discussions of programs for girls in John and Evelyn Dewey, *Schools of Tomorrow, op. cit.,* pp. 212–215; F. J. Howe, "Rural-School Extension Through Boys' and Girls' Agricultural Clubs," in *The Rural School as a Community Center,* 10th NSSE Yearbook, Part II (Bloomington, Illinois, 1911), pp. 20–28; and O. N. Benson, "Organization and Instruction in Boys' and Girls' Clubs in 1912," Circular No. 803, U.S. Department of Agriculture (Washington, D.C., 1913).

[4] A variety of these additional activities are described in *The City School as a Community Center,* 10th NSSE Yearbook, Part I, *op. cit.* Morris I. Berger discusses many of the same practices in "The Settlement, the Immigrant, and the Public School," unpublished Ph.D. dissertation, Columbia University, 1956.

[5] Anna Marie Keppel, "Country Schools for Country Children: Backgrounds of the Reform Movement in Rural Education, 1890–1914," unpublished Ph.D. dissertation, University of Wisconsin, 1960, is a good sampling of individual rural school reforms, but the author makes little effort to tie the reforms in rural education to other contemporary educational reforms. Other helpful accounts are *The Rural School as a Community Center,* 10th NSSE Yearbook, *op. cit.;* Mabel Carney, *Country Life and Country School* (Chicago, 1912); and Evelyn Dewey, *New Schools for Old* (New York, 1919).

[6] The two standard contemporary accounts of the Gary schools are Abraham Flexner and Frank P. Bachman, *The Gary Schools* (New York, 1918) and Randolph Bourne, *The Gary Schools* (Cambridge, Massachusetts, 1916). Of the two the former is much more critical.

World War I years, the Gary schools were largely the creation of a Bluffton, Indiana, school principal, William Wirt, who went to the dune wasteland of northern Indiana to create a school system uniquely fitted to the needs of an industrial city built from scratch. Gary was the classic company town. Organized by United States Steel, it had been built on the southern shore of Lake Michigan where the great steel plant drew thousands of unskilled workers. As a result, most of the pupils in the Gary schools were laborers' children, 57 per cent of whom were of foreign stock. Absence of an established school system or even a common educational tradition opened every opportunity for experimentation in the new schools. Wirt planned and implemented all sorts of programs requiring the schools' active participation in the pupils' daily lives. Schools were open all day and all year; vocational programs abounded, health activities flourished, parents and other adults of the community were caught up into many school activities. All these arrangements were conducted with surprising efficiency, a fact quickly interpreted by carpers to mean that economy, not education, was their goal.[7] The Gary schools had their critics in the prewar years, but their voices were feeble compared to the cheers of Wirt's admirers. Randolph Bourne gave the Gary schools his ultimate accolade in 1916 by describing them as "the most complete and admirable synthesis of Dewey's philosophy yet attempted."[8]

The results of urbanization and immigration, then, in tandem with compulsory school laws, forced the pre-World War I schools to expand their traditional role to include many additional functions—vocational training, health programs, and other community services.[9] Nevertheless, the fundamental mission of the school remained essentially unchanged. It was didactic. School authorities continued to make the basic decisions about what should be taught. The children came to the school as a place of instruction, and in that place they were indeed instructed. From time to time the methods of instruction were changed, even refreshed, but the end in view was the same. The teacher dispensed knowledge, and the children (it was hoped) duly acquired it. The primary concern was for subject matter, the material trans-

[7] Raymond E. Callahan is especially critical of the Gary Plan in *Education and the Cult of Efficiency* (Chicago, 1962), Chapter VI, "The 'Factory System' in Education."

[8] Bourne, *The Gary Schools, op. cit.*, p. 100.

[9] In *The Transformation of the School* (New York, 1961), Lawrence A. Cremin cites the willingness of the schools to assume additional responsibilities as a distinguishing characteristic of the progressive education movement, p. viii.

mitted in the classroom; important but still auxiliary concerns had for their object the elimination of certain overt obstacles to successful transmission—illness, malnutrition, foreigness, language ignorance.

Urbanization and immigration had quite observable effects on American society in the early 1900s. Ideological factors are harder to gauge. It has been persuasively argued that Darwinism and the "new psychology" were important factors in the shift of the center of gravity of educational thinking of the early twentieth century.[10] The second of these is easier to assess than the first, for there is rather specific evidence of the influence of psychologists such as William James, G. Stanley Hall, and Edward L. Thorndike on the educational thinking of the epoch. The matter is made more complex by the fact that Darwinism tends to blur into the "new psychology"; there is considerable testimony that psychologists, particularly James, were themselves "influenced" by Darwin or Darwinism.[11] Dewey gave a course of public lectures on Darwin and his influence on science at Columbia University in 1909, and one of these lectures, "The Influence of Darwinism on Philosophy," appeared the following year as the first essay in a book of the same title. In concluding the essay, Dewey said, "Doubtless the greatest dissolvent in contemporary thought of old questions, the greatest precipitant of new methods, new intentions, new problems, is the one effected by the scientific revolution that found its climax in 'The Origin of Species.' "[12] It is risky to argue from eulogies to influence, and it may well be that Dewey's admiration for Darwin stemmed more

[10] Notably by Cremin, *ibid.*, Chapter IV.

[11] In his biography of James, Ralph Barton Perry says, "The influence of Darwin [on James] was both early and profound and its effects crop up in diverse and unexpected quarters." *The Thought and Character of William James* (2 vols., Boston, 1935), I, p. 469. Philip P. Wiener follows Perry's lead on James's link to Darwin in his *Evolution and the Founders of Pragmatism* (Cambridge, Massachusetts, 1949), Chapter V. William Heard Kilpatrick says that Dewey told him that he (Dewey) was indebted for his organism-environment metaphor to James who, Kilpatrick adds, "in turn (we must believe) had built it by development out of Darwin." Kilpatrick does not give reasons why we must believe it. "Dewey's Influence on Education" in P. A. Schilpp, ed., *The Philosophy of John Dewey* (New York, 1951), p. 456. Reading *The Origin of the Species* in his junior year at Mercer (Georgia) University triggered a "cataclysmic upheaval" in Kilpatrick that led to his rejection of traditional religion and subsequent ouster from Mercer where he was professor of mathematics. Samuel Tenenbaum, *William Heard Kilpatrick: Trail Blazer in Education* (New York, 1951), p. 13.

[12] John Dewey, *The Influence of Darwin on Philosophy* (New York, 1910), p. 19.

from the fact that he found in Darwin's work a confirmation of his own conviction of the primacy of change and development over fixity (a conviction at least equally derivable from Hegel) than from any Darwinian conversion experience. At any rate, he said, "The influence of Darwin upon philosophy resides in his having conquered the phenomenon of life for the principle of transition, and thereby freed the new logic for application to mind and morals and life."[13] In Dewey's idiom, application to mind, morals, and life meant relevance to education.

Generally, a significant result of the acceptance of Darwinism in the United States was the gradual acceptance of the legitimacy and even the necessity of questioning orthodoxy, traditional scholarship, received doctrine of any kind. The resulting pervasive skepticism about truths formerly regarded as absolute and traditions considered inviolate touched many regions of American life, not the least being the school curriculum. No longer could it be comfortably assumed that the classical studies deemed appropriate for the student of 1850 were essential for his grandson in 1910. Strictly speaking, this conclusion could be reached without help from Darwin; all the same, it was reassuring to be able to strengthen the conclusion by showing that it was deducible from evolutionary premises. More specifically, Darwinism reinforced the push toward science that helped alter the curriculum of the schools. In the years immediately preceding the First World War, more extensive offerings were discernible, and basic changes were made within the existing science courses. Chemistry, physics, and modified biology courses were brought into the curriculum of the secondary schools. Even some signs of the fledgling social sciences were visible, although it was not until after the war that extensive ventures into the social sciences were made in behalf of the high school curriculum.

The implications of contemporary findings in psychology had quite direct effects upon American pedagogy. The "new psychology" challenged the old concepts; mental discipline and faculty psychology went to the wall. Dewey's reading of William James's *Principles of Psychology* stimulated him to formulate the instrumentalist role of the inseparability of thought and action, knowing and doing; ideas were seen no longer as objects of contemplation but as instruments of action.[14] James's pupil Edward L. Thorndike dedicated his work to

---

[13] *Ibid.*, pp. 8, 9.

[14] In a letter to James in March, 1903, Dewey referred to James's *Principles of Psychology* as "the spiritual *progenitor* of the whole industry" (italics Dewey's) quoted in Perry, *Thought and Character of William James, op. cit.*, p. 521. For more extensive accounts of Dewey's view of his indebtedness to James see Jane M. Dewey, ed., "Biography of John Dewey," in **P. A.**

the quantitative and the measurable; his stimulus-response connectionism, as well as more specific applications of his work to learning theory and reading, were taught to two generations of teachers.[15] Another of James's pupils, G. Stanley Hall, explored children's psychological development and its implication for their education.[16] His achievements earned him the title "father of the child study movement." Thus, through the work of James and two of his students, Thorndike and Hall, the foundations of twentieth-century educational psychology were laid. The followers of Thorndike would differ violently with the the disciples of Hall in subsequent years, but both could trace their intellectual heritage to William James.

The influence of Sigmund Freud on American educational practice was never so explicit as that of either Thorndike or Hall. True, Freud had lectured at Clark University (Worcester, Massachusetts) on Hall's invitation in 1909, and his lectures had been written up and discussed. Moreover, Freudianism was highly fashionable in New York during the war, particularly in Greenwich Village intellectual and art circles. But books applying Freudian concepts to child study and schooling did not appear in this country until after the armistice. During the twenties and thirties psychoanalysis would play a certain part in alerting teachers to the importance of nonintellectual factors in determining a child's academic program. Nevertheless, the Freud-oriented school (some of its partisans went so far as to think of them as "therapy centers") was always a rather special case, and the psychoanalytic movement never penetrated deeply into the ideology or methods of American pedagogy.

Schilpp, ed., *The Philosophy of John Dewey, op. cit.*, p. 23; and John Dewey, "From Absolutism to Experimentalism," in George P. Adams and William Pepperell Montague, eds., *Contemporary American Philosophy* (2 vols., New York, 1930), II, pp. 14–27.

[15] No complete biographical study of Edward L. Thorndike exists, although Geraldine M. Joncich discusses Thorndike's work at considerable length in "Science, Psychology and Education: An Interpretive Study of Edward L. Thorndike's Place in the Scientific Movement in Education," unpublished Ed.D. project, Teachers College, Columbia University, 1961.

[16] The best published study of Hall's work as an educator remains Merle Curti's essay in *The Social Ideas of American Educators* (New York, 1935), Chapter XII. Wilbur Harvey Dutton includes some material on Hall in "The Child-Study Movement in America From Its Origin (1880) to the Organization of the Progressive Education Association (1920) [sic.]," unpublished doctoral study, Stanford University, 1945, pp. 45–50. See also Hall's autobiography, *Life and Confessions of a Psychologist* (New York, 1923).

Educational Reforms after the First World War

The response of the schools to the "new psychology" was a post-World War I phenomenon, although the way had earlier been prepared by theoretical works justifying a new approach to education. Hall's classic study on adolescence appeared in 1904, and Thorndike's major work in educational psychology was done between 1913 and 1918. More general studies included Abraham Flexner's brief, *A Modern School,* of 1916 and Dewey's most explicit statement of his philosophy of education, *Democracy and Education,* of 1916. Already in the early postwar years, the American educator's conception of his role had begun to shift away from the enlightened didacticism that persisted throughout the educational reforms prior to the war. As Armistice Day receded further into the past, major differences between the eras divided by the war became more apparent. Before the war, educational reform had been pretty much a part of that generalized progressivism whose symbol was Jane Addams' Hull House. Reforms in school arrangements were directed toward the poorer classes whose members, both native and foreign born, were crowding the cities that were booming with industrialization. The school's primary role as a place of instruction was not essentially changed by these prewar reforms; its didactic function was *supplemented* by enlightened measures designed to improve the condition of the poor children, to equip them better so that they might more easily enter American society and enjoy its traditional values and benefits. Hence the vocational schools, the health and nutrition programs, the hot meal schedules, and the rest.

Social class and economic divisions mark the break in the two periods of educational reform. Prewar progressivism was largely an affair of the public schools, particularly those attended by working class children. The more typical "progressive education" manifested itself after the war in private schools or in public schools in comfortable suburbs; the pupils were well-brushed children of the middle or upper middle classes. The American 1920s saw the appearance of much new wealth. Many of the recently affluent whose family backgrounds were not quite up to Exeter or St. Paul's sent their children instead to a country day school or to a public school in a wealthy suburb.[17] These

[17] Lloyd Marcus, "The Founding of American Private Progressive Schools, 1912–1921," unpublished senior thesis, Harvard College, 1948, provides the most nearly complete information available on the motives and backgrounds of the founders of nine important private schools: Park School,

parents were positively not interested in free hot lunch programs, vocational training, or hygiene instruction for personal cleanliness. They were, however, impressed by the new psychology and social studies. Educators' talk about child-centeredness, individual expression, and creativity caught their ear, and they liked what they heard. These were the areas of educational reform they wished to see extended in *their* children's schools, and in large measure they achieved this objective.

Some of the new "progressive" schools were organized by parents concerned about the quality of education existing in the public schools.[18] One of the best of these was Shady Hill School in Cambridge (Massachusetts) established by Professor William Ernest Hocking and his wife in cooperation with a number of their colleagues in order to provide a special and superior education suitable to the needs of the children of Harvard faculty members. (One of these needs was excellent instruction in Latin.) Other private schools were founded by remarkable women such as Caroline Pratt and Elisabeth Irwin who opened their establishments in New York City in the hope of enlivening and enriching local educational opportunities. Both Miss Pratt and Miss Irwin first tried to attract to their schools the children of Irish and Italian immigrants nearby, but each gradually and reluctantly came to admit that her pupils would come perforce from the families of the newly prosperous residents of the Greenwich Village area.[19]

Baltimore; City and Country School, New York; Walden School, New York; Shady Hill School, Cambridge, Massachusetts; Oak Lane Country Day School, Philadelphia; Moraine Park School, Dayton, Ohio; Chevy Chase Country Day School, Chevy Chase, Maryland; Beaver Country Day School, Chestnut Hill, Massachusetts; and Lincoln School, New York.

[18] Carleton Washburne and Sidney P. Marland, Jr., support this view in their account of the organization of the Winnetka schools, *Winnetka, The History and Significance of an Educational Experiment* (Englewood Cliffs, New Jersey, 1963), pp. 3–15. Lucy Sprague Mitchell's autobiography, *Two Lives* (New York, 1953), reveals the same concern of intelligent parents that sparked other educational experiments. Another school established largely through parents' initiative was Moraine Park Country Day School, where Charles F. Kettering's influence was clearly discernible. (Marcus, "The Founding of American Private Progressive Schools, 1912–1921," *op. cit.*, pp. 46–51.) Richard Hocking recounted his parents' concern in an interview with the author, September 1, 1965. Hans Froelicher, Jr., reported during an interview on March 3, 1960, the leading role of educated parents in creating the Park School, Baltimore.

[19] See Caroline Pratt's autobiography, *I Learn From Children* (New York, 1948) and my biographical note on Elisabeth A. Irwin in the forthcoming *Dictionary of Notable American Women*.

Still other experimental schools were established as laboratory schools in conjunction with the new faculties of education attached to the universities. Patty Smith Hill's kindergarten and the Lincoln School, both at Teachers College (Columbia), were outstanding examples of university-sponsored private schools.

In their turn, the public schools of the rich suburbs offered fertile soil for the new progressivism's seeds of experiment. Just as the Gary schools were brightly typical of educational reform prior to the First World War, so the Winnetka schools of suburban Chicago, hardly fifty miles from Gary, became prize exhibits of contemporary educational experiment ten years later.[20] While Gary had gone in for efficiency of school operation, individualized instruction stamped the Winnetka plan. Gary achieved an *expanded* curriculum including vocational courses; Winnetka featured a *revised* curriculum stressing social studies and a newly integrated subject matter. Impetus for reform at Gary had come from old-line civic progressives and local community planners who had brought in a practicing school principal to supervise the new schools. Initiative for school revision in Winnetka, on the other hand, had come from the residents and parents of the modish suburb who wanted to improve local educational opportunities for their children. When Winnetka was hunting an administrator for its school system, it looked not to an established principal as Gary had, but rather to one of the new "professional" educators, Frederick Burk at San Francisco Normal School, who had been trained under G. Stanley Hall at Clark University. Burk recommended one of his young protégés, Carleton Washburne, and the latter accepted the job at Winnetka, thereby identifying himself and Winnetka with the progressive education movement.

In addition to upper middle class parents and other educated laymen, supporters of postwar educational reforms had a powerful ally in the emerging teaching profession. Before 1920 teachers were generally prepared with only a high school education and some additional terms at normal school. After World War I, the trend in teacher education was steadily in the direction of college training for all teachers, with licensing requirements that included "professional" courses in education for accreditation of those who taught in public

[20] William Wirt had been invited to advise the Winnetka leaders in their plans for a new school and had visited Winnetka, probably in 1913, but apparently his suggestions were not accepted by the Winnetka School Board. Washburne and Marland, *Winnetka, The History and Significance of an Educational Experiment, op. cit.,* p. 5.

schools.[21] Certification requirements were taken seriously, for school teaching had become a profession. The existence of a new class of professionals was of no small importance in the postwar history of the progressive schools. While the first decade of these experimental schools was largely an epoch of private school individualists aglow with missionary fervor, the professionals would in due course take over and put their stamp on the movement.

The increase in college training and professional courses made it easy for all parties to the postwar educational enterprise to accept the new psychology and revised curricular methods. In the days before the war, educational reform had depended to a large degree on the initiative of state or local school systems working with their teaching staffs.[22] With the postwar ascendancy of large teacher-training faculties such as Teachers College (Columbia) and the various schools of education that developed at major universities throughout the United States, new ideas in education could be widely disseminated during the preparation for teaching as well as in the schools themselves. The metamorphosis of school teachers into professionals was reinforced by the growth of strong national organizations, such as the National Educational Association, which were interested in education. The Progressive Education Association would soon take its place with these organizations and, with the cooperation of professional educators, would for two decades exercise a unique influence on American educational thought and practice.

In this way the discontinuities add up. Prewar educational progressivism was a movement essentially continuous with the social and political progressivism that flourished in the last quarter of the nineteenth century. It had for a major object the expansion of public school facilities and curriculum offerings with a view to accommodating the children of the working class, removing obstacles from their path of entry into full participation in American life. Postwar progressive education bloomed in private schools and, although it was later taken over by the educational professionals, its reforms from first to last

[21] Merle Borrowman, *The Liberal and Technical in Teacher Education* (New York, 1956); Merle Borrowman, ed., *Teacher Education in America* (New York, 1965); and Charles A. Harper, *A Century of Public Teacher Education* (Washington, D.C., 1939) recount developments in the professional training of teachers.

[22] Four of the major nineteenth-century educational reformers were either state educational employees (Horace Mann in Massachusetts and Henry Barnard in Connecticut) or local superintendents (Francis W. Parker in Quincy, Massachusetts, and William T. Harris in St. Louis).

appealed primarily to the middle and upper middle classes. With the towering exception of John Dewey, people working and writing for the prewar educational progressivism (Jane Addams, Scott Nearing, Randolph Bourne, and Joseph Mayer Rice) did not as a rule belong to the professional educator class. Postwar progressive education, however, was increasingly dominated by professional educators. Those reformers active in the progressive education movement before the First World War were not the same people, nor even the same kind of people, as those active in the movement after the war. The reform movement after the war bore little resemblance to the reform movement before the war. The old generalized crusading zeal that had marked prewar progressivism died away, to be replaced after 1918 by the more constricted fervor of the postwar progressive educators.

Gary and Winnetka were very different kinds of schools, but both were designated "progressive" by their contemporaries and by historians. Use of the term "progressive education" to apply to such different educational enterprises suggests not only the vagueness of the term but a major shift in its meaning. Before World War I, "progressive schools" were often ones that embodied in education the political and social views of prominent figures in American life, men and women identified with the progressive movement in American politics. With the demise of progressivism as a popular social and political sentiment after the war, the label "progressive" continued to be applied to schools, but these schools were of quite different kinds. In 1920 a "progressive" school was an experimental one, a school that attempted to include in its program some of the findings of the new psychology and to conform to the spirit of the emerging social sciences.[23] These methods were tightly correlated with a sharp focusing of attention upon the individual child in the schoolroom. By the 1930s, when a quite different social reformist sentiment had boiled up as a result of the Depression, a "progressive" school could be either one bearing down hard on individual development and creativity or one that emphasized the schools' responsibility in society.[24] In the late 1940s, the term "progressivism" would take on still another shade of meaning, returning very briefly

[23] George Mirick, *Progressive Education* (New York, 1923) includes a discussion of individualized and socialized study, "discipline as adjustment," projects, and testing as characteristics of progressive education.

[24] To have applied to education the term "liberal," so frequently identified with the dominant political sentiment of that period, would have seriously confused the educational term since "liberal" in education already had a distinct meaning. The very absence of an established substantive meaning for "progressive" allowed it to be used so widely in a variety of educational reforms.

to an identification with the social views of an existing political party. But the radical progressivism of presidential candidate Henry Wallace, while drawing the support of those liberal and left-wing elements so articulate in post-World War II United States, never achieved the broad-based national backing that political progressivism had enjoyed in the early 1900s. The late 1940s, too, were the years of progressive education's final decline.

Throughout the ideological oscillations of the concept "progressive," at least two elements remained constant: an appreciation of innovation in education and an acknowledgement of John Dewey's status as prophet and elder statesman of the progressive education movement. The eminent Columbia philosopher was an old-line progressive in the broad sense of late nineteenth-century social reform. He was a friend of Jane Addams, frequented Hull House, and even named one daughter for Miss Addams. He was also the founder of one of the most renowned early experimental schools, the "Laboratory School" at the University of Chicago, as well as the author of *Schools of To-Morrow*, a classic description of early progressive schooling in America. As early as 1884 Dewey was writing on "the new psychology."[25] Through fifty years of the new century he wrote indefatigably on philosophy and education. It is not an easy task to try to isolate key concepts of progressive education, as that kind of education was understood in the 1920s and 1930s, in order to compare these concepts with their likely origins or equivalents in Dewey's published educational ideology. One of these concepts is the idea of continuity between school and society, a characteristic progressivist doctrine recently identified by a prominent American educator as part of the "stultifying mythology" devised by professional education studies in which "schools have been seen as examples of society in miniature."[26] Before the century turned, Dewey had proclaimed with evangelic fervor his conviction of the unity of school and society. "I believe that the school is primarily a social institution," he stated in his pedagogic credo of 1897. "I believe that the school, as an institution, should simplify existing social life; should reduce it, as it were, to an embryonic form."[27]

[25] John Dewey, "The New Psychology," *Andover Review* 2 (September, 1884), pp. 278–289.

[26] President Nathan M. Pusey of Harvard University referring to the annual report of Dean Theodore Sizer of Harvard Graduate School of Education. *Harvard University: The President's Report, 1965–1966* (Cambridge, Massachusetts, 1967), p. 3.

[27] John Dewey, "My Pedagogic Creed," *The School Journal* 54 (January 16, 1897), pp. 77–80. Reprinted in Martin S. Dworkin, ed., *Dewey on Education* (New York, 1959), pp. 22–23.

Fifty-four years later Dewey appears still to be sticking to it: "One of the soundest and most valuable features of the genuine progressive education movement has been that it strives to break down the walls erected to shut off the schoolroom from almost everything outside the school building."[28] Yet Dewey never wholeheartedly supported the social reconstructionist movement in progressive education that sprang into being in the mid-thirties under the leadership of George S. Counts. He showed little interest in the prospect of the school leading the way to "reconstruct" (a favorite Deweyan word) even an ailing social order, as that of the United States seemed to be in the Depression years. Counts' summons to the schools to "indoctrinate" students to build a new social order left Dewey particularly unenthusiastic.[29]

Dewey stressed the importance of linking the school to life but distinctly criticized using schooling to prepare youngsters for a particular trade,[30] thereby discomfiting some of the old Gary-style pro-

[28] John Dewey in Introduction to Samuel Tenenbaum, *William Heard Kilpatrick, op. cit.*, p. ix.

[29] "There is a small but growing number of educators who think the remedy for the drift and aimlessness, which undoubtedly results, is to pursue a policy of deliberate indoctrination on the basis of a new social order. They are perhaps moved by what is going on in European countries where the schools are a definite instrumentality of promoting new social and economic orders. They are doing a valiant work in arousing teachers to think more about existing conditions, and in exposing the kind and amount of indoctrination for a reactionary social order that now goes on in the schools. I should not wish any words of mine to encourage teachers in a state of complacency and lethargy and I fear that considerable opposition to the group in question proceeds from just such sources. But I think it ignores the fact that indoctrination for a new order works in European countries just because a great change has already taken place in their political structures; that, as I have already said, indoctrination works inevitably and smoothly when it is in line with what is already largely taken for granted in a community. There is an important difference between education *with respect to a new social order* and indoctrination into settled convictions about that order." John Dewey, *Education and the Social Order* (New York, 1934), p. 10.

[30] "The aims should not, of course, be immediate, highly-specialized efficiency that is so immediate and so specialized as to limit future growth or to predestine individuals to occupy simply a particular niche. It should be aimed, rather, at a discovery of personal aptitude to practice familiarly with the fundamental processes of industry and should be devoted to the development of as much initiative, as much variety, as is possible." John Dewey, *Vocational Education in the Light of the World War*, Bulletin No. 4, Convention of the Vocational Education Association of the Middle West (Chicago, 1918), p. 4.

gressives who prided themselves on enlarging student opportunities by expanding vocational programs. "Democracy" was a good word to the "new" progressives, particularly those of the late thirties and early forties, and "democracy" was the first word of the title of Dewey's most important statement of educational philosophy.[31] Yet the late progressive educators' use of "Democratic living" as a slogan did not derive from Dewey's *Democracy and Education,* but—as this book will try to show—from quite different origins, from sources that had to do with the uniting of Americans under the threat of a second world war and encroachment of foreign ideologies.

Child-centeredness rather than subject-centeredness is another key concept of post-World War I progressive education, and Dewey's attitude to this concept underwent some development. In his very early pedagogical writing, he states his belief that "the true center of correlation on the school subjects is not science, nor literature, nor history nor geography, but the child's own social activities."[32] But Dewey was always wary of the implications of child-centeredness. He urged that children be given opportunities for creative expression in the schools, but he strenuously opposed unlimited freedom.[33] To Dewey, intelligence entailed order, and he never countenanced the anti-intellectualism that passed, at certain extremes of the progressive education movement, for authentic interest in the child. A year before his death, Dewey praised Kilpatrick for a quality some educators were surprised to hear attributed to the author of the "project method." After pointing out that progressive education ("in the best sense of the words") and the work of Kilpatrick were "virtually synonymous," Dewey went on to observe that his eminent colleague had "never fallen victim to the one-sidedness of identifying progressive education with child-centered education."[34]

Dewey's interests were eclectic enough, his language imprecise enough, and his publications frequent enough for many varieties of progressivism to be sheltered under his mantle. The fundamental difficulty in assessing Dewey's own attitude toward progressivism re-

[31] John Dewey, *Democracy and Education* (New York, 1916).
[32] John Dewey, "My Pedagogic Creed" in Dworkin, ed., *op. cit.,* p. 25.
[33] John Dewey, "How Much Freedom in the New Schools?" *New Republic* 63 (July 9, 1930), pp. 204–206. Dewey's article contrasted sharply with Margaret Naumburg's "The Crux of Progressive Education," *New Republic* 63 (June 25, 1930), pp. 145–146. Both appeared in a series, "The New Education: Ten Years After."
[34] John Dewey in Introduction to Samuel Tenenbaum, *William Heard Kilpatrick, op. cit.,* p. viii.

sults from his apparent unwillingness in his later years to criticize specifically those who called themselves his followers and who justified their work by his phrases. In particular, his relationship with Kilpatrick, perhaps the most prominent exponent of progressive education for the period between the wars, has never been adequately clarified. But discontinuities between Dewey's ideas and attitudes, and elements in the progressivist arrangements of the twenties and thirties are no more than symptomatic of the discontinuities that marked the history of educational progressivism as a whole.

In any case, it was in a milieu of contradiction and change that the Progressive Education Association emerged in 1919. Its immediate educational heritage was one of vigorous social reform movements, but the PEA initially ignored this tradition. The Association was more strongly influenced by the emphasis upon the individual child and upon curriculum revisions than it was by the activities of the school as an extension of the social settlement. The newly college-trained teachers and their instructors, desiring recognition as a professional group, became an important element in the Progressive Education Association's organizational growth. Finally, John Dewey's willingness in the mid-twenties to lend his name to the organization as its honorary president gave the infant group continuity with the past and honor in the present.

CHAPTER II

The Years of Quest

≫≪

The Founding of the Progressive Education Association

On the evening of April 4, 1919, nearly 100 persons gathered at the Washington, D.C., public library to attend the first meeting of the Association for the Advancement of Progressive Education. The chief organizer was Stanwood Cobb, a New Englander then teaching at the United States Naval Academy. The group listened to speeches extolling the "new education" by Cobb and four others: Eugene Randolph Smith, headmaster of the Park School, Baltimore; Anne George, principal of the Washington Montessori School; Otis Caldwell, director of the Lincoln School, Teachers College; and Marietta Johnson, founder of the Organic School, Fairhope, Alabama. After the meeting the leaders counted the one-dollar membership fees paid by those attending and, with an initial fund of eighty-six dollars, launched the organization.[1]

The April meeting represented a dream come true. The dreamer was Minnesota-born Marietta Johnson who had organized her "organic school" in Henry George's single tax community of Fairhope, Alabama. The Fairhope School, and subsequent organic schools in Connecticut

---

[1] The meeting was announced in the *Washington Herald,* April 2, 1919, and in the *Washington Star,* April 3, 1919. In an undated manuscript located at the Teachers College Library, Columbia University, "The Founding and Early Organization of the Progressive Education Association," Stanwood Cobb wrote that the meeting occurred in March, 1919. In "Concerning Ourselves: The Romance of Beginnings," *Progressive Education* 6 (January–February–March, 1929), p. 67, Cobb also contended that the meeting took place on March 15, 1919.

and New York, leaned heavily on the principles of natural development as basic to the educational process.[2] Mrs. Johnson had approached Cobb early in 1918, suggesting that he help her in creating a national association to support these principles. At first, Cobb demurred. He had become acquainted with Mrs. Johnson's educational ideas through Gertrude Stevens (Mrs. Milan V.) Ayres' Washington School that was modeled on the one at Fairhope. Cobb noted that although he himself was sympathetic with the Fairhope experiment, he doubted the wisdom of a national organization committed to a single educational philosophy. He recalled Alexander Graham Bell's failure with the group based on advancing the Montessori method. Shortly afterward, Mrs. Johnson approached Cobb again, this time with a proposal to establish an educational association devoted to publicizing current experiments in education. This idea was more appealing to Cobb, and he showed considerable interest in it.[3]

There was genuine reason for this interest. Born in 1881 in Newton, Massachusetts, Cobb spent all his adult life in the field of education. He took his A.B. from Dartmouth and his A.M. from Harvard Divinity School. He then taught English and Latin at Robert College, Istanbul; English at St. John's College, Annapolis; English at the Asheville School for Boys, Asheville, North Carolina; and English and history at the United States Naval Academy, Annapolis. In 1919, after having spent the three preceding years drilling the midshipmen at what he termed "the acme of educational bureaucracy and Prussianism," Cobb conclusively broke with traditional formal education, helped establish the Progressive Education Association, and founded his own progressive school, the Chevy Chase Country Day School in

[2] Marietta Johnson recounted the development of her school and her educational ideas in an autobiographical essay, *Thirty Years With an Idea,* unpublished manuscript (1939?), Teachers College Library, Columbia University. Mrs. Johnson felt her principal pedagogical debt was to C. Hanford Henderson.

[3] Cobb described the early history of the PEA in an article in *The Baltimore Sun,* June 1, 1919, and in "Concerning Ourselves: The Romance of Beginnings," *op. cit.* He also reported his role in the founding of the PEA (in a number of undated manuscripts): "Biographical Notes," "Progressive Education after Twenty Years," "The Founding of the Progressive Education Association," and "The Founding and Early Organization of the Progressive Education Association," which are located in the Teachers College Library, Columbia University. Cobb's spelling, particularly of proper nouns, was frequently erratic; for example, he often referred to both Mrs. Milan and Mrs. Millan Ayres and Ayers. In her later reports as Executive Secretary, she signed herself Gertrude Stevens Ayres (Mrs. Milan V.).

Chevy Chase, Maryland.[4] He completed his activities for the year by marrying a Canadian, Nayan Whitland. During the following years Cobb, a prolific author, wrote a number of books, ranging from critiques of progressive education—*The New Leaven* and *New Horizons for the Child*—to mystical and philosophical discourses like *What is Love?* and *Character, A Sequence in Spiritual Psychology.*

In Cobb, perhaps more clearly than in any other twentieth-century leader of progressive education, the influence of American transcendentalism is apparent. Religious influences had been strong in Cobb's New England youth; his grandfather Sylvanus Cobb had been a leader in the Universalist Church movement. The mystical romanticism and utter impracticality of Bronson Alcott's Fruitlands days found their twentieth-century counterpart in the rambling three-story house that enclosed Cobb's school in suburban Chevy Chase.[5]

Mrs. Johnson's ideas succeeded in capturing the imagination of the peripatetic Cobb, but his enthusiasm was an inadequate practical base for a national educational organization.[6] In the winter of 1918–1919 Cobb met Eugene Randolph Smith at one of Mrs. Johnson's lectures in Baltimore. Smith told Cobb about the new Park School in Baltimore, and Cobb waxed enthusiastic about Smith's novel program there. Cobb talked with Smith about forming an educational organization committed to publicizing and promulgating such similar educational experiments as Mrs. Johnson's and Smith's. A practical man, Smith was at first somewhat skeptical about the future of an organization that had only Cobb's zeal for support. But Cobb's promise of financial aid from a rich Washington matron, Mrs. A. J. Parsons, finally convinced Smith of the feasibility of forming the educational association.[7]

A nucleus of the leaders of the April meeting held regular Satur-

---

[4] Cobb, "Biographical Notes," *op. cit.,* p. 3.

[5] Cobb himself looks back upon the early years of his school when creativity was the ideal and traditional marks anathema as an ill-advised pedagogical approach. Such a system is appropriate for a utopia, he has contended, but Chevy Chase was not that. Interview with Stanwood Cobb, October 29, 1962.

[6] Cobb did not remain a permanent disciple of Mrs. Johnson's. He later described her as being "on the radical edge, the fanatic fringe, she just lapsed into one of the also-rans." Interview, October 29, 1962.

[7] Eugene Randolph Smith recalled his hesitation in supporting Cobb in an undated manuscript in the Teachers College Library, Columbia University, "Educational Experimentation and Advances 1894—As Observed or Taken Part In," p. 5.

day sessions throughout the winter of 1919–1920 at the home of Mrs. Laura Williams, another affluent Washington lady. Those attending usually included Cobb, Smith, Miss Anne George, Mrs. Ayres, Mrs. Parsons, and Miss May Libbey, a kindergarten teacher whom Cobb identified as one interested in the educational aspects of theosohy. In Arthur E. Morgan, headmaster of the Moraine Park School of Dayton, Ohio, Cobb found a dedicated supporter of the new association. Subsequently, Morgan became president of Antioch College (1920), and in this way the association achieved an early link with new experiments in higher education. An engineer by training, Morgan was one of the first directors of the Tennessee Valley Authority. He became the first president of the Progressive Education Association, serving in that office from 1920 to 1922.

The Search for a Name

The earliest years of the PEA were years of search. The Association hunted for additional members, for adequate funds, for common goals, and for a suitable name. The last was not hard to find, but seeds of future trouble lay in the name chosen. By the 1919 organization meeting, the label "Association for the Advancement of Experimental Schools," the founders' first choice, had been discarded in favor of "Association for the Advancement of Progressive Education." Cobb recalled that the group feared the public would not support an association devoted to "experimental education" because, as he said, "mothers don't want their children to be guinea pigs." The earlier title, Cobb and others believed, might limit the organization to particular schools, while the term "progressive education" allowed for a much broader range of interests and activities.[8] At the 1920 convention, the name was shortened to "Progressive Education Association."

The choice of the term "Progressive Education" was fortuitous and ultimately fatal. In selecting it, Cobb and his followers hit upon a name that would one day be used to label the entire educational reform movement of the late nineteenth century and the first half of the twentieth century. As a result, the Association benefited from the general popularity of "progressive education" in the twenties and thirties and suffered from its decline in the forties and fifties. The relationship between the Association and the progressive education

[8] Cobb, Interview, October 29, 1962. Cobb, "Concerning Ourselves: The Romance of Beginnings," *op. cit.*, p. 67; Cobb, "The Founding of the Progressive Education Association," *op. cit.*, p. 2.

movement as a whole was so close in the public mind that the Association changed its name to "American Education Fellowship" in 1944 substantially to disassociate the organization from the (by then) pejorative term "progressive education." As things turned out, this action did not improve the Association's declining fortune, and in 1953 the group shifted back to its former name "Progressive Education Association" in a desperate but unsuccessful effort to regain its previous esteem.

Simply because of the similarity of labels the Progressive Education Association has often been considered—not just by the public but also by professional educators—synonymous with the entire progressive education movement. Such an assumption is inaccurate on several counts, the most striking of which is that the Association was established when the reform movement in education was already well under way. Cobb himself emphasized this point. "The 'new education,'" he said, "was twenty years old in 1919, the year the PEA was founded."[9]

Undoubtedly the name "Progressive Education Association" was an asset in the earliest and most crucial years when the group was trying to attract national support. During these years the name meant more to the "interested laymen" whom the Association ostensibly sought out than to the university professors of education who later dominated the organization. But, years later, it was the public image, to which the name "progressive education" contributed to such an important degree, that suffered lacerating attacks in the forties and fifties. Perhaps the Association would have fared no better with another name, but certainly the tag "progressive education" lost it supporters in its declining years. Many of the leaders of the Association in the forties and fifties believed the name had, in fact, limited the organization's opportunities for future development after "progressive education" had come to be

---

[9] Cobb also took pains to point out that the Association "did not create the 'Progressive Education' movement, but it gave it form and body." "The Founding of the Progressive Education Association," *op. cit.*, p. 2. Frederick L. Redefer, executive secretary and director of the PEA from 1932 to 1943, reached the same conclusion in an undated manuscript in the Teachers College Library, Columbia University, "Between Two Wars, An Interpretation of Progressive Education in the United States of America," pp. 1, 160, and 197. The general view frequently has not distinguished between "creation" and "form and body" as such apologists as Cobb and Redefer did (Cobb, Interview, October 29, 1962). Cobb emphasized the influence of Parker and minimized that of Hall. Although this emphasis may have been true for Cobb, it was not true of the movement.

regarded as a fixed mode of education rather than a continuing experimental search.[10]

The Search for Members

Having decided upon a name for the organization, the PEA began
a campaign for members. Although nearly all the early leaders were
either teachers or private school administrators, the Association maintained that it tried to attract laymen. Stanwood Cobb noted that
approximately half the people at the 1920 Washington convention, the
Association's first national meeting, were laymen.[11]

> In this early romantic period of the Association, it was . . . chiefly lay
> support that came to our aid—a lay support naturally centering around
> the experimental and private schools then in existence . . . The move-
> ment seemed then to all of us a Cause. It was as such that we appealed
> for membership.

This high sense of mission was almost all that kept the Association
going at first. Cobb continued,

> Great enthusiasm was shown in these early days, both in our corre-
> spondence, literature and conventions. The Association had been
> accused by some of having been too romantic in this earlier period.
> Whatever be the truth of such a statement, the fact is that this ro-
> mantic atmosphere of a cause being promoted for humanitarian bene-
> fits was the only thing that made it possible for us to keep going. We
> had no inducements of any kind, no large gifts, no backers—we de-
> pended wholly upon the enthusiasm and good will of our membership.
> Later the time was to come when the Association could sober down
> and command the support of wealthy individuals and great founda-
> tions.[12]

The decision to attract laymen was understandable, for such a
small and largely unknown group of enthusiasts had little hope of
gaining the attention of leading professional educators immediately.
To achieve their ultimate objective, which Cobb modestly reports was
"reforming the entire school system of America,"[13] the backing of the

---

[10] Interviews, Frederick L. Redefer, November 1, 1962; Theodore Brameld,
January 3, 1963; and John J. DeBoer, March 11, 1963.
[11] Progressive Education Association, Bulletin No. 2 (July, 1920), p. 47.
[12] Cobb, "The Founding and Early Organization of the Progressive Education Association," op. cit., pp. 7–10.
[13] Ibid., p. 12.

new education profession was essential. But this could not be gained by a direct confrontation. Consequently, the early appeals were to the laymen, most frequently to the parents of youngsters in private "progressive" schools. With the PEA, unlike the family-oriented Child Study Association, the overture to "interested parents" seems to have been for support, preferably financial, but not for leadership. When the first Executive Committee of the PEA was announced in 1920, only four of the twenty members were laymen. Of the four, two— Mrs. Williams and Mrs. Parsons—were known patronesses of the Association. This early trend toward domination of the Association's activities by professional educators, in the 1920s by private school teachers and administrators, continued throughout the history of the Association. Although the PEA frequently appealed to the lay public for backing, laymen rarely achieved important positions within the organization.

Whatever the attitude toward laymen, the actual membership figures of the Association grew steadily, if slowly. From the first meeting in April, 1919, with eighty-six members, the Association grew so that by April 1, 1920, the membership rolls showed 491. Thirty-six states, Hawaii, and Canada were represented.[14] In 1920–1921 the membership had risen to approximately 800, and the following year it doubled.[15] For the next few years the membership figures rose fairly regularly, reaching a peak (7,400) for the decade in 1930.

The presence of well-known personages is always a significant inducement to membership in organizations. One of the Association's earliest coups was obtaining retired Harvard president Charles William Eliot's consent to serve as honorary president. Cobb and the other leaders had originally wanted Eliot to be the active president of the Association, but Eliot, who was eighty-five years old when Cobb approached him in 1919, declined that position for reasons of health and offered instead to function as honorary president.[16] Eliot's acceptance

[14] Progressive Education Association, *op. cit.*, p. 1.
[15] Gertrude Stevens Ayres, "Report of the Executive Secretary for the Year Ended March 31, 1922," unpaged, in the Teachers College Library, Columbia University.
[16] Berdine J. Bovard contends in "A History of the Progressive Education Association, 1919–1939," (unpublished doctoral dissertation, University of California, Berkeley, 1941, p. 61) that the leaders of the Association offered the presidency to John Dewey and after his declination they sought Eliot. Bovard does not document this assertion, and Cobb reports only the invitation to Eliot and Eliot's acceptance, "Yes, I believe in your principles and aims, I believe in the kind of education you advocate, and I shall be glad to serve as your honorary president." In an interview on

undoubtedly gave the infant organization considerable prestige. It also reinforced the impression that the PEA would pursue educational reform on the college, secondary, and elementary school levels, as Eliot had done in his own career.

Eliot had been very active in the affairs of the secondary schools as chairman of the NEA's Committee of Ten in 1893. He was known as well as the author of *The Changes Needed in American Secondary Education,* published by the General Education Board in 1916. But it was as the instigator of the elective system while he was president of Harvard that Eliot was most renowned. To what more prestigious institution than Harvard could the PEA hope to be identified? Once Eliot had accepted the honorary presidency, his name appeared prominently on all PEA materials, and a full-page photograph of him was included in the first issue of the Association's quarterly, *Progressive Education.*

The Search for Funds

After the Association found a suitable name and adequate membership, the next pressure was for funds. The need for more money was one of the persistent characteristics of the Association. Throughout its history it sought funds from members, wealthy individuals, advertisers, foundations, and universities. The earliest sources that the Association tapped were its members and interested patrons.

As in many such organizations, memberships were of several varieties; in the early years the minimum annual fee was one dollar, but two- to five-dollar memberships also existed. A "contributing member" paid between five and fifty dollars annually, and "sustaining members" supported the Association with payments in excess of fifty dollars annually. The staunchest of these contributors, such as Mrs. Parsons and Mrs. Williams, usually found themselves on the Executive Committee. In May, 1920, there were fifty-five "contributing members," including Charles W. Eliot and Arthur E. Morgan, and six "sustaining members": Gertrude Stevens Ayres, Stanwood Cobb, Mrs. and Mrs. George Paul Cooke, Mrs. A. J. Parsons, and Mrs. Laura C. Williams.[17]

The Association had been formed with the first membership fees

---

October 29, 1962, Cobb reported that he believed Eliot agreed to join Cobb's group because of the long and apparently cordial relationship between Cobb's grandfather and Eliot.

[17] Progressive Education Association, *op. cit.,* back cover.

in the treasury as well as grants from Mrs. Parsons and Mrs. Williams. In addition to these monetary aids, the Association had the indispensable help of both Cobb's and Mrs. Ayres' time and effort. This help was crucial. Nevertheless, "inspired enthusiasm" alone was not enough, and the leaders of the Association recognized the need for more tangible assets. As Cobb recalled:

> Many enthusiastic friendly letters were received. The kind which pleased us most read like this: "I have been contributing regularly to over thirty different organizations. I am, for certain reasons, now discontinuing these contributions to all except the Progressive Education Association. This, to my mind, is the cause the most productive of benefit to future generations."[18]

Here was the perfect PEA supporter: one who shared the evangelistic militancy of the leaders and one willing to support it financially to the point of forsaking all others.

But such letters and contributions were scarce, so scarce in fact that in the fall of 1920, Mrs. Williams, one of the chief supporters, called a meeting of the leaders of the PEA to consider dissolving it. Her sense of defeat stemmed from a discussion with another member of the Executive Committee, Michael V. O'Shea, a professor of psychology at the University of Wisconsin, who was surprised to discover the insecure financial backing of the Association and advised Mrs. Williams that the group should disband forthwith because it was "not a feasible enterprise." At the meeting, Mrs. Williams recounted her misgivings and questioned whether the members were receiving their dollar's worth for their membership fee. Cobb replied, "It is not what we are giving our members but what our members are willing to give us."[19]

The organization, while not affluent, did steadily improve its financial situation. During the first year, 1919–1920, with a membership of approximately 500, the Association's total income was $1,270.35. The following year, the income had increased to $2,412.53, and in the third year, 1921–1922, to $3,267.00.[20] In 1922–1923 the total receipts were $3,691.95, again an increase, but that year an extra appeal for funds had been necessary.[21]

[18] Cobb, "The Founding and Early Organization of the Progressive Education Association," *op. cit.* p. 17.

[19] *Ibid.*, p. 8.

[20] Gertrude Stevens Ayres, *op. cit.*

[21] James S. Howe, "Report of the Assistant Executive Secretary-Treasurer, 1923," unpaged, in the Teachers College Library, Columbia University.

Although these increases were not enough to encourage unbridled optimism among the officers, they did represent a trend that encouraged PEA leaders to think seriously of replacing Gertrude Stevens Ayres with a professional executive secretary, trained in the skills of publicity. Eager as they were for such a person, they could find neither a suitable candidate nor the funds to pay him until 1926. Apparently the Association leaders realized that widespread recognition of their ideas would be possible only with much broader publicity coverage than they could now afford. James S. Howe, assistant executive secretary-treasurer in 1923, suggested that a full-time professional executive secretary would pay his own way with the additional members he would enroll. Howe also bluntly pointed out to the Association that contributions from wealthy individuals were the most likely means of immediate support.[22] The implication was that such persons should be sought and approached at once. A donor meeting the specifications was found in 1924: Queene Ferry Coonley (Mrs. Avery), who financed the Association's handsome new journal, significantly entitled *Progressive Education.*

The Search for a Program

With a name, members, and money, the organization lacked only one thing—a program. On a single point the leaders agreed: the traditional schools were inadequate. Beyond that, consensus was difficult to achieve. Having made the initial decision to support "progressive education," the PEA leaders now had to delineate the organization's objectives more clearly and to clarify just what the Association meant by the term that gave the group its name. This task fell to a committee headed by Eugene Randolph Smith.

Smith was an excellent choice for the job because, of all the early leaders of the Association, he had the most balanced and systematic educational philosophy. A principal mark of Smith's pedagogical beliefs was a rejection of any single method of education as universally superior to all others. While many progressives of his era minimized the significance of the scientific movement in education, Smith recognized its importance and contributions. He wrote:

The psychologists, Thorndike, the students of testing, etc., were an important influence in the development of more complete understand-

---

[22] *Loc. cit.*

ing of students and the development of better methods. Whether or not they were members of the Progressive or any other association devoted to educational improvements, they contributed to the movement.[23]

Smith had gone to the Park School, Baltimore, from the chairmanship of the mathematics department of the Polytechnic Institute of Brooklyn. In 1922 he left the Park School to assume the headmastership of the newly reorganized Beaver Country Day School in Chestnut Hill, Massachusetts, a suburb of Boston. He soon became a member of the Headmasters' Association, a select group of 100 guardians of such bastions of tradition as Exeter, Andover, and St. Paul's. Smith also held important positions in the new American Council on Education and the Educational Records Bureau, neither of which was so frankly committed to progressive education as the PEA. One of Smith's activities with the ACE was helping to prepare the standard cumulative record form, which chronicles a student's scholastic activity from kindergarten through high school, a record which has become a fixture of most high school files. He was president of the PEA from 1923 to 1925.

Smith, then, was well qualified to translate the PEA's enthusiasm, the expression of which often was understandable only to the inner PEA circle, into lucid prose. The flyer that introduced the PEA to the public contained excerpts from three books: H. G. Wells's *The New Education,* John Dewey's *Democracy and Education,* and C. Hanford Henderson's *What Is It To Be Educated?* The citation from Henderson was doubtless a concession to Cobb, who considered Henderson a leading educational philosopher on a par with Dewey and Pestalozzi. Cobb had been introduced to Henderson by Marietta Johnson, who believed Henderson and Nathan Oppenheim to be the most important pedagogical thinkers of her era.[24] Oppenheim's *The Development of the Child* became her "educational Bible."

The aims of the Association were listed on the cover of each bulletin, and they revealed the group's eagerness to make the organization a clearing house through which all information about educational reform might pass. These aims were:

[23] Eugene Randolph Smith, "Educational Experimentation and Advances 1894—As Observed or Taken Part In," *op. cit.*, p. 13.

[24] Cobb revealed his enthusiasm for Henderson in an article on the PEA in *The Baltimore Sun,* June 1, 1919. Mrs. Johnson chronicled the development of her philosophy of education in *Thirty Years With an Idea, op. cit.*

1. To propagate the principles of progressive education by means of
   (a) a periodical publication to serve as the official organ of the Asso-
       ciation, issued free to all members;
   (b) newspaper and magazine articles;
   (c) lectures.

2. To influence public education toward progressivism by educating
   the public to demand it.

3. To be of service to laymen and educators through:
   (a) an exchange bureau;
   (b) counseling and cooperating with parents in solving their edu-
       cational problems;
   (c) encouraging the training of teachers in the principles and
       methods of progressive education;
   (d) giving field aid to those who are organizing or developing pro-
       gressive schools.

The aims that were included in Article II of the PEA Constitution in
1920 were much the same as these listed above. Perhaps the most
striking feature of the aims is the group's determined reluctance to
promote any particular educational point of view. Undoubtedly the
leaders wanted to attract as large a following as possible, and it might
easily be concluded that such a desire led them to minimize their
principles. In this case, however, they genuinely believed that any
single system or method of education was antithetical to the spirit of
the Association. This attitude was consistent with their rejection of
ultimate or absolute standards in education and their advocacy of adjusting the program to the individual child. In these early years of
"child-centered" schools, teachers and administrators were unwilling to
accept general pedagogical guides but insisted upon treating each child
individually to "unleash his creativity." That such a total rejection of
absolutes might itself become an absolute apparently did not occur to
these educators of the twenties.

The stated aims, however, would not stand alone as guides to
the Association's activities or as sufficient explanation of the Association's interests. Further comment was necessary in the Seven Principles
of Progressive Education:

The aim of Progressive Education is the freest and fullest development
of the individual, based upon the scientific study of his physical,
mental, spiritual, and social characteristics and needs.
    Progressive Education as thus understood implies the following
conditions, old in theory but rare in application:

I. Freedom to Develop Naturally.   The conduct of the pupil should be governed by himself according to the social needs of his community, rather than by arbitrary laws. This does not mean that liberty should be allowed to become license, or that the teacher should not exercise authority when it proves necessary. Full opportunity for initiative and self-expression should be provided, together with an environment rich in interesting material that is available for the free use of every pupil.

II. Interest, the Motive of All Work.   Interest should be satisfied and developed through:

1. Direct and indirect contact with the world and its activities, and the use of the experience thus gained.

2. Application of knowledge gained, and correlation between different subjects.

3. The consciousness of achievement.

III. The Teacher a Guide, Not a Task-Master.   It is essential that teachers should believe in the aims and general principles of Progressive Education and that they should have latitude for the development of initiative and originality.

Progressive teachers will encourage the use of all the senses, training the pupils in both observation and judgment; and instead of hearing recitations only, will spend most of the time teaching how to use various sources of information, including life activities as well as books; how to reason about the information thus acquired; and how to express forcefully and logically the conclusions reached.

Ideal teaching conditions demand that classes be small, especially in the elementary school years.

IV. Scientific Study of Pupil Development.   School records should not be confined to the marks given by the teachers to show the advancement of the pupils in their study of subjects, but should also include both objective and subjective reports on those physical, mental, moral and social characteristics which affect both school and adult life, and which can be influenced by the school and the home. Such records should be used as a guide for the treatment of each pupil, and should also serve to focus the attention of the teacher on the all-important work of development rather than on simply teaching subject matter.

V. Greater Attention to All that Affects the Child's Physical Development.   One of the first considerations of Progressive Education is the health of the pupils. Much more room in which to move about, better light and air, clean and well ventilated buildings, easier access to the out-of-doors and greater use of it, are all necessary. There should be frequent use of adequate playgrounds. The teacher should observe closely the physical condition of each pupil and, in co-operation with the home, make abounding health the first objective of childhood.

VI. Co-operation Between School and Home to Meet the Needs of Child-Life.   The school should provide, with the home, as much as is possible of all that the natural interests and activities of the child demand, especially during the elementary school years. These conditions can come about only through intelligent co-operation between parents and teachers.

VII. The Progressive School a Leader in Educational Movements. The Progressive School should be a leader in educational movements. It should be a laboratory where new ideas, if worthy, meet encouragement; where tradition alone does not rule, but the best of the past is leavened with the discoveries of today, and the result is freely added to the sum of educational knowledge.[25]

Judging from their respective publications, one suspects that Cobb or Mrs. Johnson would have prepared a set of principles with quite a different tone. While Smith's wording of the manifesto accents the leitmotiv of freedom for the child, it avoids the tone of messianic fervor that sounds in Mrs. Johnson's *Thirty Years With an Idea* or Cobb's various early statements of essentials of progressive education.[26] Moreover, each official "principle" is softened by the defining paragraph that follows: for example, the initial line of the creed's first item, "Freedom to Develop Naturally," is qualified by the proviso that the teacher may exercise necessary authority and the caution that liberty should not be allowed to become license. Too many who announced themselves as supporters of progressive education failed to read and accept the qualifying explanations of the Association's published principles.

The inclusion of "Scientific Study of Pupil Development" as one of the basic features of progressive education probably reflects Smith's own interests. In *Education Moves Ahead*, Smith's 1924 survey of progressive education, he devoted two of twelve chapters to the "scientific" influences, the I.Q. tests and methods of marking.[27] In the

[25] These Seven Principles of Progressive Education appeared on the inside cover of each issue of *Progressive Education* from 1924 to 1929. They were originally adopted in 1920.

[26] Cobb's two major books on progressive education are *The New Leaven* (New York, 1928) and a later mild critique of the progressive education movement's emphasis on social reconstruction, *New Horizons for the Child* (Washington, D.C., 1934).

[27] Eugene Randolph Smith, *Education Moves Ahead* (Boston, 1924), Chaps. 7, 8.

early twenties, intelligence and achievement testing were in their greatest vogue. These were days of belief in the immutability of the I.Q.; the extreme claims of such testing experts as Lewis W. Terman were just beginning to be challenged by astute critics like Walter Lippmann in a series of articles in the *New Republic* of 1922.[28] As a group, the enthusiasts of the country day schools, such as Cobb's in Chevy Chase, the Oak Lanes, and the Moraine Park, refused to accept these tests as valid educational aids.[29] They saw the tests as just another form of artificial categorizing of the students. Pigeonholing of students was exactly what these teachers had been fighting in their attacks on traditional schools. In addition, the tests allegedly favored intellectuality over creativity; "tyranny of the intellect" was a choice target of these pedagogues.

The standardized achievement tests, which paralleled the I.Q. tests in popularity, were particularly odious to the progressives, for these tests raised mastery of formal subject matter to a perilous level of importance. Testing enthusiasts played a dominant role in the scientific movement in education during the 1920s, but in the PEA statement on "scientific study" only school records of pupils' development are mentioned. Both "objective and subjective reports" of students' behavior are encouraged, but nothing is said about tests, the most common tool of "scientific study" in education.

The seventh principle and its accompanying rubric should have provided the ideal for the progressive movement in education. If these early schools had indeed been laboratories "where new ideas if worthy meet encouragement; where tradition alone does not rule, but the best of the past is leavened with the discoveries of today," their chances of success and survival would have been greater. Too often they reversed the recipe and used as leavening only a pinch of the past, concentrating

[28] Walter Lippmann's critical series on the testing fad appeared in six consecutive issues of the *New Republic:* "The Mental Age of Americans," 32 (October 25, 1922), 213–215; "The Mystery of the 'A' Men," 32 (November 1, 1922), 246–248; "The Reliability of Intelligence Tests," 32 (November 8, 1922), 275–277; "The Abuse of Tests," 32 (November 15, 1922), 297–298; "Tests of Hereditary Intelligence," 32 (November 22, 1922), 328–330; and "A Future for the Tests," 33 (November 29, 1922), 9–11. Lewis W. Terman replied to Lippmann, "The Great Confusion or The Impulse Imperious of Intelligence Testers, Psychoanalyzed and Exposed by Mr. Lippmann," *New Republic* 33 (December 27, 1922), 116–120. Lippmann, however, had the last word in this round, "The Great Confusion," *New Republic* 33 (January 3, 1923), 145–146.

[29] The rejection of external, standardized means of evaluation is implicit in Cobb's statement of his credo of progressive education, *The New Leaven, op. cit.*, pp. 17–25.

instead on an indiscriminate batter of "the discoveries of today." Those schools that followed the seventh principle's recommendations and preserved much that was viable in educational tradition, frequently were unsympathetic with the more radical announcements of the PEA.

Certainly the typical progressive educator of 1910 would have found little in the early principles of the PEA that he would unqualifiedly support. The exception would be an early child study enthusiast; the PEA's views in the twenties resembled those of G. Stanley Hall's followers more closely than any others, although there is no known contact between Hall and the Association despite the fact that he remained active in educational circles until his death in 1924, five years after the Association had been established.[30] The 1910 progressive would have looked to the Association's program in vain for attention to the child's vocational needs, his intellectual development, his cultural awareness, but he would certainly have sympathized with his 1920 successor's interest in the child and his aversion to traditional school methods. The earlier progressive might have feared, however, that *the child* was in danger of replacing *the subject* as the tyrant in the school.[31]

The Association accepted the seven principles at some time prior to 1924 and retained them until 1929, when a revised set of ten principles was published. For many educators the earlier statements were more than a published explanation of the Association's aims; they were the key beliefs of progressive education in the twenties. Certainly it was much easier to read these seven principles than to plow one's way through Dewey's *Democracy and Education.* Even William Heard Kilpatrick's *The Project Method,* widely read as it was, did not provide the simple set of guidelines offered by the PEA's seven principles.

Conventions

Although the Association spent much time and considerable effort searching for aims, money, members, and principles, these activities were soon superseded by other concerns. Beginning in 1920, the Association sponsored annual conventions, the first in Washington; in 1921, Dayton, Ohio; in 1922, Baltimore; in 1923, Chicago. With their

[30] Cobb discounted Hall's influence; but that influence was certainly present in Cobb's writing although it may have been indirect.

[31] John Dewey had warned of such a development as early as 1902 in *The Child and the Curriculum* (Chicago, 1902).

attendant local and subsequent national publicity, the conventions helped popularize the increasingly self-conscious progressive education movement in general, and the PEA in particular. Both in Baltimore and Chicago, faculty members and students in schools of education of the major universities attended the convention conferences, and the progressives, who had been little known educators and laymen, now found themselves a power and an influence in academe, especially among professors of education.

The January, 1922, bulletin of the PEA published a description of a fictitious PEA New Year's party, a gentle and amusing spoof of some of the leading members of the Association. But the piece contained one prophetic—and for these members, portentous—section, "Where are the people from Teachers College, Columbia? There are two or three here but the rest refused to come without their caps and gowns. They don't seem to understand the word 'popularize' as we use it."[32] Teachers College faculty may not have understood or been interested in "popularizing" in 1922, but by the end of the decade they did and were. By 1930, control of the PEA was in the hands of well-known professional educators at Teachers College and elsewhere, a fact that the bulletin's editor, Gertrude Stevens Ayres, and her associates, profoundly regretted.

Both the meetings of the PEA and its periodic bulletins accurately reflected the aims of the Association, although the term "progressive education" was taken more broadly than in the definitions of the early leaders. At the 1920 convention, Frank F. Bunker, Chief of the City Schools Division, Federal Bureau of Education, discussed "Reaction of the Public Schools to Progressive Education." As positive examples of such reaction, Bunker cited the establishment of ability grouping, health programs, year-round schools, and adult education.[33] Marietta Johnson followed Bunker on the program; in her address, "The School and the Child," she described children's need for greater freedom of mind, spirit, and body and decried standardization in the schools.[34] Variations in points of view of the educators, all of whom wanted more attention to the child than had previously been the case, dominated the early meetings and bulletins. Later in the 1920 convention, Frank D.

---

[32] Progressive Education Association, Bulletin No. 11 (January, 1922), p. 7.
[33] Frank F. Bunker, "Reaction of the Public Schools to Progressive Education," Progressive Education Association, Bulletin No. 2 (July, 1920), pp. 2–7.
[34] Marietta Johnson, "The School and the Child," Progressive Education Association, Bulletin No. 2 (July, 1920), pp. 7–12.

Slutz discussed "The Moraine Park School and the Progressive Movement in the Middle West." He noted that a principal feature of this Dayton, Ohio, school was student self-government, a rule that extended even to academic standards. In Moraine Park's efforts to avert the evils of standardization, traditional report cards were eliminated and replaced by cheerful evaluations of the student's progress in the "Ten Arts of Life": body building, spirit building, opinion forming, truth discovering, society serving, man conserving, comrade and mate seeking, wealth producing, thought expressing, and life refreshing.[35]

Sharing the 1920 convention dais with Slutz was another reform-minded educator, Persis K. Miller, principal of a public school located in a Baltimore slum. Speaking on "The Sunrise Zone between Public Schools and Industry," she described her school's efforts to allow for substantial vocational training of the youngsters from grade 5 on, an effort to meet a most pressing need of her students for salable skills. Miss Miller reported that half the school day was spent in class instruction, a fourth in school and community shops, and a fourth in health and recreational activities. She made it clear that the psyche of the child was not the first consideration, but rather his usefulness as a productive member of society.[36]

Such was the initial diversity of the PEA that speakers of such different educational outlooks as Bunker and Slutz, Miss Miller and Mrs. Johnson, could all comfortably be accommodated on the same program. Later on, as the Slutz-Johnson view became more modish, the PEA heard less and less about the kind of educational innovations Bunker and Miss Miller stood for. Both of them represented the thought of the prewar education reformers, and by 1920 most of the leaders of the PEA had already put considerable distance between them and their immediate predecessors in the progressive movement.

At the 1923 convention, Patty Smith Hill, then director of the department of kindergarten and first grade education at Teachers College, Columbia University, tried to give the PEA the first of many attempted syntheses of the contradictory elements in the progressive education leadership. She contended,

[35] Frank D. Slutz, "The Moraine Park School and the Progressive Movement in the Middle West," Progressive Education Association, Bulletin No. 2 July, 1920), pp. 19–28.

[36] Persis K. Miller, "The Sunrise Zone Between Public Schools and Industry," Progressive Education Association, Bulletin No. 2 (July, 1920), p. 29. Miss Miller's speech is one of the few evidences of a link between the socially conscious pre-World War I educators and the early PEA supporters.

The two movements in circulation in education today which must be brought together, if we are to get the benefits of both, are the liberating objectives set up by Dr. Dewey in the early '90's, and this present movement in psychology with its emphasis upon the scientific approach to the mechanics and techniques of school subjects. . . . From my point of view these two great movements are not irreconcilable, and if we can utilize the contribution from both, great good will come to education and to the children in our care.[37]

A look into contemporary numbers of the *New Republic* or the yearbooks of the National Society for the Study of Education shows that many responsible educators of the twenties noted the conflict of educational theories in PEA and commented on it. But the organization chose to ignore Professor Hill's mediating recommendations and resolutely determined to follow Dewey's—or what it conceived to be Deweys—"liberating objectives" and to ignore the conflicting claims of the "scientists" of education.[38]

The New Education Fellowship

Early on, the PEA had taken an interest in the new school movement in Europe.[39] Although founded independently of PEA, the New

[37] Patty Smith Hill, "Liberalizing Movements in Elementary Education During the Last Generation," Progressive Education Association, Bulletin No. 16 (1923), pp. 11, 16.

[38] Among the topics discussed in the yearbooks of the National Society for the Study of Education, an organization that investigated current educational questions, during the 1920s, were: new materials of instruction (1920), intelligence testing (1922, 1928), social studies in the elementary and secondary school (1923), education of gifted children (1920, 1924), adapting the schools to individual differences (1925), extra-curricular activities (1926), curriculum construction (1927), and preschool and parental education (1929). The *New Republic,* which also dealt with contemporary disputes in education, devoted considerable space to the intelligence testing controversy, beginning October 25, 1922; the American college and its curriculum, October 25, 1922; the American high school, November 7, 1923; a series on experimental schools (Dalton, Lincoln, Elisabeth Irwin's) February 13, February 20, and April 9, 1924; the elementary school, November 12, 1924; the learned societies, February 4, 1925; revision in college curriculum, April 14, 1926; on understanding children, May 5, 1926; adult education; February 22, 1928; and a query, "Can Education Save Democracy?" December 26, 1928.

[39] Among the valuable contemporary accounts of the new education movement in Europe are Ernest Young, *The New Era in Education* (London, 1923?); Frederick W. Roman, *The New Education in Europe* (New York,

Education Fellowship was established shortly afterward, 1921. The NEF set itself to do for all Europe (and later even other areas of the world) what the PEA dreamed of doing for America—reforming the entire school system in accordance with the standards and values of the new education.

The PEA's dream more nearly achieved fulfillment than did NEF's. Although NEF outlived the Progressive Education Association, it has never attained the national significance in any of its member countries that the PEA enjoyed in the United States in the thirties.[40] The only other nation that attempted national education reforms along "progressive" lines was the Soviet Union, where the pedagogical experiments were limited to the most radical years following the Bolshevik revolution. The Soviet Union never had a national organization of the NEF within its borders, and the Bolshevik educational reforms were much more directly linked to the work of Dewey and Kilpatrick in America. In the introduction to the American edition of his standard work on Soviet education, A. P. Pinkevitch wrote:

> The mere enumeration of the names of Hall, Dewey, Russell, Monroe, Judd, Thorndike, Kilpatrick and many others, known to every educator in our country, is a sufficient reminder of the tremendous influence which American education has exerted upon us. . . . We have found in the works of American pedagogues and pedologists a rich source

---

1923); John Adams, *Modern Developments in Educational Practice* (New York, 1922?); Carleton Washburne, *New Schools in the Old World* (New York, 1926); *Progressive Tendencies in European Education,* Bulletin No. 37, Department of Interior (Washington, D.C., 1923); Michael J. Demiashkevich, *The Activity School: New Tendencies in Educational Method in Western Europe* (New York, 1926); and Adolph Meyer, *Modern European Educators,* (New York, 1934). A later study, Kalevi S. Kajava, "The Traditional European School and Some Recent Experiments in the New Education" (unpublished Ph.D. dissertation, Columbia University, 1951), discusses four prominent European reformers: Hugo Gaudig, A. S. Neill, Ovide DeCroly, and Georg Kerschensteiner. All but the Demiashkevich study deal principally with individual educators and schools. Demiashkevich has a more general philosophical approach.
[40] Undoubtedly the greater success of progressive education in the United States than in Europe was a reflection of the differing educational traditions. The secondary modern schools in England, largely a product of the last twenty years, may be partially attributed to progressive reforms. Their success has not been striking, however. Individual schools, such as A. S. Neill's Summerhill, have gained substantial attention, but the movement never reached the proportions in Europe that it did in the United States.

of materials. Let us but recall the Dalton Plan, the project method, standard tests and measurements.[41]

The PEA's early bulletins publicized many of the NEF's activities and reprinted articles by such devotees of the European new education as Roger Cousinet.[42] Another bulletin included an article from *The New Era,* the journal published by the English section of the NEF, listing thirty distinguishing features of the new schools.[43] With the exception of a few clearly European influences (an emphasis on private boarding schools, for example) these characteristics were remarkably similar to those of such American schools as Moraine Park, Beaver Country Day, or the Lincoln School. Finally, Carleton Washburne, superintendent of schools in Winnetka, Illinois, and long an enthusiast of greater international understanding through studies of foreign educational systems, prepared an article for the PEA bulletin on "Progressive Schools in Europe."[44] This piece was based on a recent European trip, and in it Washburne described the use of individual instruction and the Dalton Plan in a number of English schools, and the emphasis on an individual rather than an institutional attitude in a Czechoslovakian orphanage. To judge by PEA's bulletins, American interest in the new education in Europe in the twenties seemed to be focused rather narrowly upon DeCroly and the application of Helen Parkhurst's Dalton Plan, an American innovation.

Thus the first five years of the Association's history were years of quest and uncertainty. By 1924 the leaders of the PEA could agree with some security that their effort to popularize progressive education had met with some success. They had a name, increasing membership

---

[41] A. P. Pinkevitch, *New Education in the Soviet Republic,* Nucia Perlmutter, trans. (New York, 1929), p. vi. Other studies of Soviet education by American observers stressed polytechnical education (a Soviet version of "learning by doing") and the Soviet educational system's integral relationship with Soviet society. See John Dewey, "Impressions of Soviet Russia: New Schools for a New Era," *New Republic* 57 (December 12, 1928), pp. 91–94; George S. Counts, "The Educational Program of Soviet Russia," *NEA Addresses and Proceedings* (Minneapolis, 1928), pp. 593–602; and George S. Counts, "Education and the Five-Year Plan of Soviet Russia," *Education and Economics,* Yearbook of the National Society for the Study of Educational Sociology (New York, 1931), pp. 39–46.

[42] Progressive Education Association, Bulletin No. 12 (1922).

[43] Progressive Education Association, Bulletin No. 10, "The New Schools," (1921).

[44] Carleton W. Washburne, "Progressive Schools in Europe," Progressive Education Association, Bulletin No. 17 (1923).

rolls, a rich benefactress, and a tentative program. The Progressive Education Association had demonstrated by its well-attended conventions that it was not just the few reformers who had initially met in Washington who were interested in these yeasty educational activities. Moreover, the PEA leaders had discovered that theirs was not simply an American interest but one with international ramifications, and they had established some contact with Europeans with similar interests in educational change. Cobb and his colleagues could justly conclude that they had made a promising beginning.

CHAPTER III

From Local to National Recognition

≫⊰⊱≪

Stanwood Cobb's optimism about the Progressive Education Association's growth during its first five years was dampened in 1924 when Gertrude Stevens Ayres left Washington, D.C., then the center of PEA's activities, to move permanently to Chicago. Mrs. Ayres had performed an essential function as volunteer secretary for the struggling organization, and her departure sharply called attention to both the Association's need of professional office assistance and its inability to pay for it. The loss of Mrs. Ayres, however, was more than compensated by the timely arrival of Queene Ferry Coonley in Washington that year. Like Mrs. Ayres, Mrs. Coonley had sponsored a private progressive school, and now she agreed to give a substantial portion of time to the work of the PEA whose principles she enthusiastically endorsed. Moreover, on Cobb's urging, Mrs. Coonley promised a grant of funds to cover the expenses of a new journal for two years.[1] This magazine became the quarterly *Progressive Education*. After donating the money for the periodical, Mrs. Coonley observed that Gertrude Hartman, who had published several articles and books on progressive education, would be an excellent choice as editor.[2] The Executive

[1] According to Cobb, Mrs. Coonley's philanthropy was made possible by her inheritance from her father of the Ferry seed fortune.
[2] Gertrude Hartman's *Home and Community Life* (New York, 1924) stressed the need to develop an education in which the ideals of liberal culture and social service would be harmonized. Miss Hartman was also interested in the international new education movement and was, with Marietta Johnson, an American delegate to the 1925 NEF conference in Heidelberg. In 1926 she was a member of a PEA committee that considered the NEF's application for cooperation with the PEA.

Committee accepted both the grant and the suggested editor. Cobb noted that the committee's ideal in establishing *Progressive Education* was to do for education what *National Geographic* had done for geography.

Evidences of Domestic Tranquility

The PEA was more successful in its sponsorship of *Progressive Education* than in any other of its early projects. The first number of the periodical appeared in April, 1924. From the beginning, the issues were attractive and imaginative in format. They were printed on good paper, with proper attention to typography, and included a number of interesting illustrations. The April–June, 1926 number, titled "Creative Expression through Art," contained a series of children's drawings and paintings reproduced both in black and white and in color.[3] This issue was later published as a separate book under the title *Creative Expression* (1932). The journal gave every outward appearance of the organ of a prosperous association, and there is no doubt that this editorial respectability was an important factor in establishing the PEA's reputation nationally.

Another significant factor in the increasing popular acceptance of the Association was the appointment of Morton Snyder in 1926 as executive secretary, PEA's first professional appointment to that post. Snyder had been on the faculty of Newark Academy, the Park School in Baltimore, and most recently the Scarborough School in Scarborough, New York. He was the Association's third choice for executive secretary, the position having been earlier offered to W. Carson Ryan, Jr., who at that time taught at Swarthmore College, and to Frank Slutz, headmaster of the Moraine Park School, Dayton, Ohio.[4] Snyder stayed with the PEA only two years, from October, 1926, to September, 1928, but during that time the Association's membership increased from 3,547 to 6,621.[5]

When he accepted the job of executive secretary, Snyder reported to the Executive Committee on the problems of the Association as he saw them. He recommended a number of promotional ideas, then recommended that the Association

[3] It was also expensive; according to Cobb, the art issue cost $10,000. Mrs. Coonley, whom Cobb estimated had a fortune of eleven million dollars before the Depression, paid the bill. Interview, October 29, 1962.

[4] Executive Board Minutes, January 8, 1926, and March 25, 1926.

[5] Executive Board Minutes, October 16, 1926.

. . . retain the seven principles and the emphasis on creative effort, the fine enthusiasm and sentiment of it all, but recognize more definitely the scientific and objective phases of educational work, the practical adaptations and the progress being made under conditions not ideal. . . . Enlarge upon the Association as an independent-public service agency in education, operating under a unified executive, with its magazine as its organ, worthy of co-operation and support.[6]

While deferring to the early leaders' zeal, Snyder had nevertheless suggested two drastic changes in the focus of the organization: to take in the scientific movement in education, and to direct attention away from private experimental schools and toward the public schools. Ultimately the Association accepted the latter recommendation entirely, but, while it certainly recognized the science-oriented work in education as an important development, it failed to effect any genuine rapprochment with the scientists. Both these results manifested themselves long after Snyder had left his executive role in the PEA. Snyder resigned in 1928 to become headmaster of the Rye Country Day School in Rye, New York. He was succeeded by one of his former colleagues at the Scarborough School who had headed the English department there, J. Milnor Dorey. Dorey remained executive secretary of the PEA until 1932.

Charles William Eliot died in 1926, thus creating a vacancy in the position of honorary president of the Association. Eliot's acceptance of this formal role and his occasional statements of support had been precious assistance to Cobb and the other early leaders. The Executive Board, which in effect governed the Association in the twenties, searched for a successor to Eliot who would be of comparable prestige, a leader who would also symbolize the interests of the PEA and the progressive education movement as the board envisioned them. The man they selected was John Dewey. In inviting him to become honorary president, they said, "More than any other person you represent the philosophic ideals for which our Association stands."[7] Dewey accepted the invitation and assumed the honorary presidency, thus cementing his most formal tie to the progressive education movement.

The impressive appearance of *Progressive Education,* the energy of the executive secretary, and Dewey's acceptance of the honorary presidency all combined to elevate the PEA's prestige and build up its prominence as a national educational organization in the middle and late 1920's. One result of this increased significance was that other

[6] Executive Board Minutes, October 1, 1926.
[7] Executive Board Minutes, April 30, 1927.

educational organizations sought out the PEA and invited it to participate in their activities. One group's recognition of the PEA stimulated the awareness of another; the spiral was set in motion and the Association found itself the object of growing national attention.

Since both the New Education Fellowship abroad and the PEA at home were struggling neophytes sharing a number of pedagogical interests, it is not surprising that the two groups frequently considered a merger. By 1924 the PEA was urging Mrs. Beatrice Ensor, Cobb's opposite number with the NEF in England, to speak at the PEA's next convention.[8] A few months later the PEA Executive Committee suggested that "Miss Hartman and Mrs. Marietta Johnson, who are to be at the Heidelberg Conference [of the NEF] this year, can do missionary work toward the end of bringing an international conference here in 1926."[9] Although the group was unable to arrange such a conference, it did succeed in bringing to the United States Mrs. Ensor, who spoke to the 1926 annual convention in Boston on "Release of the Creative Energy of the Child."

Mrs. Ensor also spoke informally to the PEA leaders in 1926, urging an affiliation between the NEF and the PEA. Union of the two groups had been suggested to Gertrude Hartman when she attended the 1925 conference in Heidelberg. The PEA had then declined, ostensibly because it believed that the NEF sponsored only one plan of education while the PEA was (so it thought) more eclectic in its interests and pluralist in approach.

Probably the most important factor preventing the merger between the PEA and NEF was the animosity Cobb felt toward Mrs. Ensor. Thirty-five years after Mrs. Ensor's visit to these shores, Cobb still spoke heatedly about her. "Mrs. Ensor," he said, "was ambitious to have the whole world under her banner. Why should we be swallowed up?"[10] Cobb referred to her undependability and to her socialistic views, stating that they were primarily responsible for his antipathy toward her. He admitted that others, particularly Harold Rugg, had urged a merger because they believed PEA's membership in an international organization would help the Association gain the foundation grants it sought.

Both the German and French sections of the NEF were in serious financial straits and wanted assistance from the PEA, and undoubtedly this circumstance also discouraged a possible merger at that time. In

[8] Executive Committee Minutes, October 16, 1924.
[9] Executive Board Minutes, April 23–25, 1925.
[10] Cobb, Interview, October 29, 1962.

any event, as a result of Mrs. Ensor's 1926 discussion, a committee of three—Francis M. Froelicher, Lucia Burton Morse, and Gertrude Hartman, all active members of the PEA's Executive Board—was appointed to look into ways of cooperating, but not affiliating, with the NEF. The major effect of the new arrangement seems to have been that at the request of NEF, the PEA sent representatives to various international conferences and, in particular, to the NEF's conferences at Locarno, Italy, in 1927 and at Elsinore, Denmark, in 1929.

In January, 1929, again at the insistence of the NEF, the PEA Executive Board reconsidered its relationship with NEF, but the Committee concluded it was "not a wise policy" to affiliate with the European organization.[11] Later in 1929 the NEF again proposed a closer tie with the PEA. W. Carson Ryan, Jr., and Harold Rugg, who with over 200 other Americans had attended the 1929 NEF conference at Elsinore, reported to the PEA that the Americans at the conference favored a closer tie with the NEF and believed the PEA was the most logical organization to make this connection. The Executive Board was still not enthusiastic, and throughout the fall the special committee on the NEF met regularly in an attempt to reach some agreement. A principal problem was financial; the NEF wanted to use PEA office facilities and the PEA thought this would involve an unwarranted outlay of PEA funds.

In its earliest years the PEA had included in its publications a substantial amount of news about educational experiments in Europe, but as the PEA itself became better known nationally, its interest in international educational affairs diminished. The "Foreign Notes" section of *Progressive Education,* which appeared regularly in 1924, 1925, and 1926, was dropped in the late twenties. Between 1921 and 1923 three of the eight bulletins published by the PEA dealt with European educational experiments, and two of the first three issues of *Progressive Education* contained a number of articles on European schools. After 1925 there were only occasional articles on foreign education. From the mid-twenties until the forties, it was always the NEF who took the initiative in activities with the PEA, although some individual PEA members, such as Carleton Washburne, Harold Rugg, and W. Carson Ryan, Jr., were active in both organizations.[12]

The NEF was not the only organization that had become interested in the PEA by the mid-twenties. The American Association of Univer-

[11] Executive Board Minutes, January 18, 1929.
[12] Interestingly enough, when the PEA lost national stature during and after the war years, its relationship with the NEF became a closer one.

sity Women agreed to cooperate with the PEA in sponsoring Mrs. Ensor's lecture tour of the United States in 1926.[13] The PEA reported with pride that "hundreds of representatives of leading progressive schools, colleges, and other institutions" had invited them to hold their annual convention in New York in 1928.[14] Although PEA may have overstated this cordiality, the genuine interest behind it was in marked contrast to the reserve the Association met a few years before when it was hunting for a congenial location for a convention. Other educational groups began to invite the PEA to set up exhibits and to send representatives to their conferences. The PEA accepted a number of these offers, including that of the Philadelphia Sesquicentennial Exhibition in 1926.[15]

In 1929 the New York Society for the Experimental Study of Education began to petition the PEA to establish a closer mutual relationship. The Society suggested a merger, and when that idea obviously failed to engage the PEA Executive Board, the Society suggested that it might "affiliate" with the New York branch of the PEA.[16] The Society included among its members most of the outspoken advocates of progressivism in the New York area, including Caroline Pratt, Lucy Sprague Mitchell, Harriet Johnson, Margaret Naumburg, and Elisabeth Irwin. Although these women represented various shades on the spectrum of progressivism, they all agreed that the child and his needs should form the basis of the curriculum. For this reason they naturally turned to the PEA, dominated as it was in the twenties by its child-centered ideology.

The schools represented by the New York Society for the Experimental Study of Education were the ones around which much of the mythology of progressive education had already developed. Certainly, as contemporary lampoons made out, the pedagogical approach of these schools was unorthodox. But some of the secondary assumptions

[13] Executive Board Minutes, January 8, 1926.
[14] Executive Board Minutes, March 19, 1927.
[15] Executive Board Minutes, June 30, 1926. The Association had developed in 1926 an interesting rationale to decide whether to cooperate with other associations: "There was some discussion as to how far this Association should work with committees in other Associations, for the demand was becoming large now that the Association is somewhat popular. The sense of the meeting was that as far as the Association could help to leaven the public school work—which was the ultimate goal of progressive ideas—there should be representation on committees." Executive Board Minutes, May 29, 1926.
[16] Executive Board Minutes, September 21, 1929.

made by the critical wits were not accurate. It was not true, for instance, that the Freud-oriented schools were all to be found in Greenwich Village. The most Freudian of these havens for the young, Margaret Naumburg's Walden, was located in the (then) dignified upper West Side of New York City. Although most of the schools were private, one of them, Elisabeth Irwin's Little Red School House, had been established as a public school, and Miss Irwin was crushed when the city withdrew its support and the experiments had to be continued under private auspices.[17]

In any event, the Society's proposal to affiliate with the PEA New York City branch was either tabled or rejected informally, for the Society of the Experimental Study of Education continued as an independent organization for several years. Perhaps the PEA's Executive Board, aware of its own state of transition in 1929, was unwilling to accept any ties with other organizations that might limit the development of the Association.

Problems of the Association, 1924–1930

The Problem of Doctrine   Even though the PEA was beginning to flourish in the middle twenties, all was not peaceful within the organization. Three major problems, all of them interrelated, kept

[17] By far the most comprehensive contemporary accounts of these schools are Agnes DeLima's wholly uncritical *Our Enemy, the Child* (New York, 1926) and Harold Rugg and Ann Shumaker, *The Child-Centered School* (Yonkers-on-Hudson, 1928). Neither is very analytical. Lloyd Marcus discusses the founding of nine early leading progressive schools (Park School, Baltimore; City and Country School; Walden School; Shady Hill School; Oak Lane Country Day School; Moraine Park School; Lincoln School; Chevy Chase Country Day School; Beaver Country Day School) in a senior honors thesis, "The Founding of American Private Progressive Schools, 1912-1921," Harvard University, Cambridge, 1948. Individual experiments are discussed by their sponsors, such as Lucy Sprague Mitchell in *Two Lives* (New York, 1953) and Caroline Pratt, *I Learn from Children* (New York, 1948). Agnes DeLima described Elisabeth Irwin's experiment in *The Little Red School House* (New York, 1942). Robert Beck evaluates the City and Country School and the Walden School in an excellent dissertation, "American Progressive Education, 1875–1930," unpublished Ph.D. dissertation, Yale University, 1942. Beck subsequently published three articles based on the dissertation, "Progressive Education and American Progressivism," *Teachers College Record* 60 (1958–1959), pp. 77–89, 129–137, 198–208. The best summary is in Lawrence A. Cremin, *The Transformation of the School* (New York, 1961), pp. 202–215.

recurring: doctrine, money, and control. Of these difficulties the most crucial, at least from the point of view of understanding the Association, was that of doctrine. Although the early leaders of the PEA had steadfastly opposed a commitment to any philosophy other than a comprehensive and amorphous "progressivism" they had, in fact, become advocates of a single, rather narrow, theory. *Progressive Education,* the annual conventions, and the schools the leaders represented all made it quite plain that the PEA leadership endorsed the educational panacea known as "the child-centered school."

The most distinctive feature of a "child-centered school" was that the child—and not the traditional subject matter and values—supposedly determined the curriculum. Obviously, there was tremendous variation among the "child-centered schools" in the degree to which the child dictated the material of instruction. (Typically the child in these schools came from an upper middle class background and was likely to be bright.) In some schools, such as the Walden School in New York City, the children's expressed interest decided the topics of discussion; in others, such as the Lincoln School of Teachers College, teachers—sometimes in consultation with pupils—drew up a new curriculum based upon topics they believed would generally be found interesting and valuable to children. But the fundamental assumptions common to all these schools were that the schoolwork should be "meaningful" to the pupils and that, contrary to what was understood as traditional doctrine, subjects should not be taught solely on the basis of their intrinsic merit.

It is easier to identify what these enthusiasts of the new education disapproved than what they approved of. Typically, they opposed fixed arrangements and preferred flexible ones. They revolted against fixed grades in the schools, fixed rules for the children, and fixed furniture in the classrooms. They advocated instruction that was individual or in small groups. They favored programs stressing physical activity and often actual exposure to the elements. They objected categorically to all standards except their own rule of freedom and creativity. At first these enlightened views were most characteristic of the teachers at the elementary school level, but they became increasingly common among secondary school instructors.[18]   Later, colleges, particularly Sarah

[18] The two best discussions of these issues are in DeLima, *Our Enemy, the Child, op. cit.,* and Rugg and Shumaker, *The Child-Centered School, op. cit.;* but both books are essentially descriptions of practices in "progressive schools" and fail to evaluate seriously the new movement, although the Rugg and Shumaker book makes a brief attempt in Chapter XXIII, "In Critical Respect." The articles published in *Progressive Education* during

Lawrence, Bennington, and Antioch, endorsed the ideology of unfettered student-centered mobility.[19]

No one doubted that freedom and creativity were valuable. The emphasis that should be placed on these two liberating forces, however, remained a matter of question. Uncertainty concerning the degree of emphasis did not become a major source of trouble to the policy-makers of the PEA until the late twenties. For the most part, this was for the PEA a rare period of near unanimity, but the very success born of the PEA's publicizing and popularizing of "child-centeredism" opened the door to the period of divisiveness in which the Association soon found itself. The "child-centered" view was by no means the only one then current in American educational circles.[20] But the attention the PEA received as a result of its promulgation of the child-centered doctrine led others to join the organization even though their pedagogical interests were somewhat different from those of the PEA's early leaders.

PEA's exaltation of child-centeredness, freedom, and creativity became nationally known via the medium of its periodical *Progressive Education.* Until 1929 each issue of the magazine was devoted to a single topic, and three of these twelve early issues dealt directly with so-called creative activities: "Creative Expression Through Art," "Creative Expression Through Music," and "The Environment for Creative Education." Other issues announced the ideal of freedom for the child: "Individual Instruction," "The Project Method," "The New Child Study," "Progressive Parents," and "The Spirit and Practice of the New Education." The April, 1925, issue was originally scheduled to be devoted to "The Public Schools" but instead reverted to more familiar themes and included some articles stressing the need for greater international understanding.[21]

PEA conferences further illustrated the group's fascination with

---

the twenties furnish another excellent guide to current attitudes toward progressive education. Cremin makes a thoughtful assessment in *The Transformation of the School, op. cit.,* particularly Chapter VI. Beck's dissertation and articles are also helpful.

[19] See Louis T. Benezet, *General Education in the Progressive College* (New York, 1943).

[20] A survey of the topics discussed by the National Society for the Study of Education in the twenties illustrates by contrast the narrowness of the PEA. The NSSE's chief interests then were revisions of the materials used in the traditional subject matter areas, intelligence tests, and gifted children.

[21] Executive Committee Minutes, October 16, 1924.

freedom and creative activity. A high spot of the 1925 convention was the debate between Carleton Washburne, Superintendent of the Winnetka, Illinois, Public Schools, and Flora J. Cooke, Washburne's former teacher at the Francis W. Parker School in Chicago. Washburne plumped for the training of the individual as the primary task of the school, while Miss Cooke countered that the development of social groups should be the fundamental emphasis of the schools.[22]

In 1926 the Executive Committee for the first (and only) time in the twenties selected a theme for an entire convention. Cobb presented the Program Committee's report, and, after discussion, the Executive Committee chose "Creative Opportunity for the Child, the Basis of the True Education" as the convention's key topic. Other possibilities were considered, but these were no more than rephrasings of the same theme —"The Necessity for Creative Opportunity for the Child," "The Child's Need for Creative Opportunity," "How Shall We Provide Creative Opportunity for the Child," and "Provision for Creative Opportunity for the Child." [23]

The limits within which some PEA leaders interpreted their commitment to "freedom" and "creative activity" in the mid-twenties was revealed at an Executive Committee meeting in October, 1924. While the group discussed plans for the 1925 convention to be held in Philadelphia, Francis Mitchell Froelicher, president of the PEA from 1925 to 1927, noted fourteen schools in the Philadelphia area that were interested in progressive education. Having cited all fourteen, he added, "Tower Hill School was perhaps nearest to our type." [24] Burton P. Fowler, president of the PEA from 1930 to 1932, was then headmaster of the Tower Hill School. Typical of Fowler's pedagogic approach was his statement in 1936 to a group of teachers that school marks and competitive examinations should be abolished: "They make children feel inferior or superior, encourage dishonesty, give a feeling of insecurity, dull the edge of intellectual curiosity, make children course-passers instead of learners, and provide in general unworthy

[22] Executive Committee Minutes, November 8, 1924.
[23] Executive Board Minutes, January 8, 1926.
[24] Executive Committee Minutes, October 16, 1924. The fourteen schools Froelicher noted were Shady Hill School, Montgomery Country Day School, Germantown Friends School, William Penn Charter, Phebe Anne Thorne School, Haverford School, Oak Lane Country Day School, Carson College for Orphan Girls, Friends Select School, Tower Hill School, Park School, Trade School for Girls, Sunnyside Nursery School, and Southern High School.

motives for hard work." [25] Today even conservative educators would agree that Fowler had a point there; the limitations show up only in the narrow conclusions progressives like Fowler drew from true premises.

In any case by the fall of 1928 the term "creative activity," if not the idea itself, was beginning to jar some of the PEA leaders. When the Executive Committee discussed plans for the 1929 conference to be held in St. Louis, the Secretary reported, "The topic 'Creative Activity' was commented on. Desire was expressed to get away from the word 'Creative' and to substitute another term for 'Activity.' Those present were requested to suggest other titles for final decision at the next meeting." [26] The report of the next meeting contained no reference to "creative activity," although there was much discussion of the coming convention, which was being arranged by Wilford M. Aikin, who in 1932 had become chairman of the PEA's Commission on the Relation of School and College. It was this group that conducted the "Eight-Year Study."

Although "freedom" and "creative activity" were close to the Association's heart, minority views were expressed. Of these Eugene Randolph Smith's was perhaps the best example. While he did not downgrade the interests of the child, Smith constantly insisted upon the need for some kind of standardized evaluation of what the schools were doing and what the children were learning. In 1928 at the PEA convention in Boston, Smith was one of a panel of three, all of whom supported in varying degrees the use of tests in the progressive schools.[27] Smith and his colleagues agreed with Patty Smith Hill that the two movements for freedom and for science in education were not irreconcilable, but this tolerant dualism was not a common attitude

---

[25] Fowler's statement was made at the annual Junior High School Conference at New York University in 1936 and quoted in his obituary in *The New York Times*, November 18, 1963.

[26] Executive Board Minutes, October 20, 1928.

[27] The views were presented in a symposium of which Eugene Randolph Smith was the leader, "The Use of Tests and Measurements in the Three R's," *Progressive Education* 5 (April–June, 1928), pp. 136–152. Other contributors to the symposium were Virginia E. Stone, Community School, St. Louis; Rebecca J. Coffin, Lincoln School, Teachers College, Columbia University, New York; Wilford M. Aikin, John Burroughs School, Clayton, Missouri; Howard E. A. Jones, North Shore Country Day School, Evanston, Illinois; Flora J. Cooke, Francis W. Parker School, Chicago; and Helen Erickson, Sunset Hill School, Kansas City, Missouri.

among the early leaders. The PEA rarely attacked the scientific movement in education; it merely ignored it.

John Dewey's speech, "Progressive Education and the Science of Education," at the 1928 conference of the PEA foreshadowed the doctrinal disputes of the Association. Dewey had just accepted the honorary presidency of the Association and thus spoke to the convention as a philosopher with a worldwide reputation and as the leader, however formal and remote, of the Association itself. Dewey did not view the "science of education" mechanistically, as Thorndike did; rather, he considered the science of education to be synonymous with "philosophy of education," and he held that both these terms described the theoretical, intellectual rationale for education. It was specifically this dimension of education in which Dewey believed the PEA and the progressive schools were most lacking.

* Dewey noted the elements common to the progressive schools: an emphasis on individuality and increased freedom, an inclination to build upon the nature and experience of the students, an atmosphere of informality, a preference for activity as distinct from passivity, and an unusual attention to human factors. Having discussed these characteristics, Dewey added, "Now I wonder whether this earlier and more negative phase of progressive education has not upon the whole run its course, and whether the time has not arrived in which these schools are undertaking a more constructive organized function." [28] Dewey then urged that the schools attempt to organize subject matter along intellectual lines and to study conditions favorable to learning.

Educators of diverse philosophical persuasions found much of interest in Dewey's speech. By stressing the importance of the *quality* of activity for teachers, Dewey effectively criticized the supporters of Thorndike's maxim that all that exists exists in quantity and can be measured. By calling for more attention to the overall intellectual program of the school, he stimulated the curriculum reformers of the thirties. By noting the schools' potential to effect social change, he awakened his listeners to ideas that George S. Counts and others developed more extensively during the years of the Depression.

Some months after Dewey's speech, the PEA selected a committee to revise the Association's Seven Principles of Progressive Education, emblazoned on every copy of *Progressive Education* from the first in 1924 to the April–June, 1929, issue. The decision to tinker with the principles so soon after Dewey's speech may have been coincidental,

[28] John Dewey, "Progressive Education and the Science of Education," *Progressive Education* 5 (July–September, 1928), p. 201.

but the most significant additions to the principles were the very ones discussed by Dewey in his speech.

Although the committee reworded nearly every "principle," the intent of the original seven remained fundamentally intact. The three additions were:

Social Development and Discipline
Group consciousness is developed in children through participation in the school as a community. Discipline should be a matter of self-mastery rather than external compulsion, and character development the result of social experience, and of the recognition of spiritual forces and resources underlying all nature, life and conduct. A co-educational student body, and a faculty of both men and women, constitute a normal life situation for character and development.

Beauty of Environment
The school should furnish an environment that is simple, natural, and beautiful.

The Curriculum
The curriculum should be based on the nature and needs of childhood and youth, with the ideas of acquiring knowledge as far as possible through the scientific method of firsthand observation, investigation, experiment and independent search for material. Through these activities the world of books and abstract ideas is entered. The School should increasingly widen the circle of the child's world, leading him not only to appreciation of national ideas, but also to a realization of the interdependence of peoples, and international good will.[29]

The section on social development and discipline deals with the conditions under which learning should take place, the second of Dewey's major points, although the rewriters failed to express the need of fundamental inquiry necessary to achieve ideal learning conditions. Lucia Burton Morse, chairman of the committee that revised the Seven Principles, had been an associate of Flora J. Cooke in Chicago. Miss Cooke had long advocated the importance of socialization and social groups in education, and this statement may be Miss Morse's attempt at a synthesis of Dewey's and Miss Cooke's positions.

It is likely that the statement on the curriculum was inspired by Dewey's remarks, although the Association's statement on this topic was more specific than anything in the honorary president's speech. The third addition to the PEA's principles, Beauty of Environment,

[29] The revised "principles" appeared first in the April, 1929, issue of *Progressive Education*. They were discarded in the spring of 1930.

was undoubtedly one that Dewey supported although he did not discuss it in his 1928 speech. For years Dewey had campaigned for the aesthetic as a pervasive character of environment rather than an isolated ingredient compartmentalized as "art."

One significant difference between the earlier statement and the revision is that the term "progressive education" appeared six times in the 1924 manifesto but only once and that only in the title of the 1929 statement. Although the phrase "progressive education" went out of fashion long before the death of the Association, it is not unlikely that the PEA leaders as early as 1929 were beginning to veer away from that phrase, just as they were already avoiding "creative activity." Such an omission from the revised principles could not have been merely accidental.

The Problem of Money   The PEA's efforts to achieve doctrinal harmony were persistent, but being practical men, not primarily theoreticians, the leaders recognized as more pressing the need for adequate financial support. Agreement on aims of the Association could wait, but bills could not be postponed indefinitely. The several patrons whose contributions had supported the PEA in the early years had by 1924 dwindled to only one, Queene Ferry Coonley. Although she was very generous, she could not assume full responsibility for PEA's expenses. Mrs. Coonley's original promise had been to underwrite the cost of *Progressive Education* for the two years, 1924 to 1926. The Association estimated that the magazine's deficit for 1924 alone was $10,000.[30] Mrs. Coonley was in a good spot from which to observe the state of PEA's finances, for she was treasurer of the Association from 1924 to 1930. As treasurer she made other occasional contributions to the Association. Her largest single gift was one of $5,000, made in December, 1926, to cover a debt of $2,469.50 accrued during that year and to assist the Association's activities during the following year.[31]

Liberal as Mrs. Coonley was with both her money and her services, the Association realized that if it were to prosper, it must devise a more permanent means of financial support. At one of the Executive Board meetings during his term as president of the Association, Francis M. Froelicher "made it plain that the Association should be put on its feet and that people should not be asked to continue to give." [32] Apparently the other members of the Executive Board agreed with him, and the Association sought alternative means of support. Four principal sug-

[30] Executive Board Minutes, April 23, 1925.
[31] Executive Board Minutes, December 31, 1926.
[32] Executive Board Minutes, January 8, 1926.

gestions were made: to conduct a fund-raising drive, to ask progressive schools for regular contributions, to increase the membership, and to solicit aid from foundations.

At its April 4, 1925, meeting, the Executive Committee decided upon a fund-raising campaign. At the time the leaders hoped to gather in $10,000, a sum they estimated would cover the annual deficit of the magazine. Because of *Progressive Education*'s handsome format, small circulation, and few advertisers, the printing cost in 1925 was forty-five cents more per copy than the subscription price. The magazine was the single greatest expense of the Association in the twenties. By 1925 the leaders realized that if the Association wanted to continue and publish the journal, some major source of income must be found by January 1, 1926, when Mrs. Coonley's subsidy of the magazine expired. The fund-raising campaign, then, was to be a short-term solution to the problem. The original goal of $10,000 was increased to $15,000 in May, 1925, when the Executive Board decided to seek a field secretary. Employment of this officer, the leaders believed, would prove valuable in publicizing the activities of the Association and of the progressive education movement.

The original plan to have the Executive Committee administer the campaign proved faulty, and in January, 1926, Francis M. Froelicher, then of the Oak Lane Country Day School, Philadelphia, agreed to become chairman of the Special Fund Committee because "all others had refused." [33] Specific amounts and local chairmen were assigned to various areas where there was believed to be favorable sentiment toward the PEA and the progressive education movement. Although few cities actually met their quotas, Boston, in place of the $1,000 that had been its goal, donated the entire cost of the 1926 convention— $2,543.32.[34] By the end of 1926 nearly $10,000 had been raised.[35] Although this sum was only two-thirds of the amount that had been hoped for, the Association's financial future looked brighter than at any previous time.

The second major source of funds in the mid-twenties was the progressive schools themselves. Although the Association continued to forbid any kind of institutional memberships, it did feel free to ask the

[33] *Loc. cit.*

[34] Executive Board Minutes, November 20, 1926.

[35] A total of $9,817.32 had been found by November 20, 1926, *Ibid.* A May 29, 1926, report revealed that Washington, D.C., Illinois, and Pennsylvania had most nearly reached the financial goals assigned them. In view of the PEA's headquarters in Washington and the concentration of friends in both Chicago and Philadelphia, the success in these areas is not surprising.

schools for money. PEA leaders thought it only reasonable that the schools should help support the Association with annual contributions since it was working specifically "for the increase of the progressive-school idea."[36] By May, 1926, Froelicher, who by that time was president of the Association, was able to report that many schools had approved the idea of contributing something regularly to the Association.[37]

The leaders of the PEA recognized that the Special Fund and even the contributions of the progressive schools were not permanent solutions to their financial predicament, helpful as these measures were at the moment. To reduce the magazine's deficit, more members and therefore more subscribers were needed. The Association always wanted to increase its membership, not merely to improve its financial status but also to achieve its higher goal of reforming American education. PEA's actual membership rose steadily after 1924. With about 2,000 members in that year, the Association gained approximately 500 new members in each of the next two years. After the appointment of the executive secretary in 1926, the membership increased by over a thousand in each of the next three years, for a total in excess of 6,000 in 1929. In that year the income from membership fees and subscriptions was more than $1,000 above what had been anticipated in the budget.[38]

In the mid-twenties the Executive Committee had considered the step of seeking a grant from an educational foundation, but rejected it for fear this would "limit the spontaneity" of the Association.[39] A year later, however, the Board had overcome its scruples and agreed that "a definite sum guaranteed by a foundation seems the only practical assistance for a time."[40] Various members of the Executive Board began to visit foundations that supported educational experiments or organizations. President Froelicher visited Otis Caldwell, director of the Lincoln School at Teachers College and a former vice-president of the PEA, but Caldwell told him that there was no possibility of aid from the General Education Board, which had financed much of the experimental work at the Lincoln School.[41] Undismayed by Caldwell's

[36] Executive Board Minutes, November 21, 1925.
[37] Executive Board Minutes, May 29, 1926.
[38] Executive Board Minutes, March 16, 1929.
[39] Executive Committee Minutes, April 4, 1925.
[40] Executive Board Minutes, June 19, 1926.
[41] Caldwell himself gave the Association $50 and told them they would do well to reverse the present emphasis of *Progressive Education* and stress content over appearance. Executive Board Minutes, October 24, 1925.

discouragement, the Board looked to other foundations. Approaches were made to the Commonwealth Fund and to the Carnegie Corporation. In September, 1928, after the Laura Spelman Rockefeller Fund had been absorbed by the Rockefeller Foundation and some of its projects assumed by the General Education Board, Stanwood Cobb wrote to see if under the new arrangement the organization might aid the Association. At that time the Rockefeller Foundation, while manifesting some interest in the PEA's exertions, declared itself unwilling to take on any new project.[42]

In 1929, when the PEA actively sought foundation money, it was able to point to a degree of affluence unknown in its past. At each monthly meeting of the Executive Board the financial reports were a little more glowing. Responsible for the improved status were the increase in number of members, success of the annual convention in St. Louis, and the contribution of the regional conferences. For the first time in its history, the PEA ended the year with a balanced budget; there was even a net surplus of $1,302.29.[43]

Lois Hayden Meek, Harold Rugg, and others who visited the foundations in 1929 seeking funds for the PEA had another bargaining advantage besides the apparent financial stability of the Association. These later leaders had little of the academic naiveté characteristic of their predecessors in the PEA. Their obvious intelligence and greater sophistication undoubtedly instilled some confidence in the PEA among the foundation directors. This taught the PEA that the foundations were generally more willing to part with their funds for specific and carefully defined educational experiments and projects than they were for general purposes like the operating expenses of a struggling organization. Consequently, in the later appeals for Rockefeller money Dr. Meek asked specifically for funds "to investigate the extent of growth of progressive education in the public schools." [44] The Foundation was apparently interested in a survey of this kind and encouraged the PEA to prepare an outline for such a project. The Carnegie Corporation also indicated to Burton P. Fowler (who became president of the PEA

---

[42] The Association's records are not altogether clear about the sources from which they sought money. The Rockefeller Foundation never made a grant to the PEA, but the General Education Board, which was totally supported by funds from the Rockefeller family, did give the PEA and its Commissions a total of $1,622,000 chiefly in the thirties, according to Raymond B. Fosdick in his history of the GEB, *Adventure in Giving* (New York, 1962), p. 248.

[43] Executive Board Minutes, January 18, 1930.

[44] Executive Board Minutes, September 21, 1929.

in 1930) and to Harold Rugg a tentative willingness to sponsor such a study. Thus, the financial future of the PEA in 1929 seemed quite bright.

The Problem of Control   If questions of doctrine and money were temporarily resolved in 1929, the problem of control of the organization was not. Before 1929 representatives of small, private, progressive schools set the course of the PEA. These schools served chiefly the upper and upper middle socioeconomic classes. Every president of the PEA from 1920 to 1932 was at the time of his election the headmaster of a private school: Arthur E. Morgan, Moraine Park School, Dayton, Ohio; Eugene Randolph Smith, Beaver Country Day School, Boston; Francis M. Froelicher, Oak Lane Country Day School, Philadelphia; Stanwood Cobb, Chevy Chase Country Day School, Chevy Chase, Maryland; and Burton P. Fowler, Tower Hill School, Wilmington, Delaware. The membership of the Executive Committee was also a roll call of private, progressive schools. But after Fowler, not another headmaster was elected president of the Association. In later years most of the presidents were either professors of education or superintendents of public school systems.

Both the executive secretaries chosen in the twenties, Morton Snyder and J. Milnor Dorey, came from the Scarborough School, Scarborough-on-Hudson, New York, a private institution founded on the Montessori method. Frederick Redefer, who succeeded Dorey as executive secretary in 1932, had taught at Oak Lane Country Day School, but he had a tour of duty as Superintendent of Schools in Glencoe, Illinois, before joining the PEA staff. After leaving the PEA, Redefer took a doctorate at Teachers College and became a professor of education at New York University.

The Executive Board also reflected the shift from private-school men to public-school men and professors of education. In 1929 Harold Rugg, a perennial member of the avant garde of the progressive education movement, began to attend regular meetings of the governing body of the Association.[45] The officers who sought foundation grants for the

[45] Rugg was a key figure in the progressive education movement and the PEA. He joined the faculty of Teachers College, Columbia University, in the year of the PEA's founding. Coming as a statistician, Rugg quickly shifted his interests from the science of education to the new curriculum and worked on efforts to integrate the social studies. With Ann Shumaker he published *The Child-Centered School* in 1928, and that volume became a standard source for the new experiments in education. By the early thirties Rugg began to take an active interest in the international new education movement and became an American representative to the

PEA at the close of the twenties were not the early enthusiasts who had feverishly sparked the first PEA meetings. Stanwood Cobb was widely regarded as the founder of the PEA. When asked about the changes in the late twenties, he lamented, "The Association was an enthusiastic well-coordinated working organization during the first decade, but then something happened." When asked what happened, Cobb replied, "Well, *they* took it away from us." Cobb identified "they" as the group from Teachers College. This was an ironic turnabout of the events described in the PEA bulletin's spoof of 1922. The group PEA had facetiously invited to its New Year's Party had now arrived en masse and, Cobb claimed, had displaced the hosts.[46]

To a large extent Cobb was right. But if the organization were to succeed, some transfer of power was inevitable. The Progressive Education Association had almost unwittingly stumbled across a soon-to-be-dominant new idea in American education at a most propitious moment when not just a handful of experimenters, but a large segment of the nation, was willing to try the new approach to education. The

---

NEF. Also in the thirties he, along with many of his colleagues in the Department of Social and Philosophical Foundations of Education at Teachers College, became interested in the school's role in the social order. In the early forties he edited *Frontiers of Democracy,* the successor to *The Social Frontier,* and presided over its final issue in 1943.

[46] Cobb's remarks are quoted in Lawrence A. Cremin, "What Was Progressive Education?" *Vital Speeches* 25 (September 15, 1959), p. 723. Undoubtedly part of Cobb's view, which he expressed to Cremin in 1959 and to me in an interview in 1962, is based not on an objective analysis of elected leaders of the Association but rather on the informal power structure. The two events that thrust the PEA into national prominence in the early thirties, the acquisition of foundation support for research activities and the speech and subsequent pamphlet urging the schools to take a more active role in the social order, were the result of Teachers College faculty leadership. Lois Hayden Meek and Harold Rugg were largely responsible for securing the grants and George S. Counts made the speech and was chairman of the committee that wrote the pamphlet, *A Call to the Teachers of the Nation* (New York, 1933). Further evidences of the shift in leadership and interests of the Association around 1930 were Harold Rugg's selection in 1929 as a member of the Executive Board; Cobb's retirement as president in 1929; Burton P. Fowler's recognition in 1932 that progressive education had entered a "second phase"; the revision of the Association's principles in 1929 to include some of Dewey's views expressed in his 1928 speech to the Association, his first address as honorary president; and Frederick L. Redefer's observation that as the decade (of the twenties) ended, progressive education was in a transitional phase (Frederick L. Redefer, "Between Two Wars: An Interpretation of Progressive Education in the United States of America," unpublished, undated manuscript at Teachers College Library, Columbia University, p. 214).

Association had assured its early success by its selection of a name that later was adopted by the movement as a whole. Such power as the PEA had thus achieved could not be left in permanent trust to little known enthusiasts like Cobb, Mrs. Coonley, and Mrs. Ayres. A few of the early guardians of the PEA, such as Eugene Randolph Smith, grew in national prominence with the organization, but most of the later leaders of the Association came to it after already having established themselves elsewhere in the educational hierarchy. In this way the PEA, though still small in size, had by 1929 become a significant "power group" in American education.[47]

The PEA was a sharp focal center of activity within the larger context of that comprehensive nationwide development we call the progressive education movement. It is no accident that political historians writing of the 1920's fail to include a discussion of the progressive education movement, for in the decade following World War I educational reform was nearly totally divorced from the political life of the nation.[48] But students of social and intellectual history cannot ignore the progressive education movement if they are interested in the cultural import of the 1920's in America. True, the movement in which PEA played so notable a part became increasingly parochial. This was due in large part to the emergence of a new "professional" group, complete with its own degrees, M.Ed. and Ed.D, who pushed and publicized the new educational ideas. But in the twenties, at least, American intellectuals thought they had a real stake in the new educational reforms. Commentators on the American scene like Malcolm Cowley and Frederick Lewis Allen have noted the interest of intellectuals in progressive education. To them, "progressive education" was the full variety of educational innovations advocated by the PEA,

[47] Fosdick, in recounting the GEB's grant to the PEA, described the Association thus: "Another of the so-called 'power groups' of professional educators was the Progressive Education Association, an organization which for many years had been working in the field of educational theory and practice and had given vitality to many educational movements." Fosdick, *Adventure in Giving, op. cit.*, p. 248.

[48] An example of the manner in which the progressive education movement has been ignored is Arthur T. Link's otherwise excellent article, "What Happened to the Progressive Movement in the 1920's?" *American Historical Review* 44 (July, 1959), pp. 833–851. Link notes certain continuities between the progressives of pre-World War I and the New Dealers of the thirties, particularly with regard to the farm bills, but omits any discussion of links between the reforms in education between 1915 and 1930.

although the PEA itself was unknown to them. Cowley cites the ideals of self-expression, psychological adjustment, and salvation by the child as three essentials of the Greenwich Village credo.[49] Allen observed that, while American intellectuals of the twenties were distrustful of all reformers, they so feared the effects of regimentation upon themselves that they accepted the variety of progressive education then dominant —the cult of creativity and freedom for the child—as an article of faith.[50]

Many of the best-known champions of "child-centered" education, such as Margaret Naumburg, Lucy Sprague Mitchell, and Harold Rugg, were also active participants in the broader intellectual life of the nation. Miss Naumburg, who founded the Walden School, had an interest in James Oppenheim's little review *The Seven Arts* through her husband Waldo Frank who was co-editor. Mrs. Mitchell, who worked with Caroline Pratt at her City and Country School and who independently established the Bureau of Educational Experiments, had important contacts in economic and business research through her husband Wesley Clair Mitchell, professor of economics at Columbia. Harold Rugg, professor of education at Teachers College and co-author of *The Child-Centered School,* had a brief but intense relationship with *The Seven Arts* review. Dewey himself, of course, seemed to the enthusiasts of progressive education a giant whose interests touched every phase of the greater national intellectual life. And indeed this was true.

Of all facets of the progressive education movement, it was the child-centered aspect that attracted followers from the greatest variety of sources. The work of the educational scientists—psychologists, psychometricians, statisticians, and others—remained of interest chiefly to professionals in the twenties, thirties, and forties. Vocational education lost its national vogue as early as the passage of the Smith-Hughes Act in 1917. In the end, the child-centered wing of the progressive education movement became parochial too, drawing its support as time went on mostly from teachers colleges and their trainees. But during the anti-authoritarian and speculative twenties, child-centeredness in education excited feverish interest and elicited partisan support from coast to coast. The grim realities of the thirties would call into question the adequacy of a philosophy based on "unleashing the child's creativity." The nation's search for an educational panacea took another direction.

[49] Malcolm Cowley, *Exile's Return* (New York, 1956), pp. 59–61.
[50] Frederick Lewis Allen, *Only Yesterday* (New York, 1931), p. 237.

CHAPTER IV

Ideological Uncertainties

⋙⋘

Unity was never a conspicuous attribute of the Progressive Education Association, but the era of the twenties was a time of doctrinal tranquillity compared with the contentious ten years that followed. During the twenties the Association had shown a certain unanimity of commitment to the doctrine of the child-centered school. But the very success of the Association in popularizing the child-centered school was an important factor leading to the ideological unrest of the thirties. For during this decade many men and women who considered themselves "progressive educators," but whose educational philosophies had widely different emphases, were attracted to the Association, which they now acknowledged as spokesman of what they considered the "new education."

By the end of the twenties, progressive education was enjoying a moderately good press. The decision of the *New Republic* to publish the series "The New Education: Ten Years After" in 1930 reflected contemporary popular recognition of the progressive education movement and of PEA's central role in it.[1] The series appeared just "ten years after" the first national convention of the Association. Already the diversity of approach and tone that marked the several articles

[1] "The New Education: Ten Years After," *New Republic* 63 (1930): Boyd H. Bode, "Apprenticeship or Freedom?" June 4, 1930, pp. 61–64; Joseph K. Hart, "Judging Our Progressive Schools," June 11, 1930, pp. 93–96; Francis Mitchell Froelicher, "A Program for Progressive Schools," June 18, 1930, pp. 123–125; Margaret Naumburg, "The Crux of Progressive Education," June 25, 1930, pp. 145–146; Caroline Pratt, "Two Basic Principles of Education," July 2, 1930, pp. 172–176; John Dewey, "How Much Freedom in New Schools?" July 9, 1930, pp. 204–206.

foreshadowed the fragmentation to which the movement later fell victim. Although the Association had labored hard in publicizing the progressive movement, the PEA had rarely commented on the state or purpose of American education as a whole. It is not surprising, then, to find that none of the contributors to the *New Republic* anniversary series was an early leader of the PEA. If the *New Republic* had seriously believed that the Association was the prime cause of the progressive education movement in the United States, then Stanwood Cobb, "father of the Association," would have been a logical, indeed, essential contributor to the series. But there was no article by Cobb. Of the authors of the series, only Francis Mitchell Froelicher had ever held an important office in the PEA. Dewey, of course, contributed and he was honorary president of the PEA, but there is little evidence that the Columbia philosopher ever considered his office to amount to much more than a title. Boyd Bode was an active member of the PEA in the thirties, but never an officer. The other three contributors, Joseph K. Hart, Margaret Naumburg, and Caroline Pratt, never belonged to the PEA's inner circle, although their particular educational views were championed by various factions within the organization.

The term "progressive education" held quite different meanings for the various contributors. Dewey and Miss Naumburg, especially, disagreed on the relative emphasis on individual students and subject matter. Dewey believed there could be too much freedom in the schools, and Miss Naumburg rejected Dewey's "group consciousness." Froelicher's article was more nearly straight publicity for the PEA and progressive education than critical analysis of either. Hart stressed the need of the school to establish a pattern for pupils to follow. Miss Pratt's article emphasized the progressive methods of her own school, rather than trends in progressive education generally. Finally, Bode anticipated the thesis of his 1938 book, *Progressive Education at the Crossroads,* by criticising the progressive education movement's lack of a program or even a sense of direction.

At the very least, the 1930 *New Republic* series demonstrated that some prominent educators were giving serious consideration to the need of a systematic analysis of the new education. The philosophically formless educational experiments of the twenties were rapidly becoming extinct. William Leuchtenburg has observed that never was a decade snuffed out so quickly as the 1920s;[2] this is certainly true of the decade's developments on the educational scence. The old free-wheel-

[2] William Leuchtenburg, *The Perils of Prosperity* (Chicago, 1958), p. 269.

ing experimentalism rapidly lost its momentum. New projects—like those of the schools participating in the PEA's eight-year study—were generally undertaken with a more nearly complete theoretical rationale.

The new decade was one of ideology. No demand was made for unified orthodoxy, but there was a definite desire for some kind of ideology. Of course, the economic depression played its part in orienting the PEA to ideology; no social organization of the thirties was exempt from that effect. But the Association's search for ideology also reflected dissatisfaction with the aimlessness, even the anti-intellectualism of the previous decade. The new commitment was for active participation in the national life. The educators, many of whom had been up to now staid and unexcitable, became fired in the thirties by the need to *do* something.[3]

What the educators wanted to do varied. Some, like George S. Counts, wanted the schools to be initiators of social change. Others, such as Alice V. Keliher, urged the schools to modify drastically their curricula, the content of the subject matter, and their teaching methods. Still others, like W. Carson Ryan, Jr., wanted development of attitudes of international understanding. Some followed Margaret Naumburg in concentrating on the psychological welfare of the youngster, and others supported Elsie Ripley Clapp's program for the use of the school as a community center. The common element among these educators in the thirties is that as a group they recognized at least the desirability of fitting their particular methods into a larger scheme. In the twenties, the method, not the rationale or philosophy, had been supreme.

But common search for rationale did not exclude radical diversity of views among the progressive educators. Given this diversity, the PEA's difficulties in achieving philosophical harmony should have been easily predictable. The Association yielded to these divergent pressures in the spring of 1930 by discarding the recently revised "Seven Principles of Progressive Education."[4] The altered set had been adopted barely a year before, but already it was obsolete in the context of the rapidly expanding interests of the Association. Although a committee

[3] Alfred Kazin discusses this drift in the national temperament in "The Bitter Thirties," *Atlantic* 197 (May, 1962), pp. 82–99. Lewis Feuer makes essentially the same point but with a different emphasis in "Travelers to the Soviet Union 1917–1932: The Formation of a Component of New Deal Ideology," *American Quarterly* 14 (Summer, 1962), pp. 119–149. See also Leo Gurko, *The Angry Decade* (New York, 1947).

[4] The omission was ostensibly made "lest any published article be regarded as rigid or universal in an association that is actually fluid and progressive." Editorial, *Progressive Education* 7 (June, 1930), p. 252.

to develop another body of principles was appointed, it did not make a report until the fall of 1936, and then its members (Theodore Newcomb, W. Carson Ryan, Jr., and Lois Hayden Meek) expressed dissatisfaction with their own statements. The Board of Directors, to whom it reported, apparently shared the committee's view of its labors and agreed that further work should be done on the project.[5] Following the traditional method of organizations in dealing with delicate problems, the Board of Directors then referred the problem to another committee. No more official statements of the organization's educational philosophy were made until 1941.[6]

Interest in Social Reconstruction

The most important and striking new doctrine proposed to the PEA during the thirties was the social reconstructionism of George S. Counts. Born in Kansas in 1889, Counts had received his Ph.D. from the University of Chicago, where he worked under Charles H. Judd and Albion Small. After an initial study of arithmetic tests, he turned his attention to social-class influences on education. After leaving Chicago, Counts taught at teachers colleges in New Jersey and Missouri, then at the University of Washington, Yale University, and the University of Chicago before joining the faculty of Teachers College, Columbia University, in 1927, where he remained until his retirement in 1955. In the late twenties Counts' interest in foreign educational systems was at its height, and he served as associate director of Teachers College's International Institute of Education. During this period, like his colleagues at Columbia, William Heard Kilpatrick and John Dewey, Counts traveled in the Soviet Union and was much impressed with Soviet society and its new educational system that, for the moment, was committed to progressive education.[7]

[5] Board of Directors Minutes, September 26–27, 1936.
[6] Both the midwestern and the western branches of the PEA prepared policy statements, the former cited in the Board of Directors Minutes, April 10–11, 1937, and the latter in the Minutes, April 24–25, 1937. In addition, various resolutions passed at the annual business meetings of the Association in the thirties contained implicit statements of educational philosophy.
[7] Counts' publications of the late twenties and early thirties reflected his interest in and appreciation of the new Soviet educational experiments. Like many other American intellectuals of the thirties who considered the excesses of capitalism as substantially responsible for the Depression of the thirties, he looked to the Soviet experiment as offering possible alterna-

Counts' only office in the PEA was that of chairman of the Committee on Economic and Social Problems, and his selection for this position was a direct result of his electrifying speech to the 1932 PEA convention in Baltimore. This speech, "Dare Progressive Education be Progressive?" and the more extreme pamphlet that followed it, *Dare the School Build a New Social Order?*, became basic works in the library of the advocate of increased social action by the schools. "The great weakness of Progressive Education," Counts began, "lies in the fact that it has elaborated no theory of social welfare, unless it be anarchy or extreme individualism." Counts contended that this lack was a reflection of the views of the predominantly middle class parents who sent their children to progressive schools, but he noted that there was now a new interest in economic and social matters among informed Americans. Presumably these new interests would be reflected in the schools. After severely criticizing the selfishness and oppressive effects of capitalism, Counts concluded, "Historic capitalism will either have to be displaced altogether or so radically changed in form and spirit that its identity will be completely lost." The alternative

---

tives to the American educational system. He was particularly impressed by the Soviet schools' close relationship with their society. See George S. Counts, *A Ford Crosses Soviet Russia* (Boston, 1930); "Education in Soviet Russia" in *Soviet Russia in the Second Decade*, Report of American Trade Union Delegation to the Soviet Union (New York, 1928), pp. 268–304; "The Educational Program of Soviet Russia," *NEA Addresses and Proceedings* (Minneapolis, 1928), pp. 593–602; "Education and the Five-Year Plan in Soviet Russia," *Education and Economics*, National Society for the Study of Educational Sociology Yearbook (New York, 1931), pp. 39–46; and *The Soviet Challenge to America* (New York, 1931). See also, "Toward a United Front," *Social Frontier* 2 (January, 1936), pp. 103–104. During the late thirties Counts became increasingly critical of the Soviet regime, and in 1940 successfully ran against John J. DeBoer as the more conservative candidate for president of the American Federation of Teachers. In 1941 Counts explained part of the changes in his political philosophy in "A Liberal Looks at Life," *Frontiers of Democracy* 7 (May 15, 1941), pp. 231–232. He observed then, "These considerations [military power, inseparability of means and ends, canons of the democratic process] have led me to the conclusion that the forces of democracy cannot cooperate or form a united front with any totalitarian movement or party however loudly it may announce its devotion to the cause of democracy." This article appeared a month prior to Hitler's attack on Russia, which severed the Hitler-Stalin pact. Counts' post-World War II publications, especially *The Country of the Blind* (New York, 1949) and, with Nucia P. Lodge, *The Challenge of Soviet Education* (New York, 1957), are intensely critical of the Soviet Union.

to private capitalism that Counts saw was "some form of socialized economy." Having pointed out the progressive school's previous narrow interests, Counts now called upon education to take in the entire range of life: leisure and recreation, sex and family, government and public opinion.[8]

Admonished in these terms to revise their schools' activities drastically, members of the PEA awaited Counts' second, more radical pronouncement: *Dare the School Build a New Social Order?* In this manifesto Counts again censured progressive education's alleged tie to the ruling upper middle class and its educational philosophy of extreme individualism. He then introduced his highly controversial "doctrine of imposition":

> If Progressive Education is to be genuinely progressive, it must emancipate itself from the influence of this class, face squarely and courageously every social issue, come to grips with life in all of its stark reality, establish an organic relation with the community, develop a realistic and comprehensive theory of welfare, fashion a compelling and challenging vision of human destiny, and become less frightened than it is today at the bogies of *imposition* and *indoctrination*. In a word, Progressive Education cannot place its trust in a child-centered school.

Here indeed was a radical break with the child-centered philosophy of the early progressives as well as with the libertarian permissiveness that was its corollary. Counts urged that there be no distortion nor suppression of facts and added that all education contained a large element of imposition. Failure to recognize this, he maintained, was an assumption that one's own prejudices were universal truth.[9]

Although Counts was the best-known exponent of the new social view of progressive education's responsibilities, he was by no means alone in decrying the schools' lack of a social philosophy. The need for the schools' active interest and participation in society had been one of Dewey's major concerns since the publication of *The School and Society* in 1899. In *The Child-Centered School* of 1928, Harold Rugg and Ann Shumaker had listed the average school's lack of interest in social questions as one of its principal weaknesses. Even *Progressive Educa-*

[8] George S. Counts, "Dare Progressive Education be Progressive?" *Progressive Education* 9 (April, 1932), pp. 257–263.

[9] George S. Counts, *Dare the School Build a New Social Order?* (New York, 1932), p. 9.

tion had announced, as early as 1930, "Our journal, to be truly progressive, should be not merely a forum for the exchange of educational ideas, but should also play a vital part in the stimulation of thought leading to social reconstruction."[10] Such statements as these indicate at least that the ground upon which Counts' statement fell had earlier been watered.[11] Counts, however, pressed further beyond the range of educational theory and penetrated far more deeply into questions of social and economic organization than any other major spokesman of progressive education.

Counts' speech to the 1932 PEA convention was one of the most exciting and controversial events in the Association's history. Ironically, on this occasion Counts shared the lecture platform with Hughes Mearns, who was a prolific contributor to *Progressive Education* in the twenties and who represented that group of educators of whom Counts was most critical: those lacking a social philosophy. Mearns' chief interest was in "fostering creativity in youth," and he set out how to do it in *Creative Youth: How a School Environment Set Free the Creative Spirit* (1925) and *Creative Power* (1929). But now few were interested in Mearns or creativity. It was Counts who caught their attention.

Frederick Redefer, who became the Association's executive secretary in 1932, described Counts' speech as a "bombshell."[12] All planned discussions for the remainder of the convention were discarded, and participants met informally to discuss Counts' proposals. A special Board of Directors meeting was called, and the Board decided to appoint a Committee on Economic and Social Problems. Its task was "to promote within the schools and their affiliated agencies thoughtful and systematic study of the economic and industrial problems confronting us today."[13] The next issue of *Progressive Education* was devoted almost entirely to comments from members about Counts' speech. Few seemed eager to admit direct opposition to the Columbia educator, but none appeared willing to support him totally. The arguments ranged from Elsie Ripley Clapp, who categorically opposed any kind

[10] Editorial, *Progressive Education* 7 (November, 1930), p. 350.

[11] Malcolm Skilbeck has argued, not altogether convincingly, that even in the twenties the progressive education movement had a vital social philosophy. He cites the Dalton, Winnetka, and Gary plans as evidences of this. "Criticisms of Progressive Education, 1916–1930," unpublished M.A. thesis, University of Illinois, 1958.

[12] Frederick L. Redefer, "Resolutions, Reactions, Reminiscences," *Progressive Education* 26 (April, 1949), p. 188.

[13] "The Association Faces Its Opportunities," *Progressive Education* 9 (May, 1932), p. 330.

of "indoctrination," to Nellie Seeds, who contended that genuine progressivism could not flourish in a middle class progressive education movement.[14]

The Board of Directors and the Advisory Board also set up a special weekend meeting that was held on the campus of Vassar College in the late spring of 1932. The topic for the first evening was "The Responsibility of Education for Social Reconstruction." William Heard Kilpatrick was chairman and opened the discussion with three questions: How shall we psychologically see the nature of educational progress? How shall we see the social function of education and the direction of social progress? How shall we administer education in the light of these insights? The group then presented a severe indictment of the school the Association had so energetically publicized throughout the past decade:

> There was general agreement that the new type of school must be more than child-centered. The progressive school in emphasizing the development of individuality has often failed to develop an adequate social outlook. It has cultivated openmindedness, but students are not moved to social action or fired by great beliefs or causes. Students are critical but undecisive, interesting and well-poised as individuals, but self-centered. Too frequently the student body of the progressive school is not sufficiently representative of conflicting social points of view to arouse keen thinking about social problems.[15]

Here agreement seemed to end; there was no such unanimity among the conferees regarding the procedures that the schools should follow

[14] "Comments on Dr. Counts's Challenge," *Progressive Education* 9 (April, 1932), pp. 264–278.

[15] Those attending the meeting were Wilford M. Aikin, Rose Alschuler, Elsie Ripley Clapp, Harold T. Clark, Queene Ferry Coonley, Rachel Erwin, Burton P. Fowler, Ellen W. Greer, Gertrude Hartman, Allan Hulsizer, William Heard Kilpatrick, Lois Hayden Meek, Clyde R. Miller, Morris R. Mitchell, Jesse Newlon, Frederick L. Redefer, Ann Shumaker, Winifred Smith, Vivian T. Thayer, Constance Warren, James B. Welles, Laura Williams, and Laura Zirbes. Only three of the early leaders of the PEA, Mrs. Coonley, Miss Hartman, and Mrs. Williams, were there, and two of them were patronesses. Of the Teachers College group committed to a drastic overhaul of the school to adjust it to the new social order only Kilpatrick and Newlon attended. Counts, Dewey, Rugg, and Childs apparently did not go. Board of Directors Minutes, April 29–May 1, 1932. The Advisory Board was an additional group that offered general suggestions to the organization but did not make policy as the Board of Directors did.

or that the Association should advance in order to educate youngsters with greater concern for these problems.

After a brief interlude during which the group discussed less explosive topics, such as the relation of progressive education to rural schools and the training of teachers for progressive schools, the participants returned to the thorny question, "The Program of the Association with Respect to Social-Economic Problems." On this occasion Lois Hayden Meek, Counts' colleague on the faculty of Teachers College and an expert on child development, was chairman. The group debated at length various possible activities for the new Committee on Economic and Social Problems but was unable to agree on any program for it. The group decided to ask John Dewey to serve as chairman, but he declined, and Counts accepted the position.[16]

Throughout 1932 and early 1933 Counts' committee met regularly to work on a draft of a statement of social policy for the schools. The committee itself was a diverse group. Counts, the chairman, was joined by two of his colleagues at Teachers College: Goodwin Watson, a social psychologist and later chairman of the PEA's Commission on Educational Freedom, and Jesse Newlon, a school administrator who later became head of Counts' Department of Social and Philosophical Foundations of Education at Teachers College. John S. Gambs, an economist, was on the faculty of New College, Thomas Alexander's short-lived experiment in teacher education at Teachers College in the mid-thirties. Merle Curti, an American historian, was then on the faculty of Smith College and was soon to write *The Social Ideas of American Educators,* a radically revisionist document (published three years later) criticizing the traditional conservatism of American educators. Charles L. S. Eaton was a member of the faculty of Burton P. Fowler's Tower Hill School and had shown great interest in Counts' speech at the annual convention. Representing the Association itself were Willard W. Beatty, the president, then superintendent of the Bronxville, New York Schools, and Frederick L. Redefer, the executive secretary.[17]

By March, 1933, at the annual convention of the Association,

---

[16] *Loc. cit.*

[17] This was the original committee appointed at the Vassar meeting. Board of Directors Minutes, April 29–May 1, 1932. A later statement about the committee failed to include Goodwin Watson as a member but did name Rexford G. Tugwell, an economist at Columbia University and one of President Roosevelt's New Deal "Brain Trust," and Beulah Amidon, an education writer for *Survey Graphic.* "News of the Association," *Progressive Education* 9 (October, 1932), p. 446.

Counts' committee had completed a tentative report. Apparently the presence of the document was known to members of the Association, for when no official mention was made of it a member of the Association moved that the committee release its report to the members "with majority and minority views, if necessary, and with the disclaimer that this does not speak for the Association."

The committee itself was meeting at the same time as the business meeting, and no representative was able to examine the report in detail at the business meeting. There was no absence of discussion, however. PEA leaders Carleton Washburne, V. T. Thayer, Harold Rugg, and Burton P. Fowler, all independently stated their belief that the present was not a propitious moment for releasing the report. Washburne feared the document might be dangerous to the well-being of the Association "through stirring up a feeling on the part of many people who are at the present time overly sensitive that the Association has gone radical." Thayer urged time "for more mature consideration" and Rugg, as well as Thayer, noted the prohibitive expense of sending copies to all the members. Flora J. Cooke, Washburne's former teacher and his frequent opponent in debates on the value of individual versus group instruction, differed with her old pupil again. She observed that there were so many garbled versions of the report now that it would be better to have the report available to members who specified their interest in it.[18]

Miss Cooke had her way, and later in the year the report of the Counts' committee was published as "A Call to the Teachers of the Nation." The report was prefaced by a statement relieving the Association of responsibility for the report and placing the burden upon the members of the committee. After a biting attack upon the social and economic order that had permitted the suffering of the Depression, the report reasserted Counts' proposition that some new form of national government must replace the present inadequate one. The report concluded,

> Progressive teachers must unite in a powerful organization, militantly devoted to the building of a better social order and to the fulfillment under the conditions of industrial civilisation of the democratic aspirations of American people. . . . To serve the teaching profession of the country in this way should be one of the major purposes of the Progressive Education Association.[19]

[18] Minutes of the Annual Business Meeting, March 4, 1933.
[19] Committee of the Progressive Education Association on Social and Economic Problems, George S. Counts, Chairman, *A Call to the Teachers of the Nation* (New York, 1933), p. 26.

The PEA was unwilling to commit itself without reservation to such a drastic proposal. The organization was just then (1933) beginning to receive large grants from the Rockefeller-supported General Education Board and from the Carnegie Corporation. Many members of the Association were reluctant to brandish at this time a controversial manifesto that might limit the PEA's future request for grants. It should be noted too that the Association still included in its membership a number of ardent supporters of the permissive progressive education characteristic of the twenties. Their *laissez-faire* attitude toward the child's educational activities extended in some cases to their own political attitudes, insofar as they had opinions on such questions. In any case, Washburne's and Thayer's efforts to calm the waters roiled by Counts' committee were successful.

The PEA had failed to respond to Counts' "call," and he and others sharing his view now looked to other groups more sympathetic to their ideas. According to Harold Rugg, a small gathering of professors in the New York City area had begun meeting in 1928 to discuss social questions, and this group formed a nucleus that supported many of Counts' proposals in the thirties.[20] Among the members were Edmund DeS. Brunner, John L. Childs, John Dewey, William Heard Kilpatrick, Eduard C. Lindeman, Lois Hayden Meek, Jesse H. Newlon, Harry Overstreet, Sidney Hook, Harold Rugg, and Goodwin Watson. In 1933 a relatively mild statement of their desire for a revised philosophy of education that would give attention to the current social and economic pressures within society was published as *The Educational Frontier*. Edited by Kilpatrick and with contributions by H. Gordon Hullfish, R. Bruce Raup, V. T. Thayer, Boyd E. Bode, Childs, and Dewey, the book established a tone for educational theorizing in the thirties much as Rugg's and Shumaker's *The Child-Centered School* had for the twenties.

When he reviewed *The Educational Frontier* for the *New Republic*, Sidney Hook called it "by far the most progressive and significant statement of the new educational philosophy which is emerging from the depression." Hook noted the rather timid suggestions in the volume—particularly in the second chapter, written by Dewey and Childs—that a national educational philosophy must be consistent with a national social and political philosophy. Hook then extrapolated from the Dewey-Childs position and stated:

> The philosophy of experimental education, then, demands the existence of the classless society. But by its own logic the experimental

[20] Harold Rugg, *The Teacher of Teachers* (New York, 1952), p. 225.

philosophy cannot stop with a proclamation of an ideal. "A goal cannot be intelligently set forth apart from the path which leads to it."

It is the discussion of the means by which the new classless society is to be achieved that the new educational philosophy reveals its greatest advance and its greatest shortcomings. The advance consists in making emphatic, to a point which ought forever to silence its professional misunderstanders, that the experimental method which it uses cannot be identified with opportunism or with sweet reasonableness. . . . The real educational question of the moment is: how is the transition from a class to a classless society to be brought about?[21]

Hook was right in asserting that the "real educational question of the moment" had not been answered by the authors of *The Educational Frontier*. As the Depression deepened, Hook and his colleagues from the discussion group came to believe that more radical and more regular statements were needed. George Counts, who had not been involved with *The Educational Frontier*, was instrumental in the development of a different publication that promised to provide a regular forum for the social reconstructionists. This was the periodical *The Social Frontier*.

The Social Frontier called itself "a journal of educational criticism and reconstruction," and throughout the thirties it presented the responsible radical position of those educators who wanted the schools to lead in social rebuilding. Raymond E. Callahan has termed it "a journal which in its short life was the most outstanding and courageous journal American education has produced."[22] Public endorsement of the new journal showed in its circulation figures. At the end of its first year, *The Social Frontier* had 6,000 subscribers, a figure it had taken PEA ten years to reach.[23] The journal's pages included articles by distinguished authors, and many of its essays were among the most arresting then being written on educational topics. John Dewey and Robert Maynard Hutchins debated the merits of their respective educational philosophies in 1936 and 1937.[24] A symposium representing the spectrum of social thought from Conservative Harry Gideonse and

[21] William H. Kilpatrick, ed., *The Educational Frontier* (New York, 1933). Sidney Hook, "Education and Politics," *New Republic* 77 (May 24, 1933), pp. 49–50.

[22] Raymond E. Callahan, *Education and the Cult of Efficiency* (Chicago, 1962), p. 203.

[23] "The First Year," *The Social Frontier* 1 (June, 1935), p. 3.

[24] "John Dewey on the Educational Ideas of Robert Maynard Hutchins," *The Social Frontier* 3 (December, 1936), p. 71. Hutchins' reply appeared in *The Social Frontier* 4 (January, 1937), p. 103.

Fascist Lawrence Dennis to Communist Earl Browder discussed "The Crisis in Education and the Social Order" (1935).[25] *The Social Frontier* and *Progressive Education* shared several members of executive boards, and this mutuality of interests became more significant in 1937 when *The Social Frontier* sought unsuccessfully to merge with the PEA.[26]

If the PEA was not so radical as *The Social Frontier* group, at least it was concerned with some of the same problems that occupied the attention of the editors of the newer publication. Willard W. Beatty, Superintendent of Schools in Bronxville, New York, and newly elected president of the Association, wrote in *Progressive Education* in 1933:

> In the substitution of integrated social planning for "rugged individualism" lies the only possible hope of preserving, in general, a social and economic structure even remotely resembling the one familiar to nations of western Europe and America. More clearly than other members of our profession, leaders in Progressive Education have seen the handwriting on the wall and have demanded that the schools reorganize their approaches to social and economic understanding, political activity, and personal adjustment. Increasingly must fall upon us responsibility for leadership in the actual remaking of education, so that it may contribute directly to the building of a new and better social order.[27]

By no means did all the readers of *Progressive Education* agree with President Beatty or committee chairman Counts. Letters and articles poured into the journal's office criticizing the Association's new attitude, particularly Counts' speech and committee report.[28] *Progres-*

---

[25] "Indoctrination: The Task Before the American School," *The Social Frontier* 1 (January, 1935), pp. 8–33.

[26] Board of Directors Minutes, February 25, 1937. The question was discussed throughout the spring of 1937, and in June the PEA Board of Directors finally decided against any merger. Approximately 27 per cent of the PEA's members were also subscribers to *The Social Frontier,* but the Association apparently believed that the remaining three-quarters of the membership was significantly out of sympathy with the journal's radical statements. Financial problems also hindered the union. Board of Directors Minutes, June 10, 1937.

[27] Editorial, *Progressive Education* 10 (October, 1933), p. 304.

[28] Ironically, Ann Shumaker, co-author with Rugg of *The Child-Centered School* (Yonkers-on-Hudson, 1928) and editor of *Progressive Education,* had suggested Counts as a speaker at the 1932 convention, thus loosing the flood of dispute within the membership and in the magazine. Frederick

sive Education, which until recently had quietly reported new artwork in the Norfolk schools or experiments with the social studies curriculum at the Lincoln School, now found itself plunged into a debate on American social and economic policies and their influence on the educational system. Among Counts' most vociferous critics were George A. Coe, James Truslow Adams, Horace M. Kallen, and Henry W. Holmes. All but Coe's statement followed publication of the report of Counts' Committee on Economic and Social Problems. Coe, a frequent contributor to *The Social Frontier,* objected both to the word and the idea of indoctrination. To attain the goal of a classless society (which Coe approved) the progressive school's original commitment to freedom should be allowed full rein. The exercise of such freedom would, said Coe, "of itself make the school a protagonist of a classless society."[29] Horace M. Kallen also attacked the idea of indoctrination but from a another point of departure. He believed that indoctrination in anything but the scientific method was inherently undesirable.[30]

James Truslow Adams also doubted the feasibility of the method of indoctrination but for a different reason. With a historian's backward glance, Adams noted that Americans were not yet willing to overhaul totally their economic system, and that, in any case, teachers of elementary and secondary schools certainly were not the ones to lead such a movement. They would, said Adams, have difficulty "fully grasping the problems." [31] Two years later Henry W. Holmes took much the same position as Adams, arguing that teachers as a group simply were not competent to build a new social order.[32]

The third major group of Counts' critics were the Marxists. They too believed that the Columbia educator had too much faith in the ability of teachers to effect fundamental changes in society.[33] They

L. Redefer reported Miss Shumaker's sponsorship of Counts in an interview with me on November 1, 1962.

[29] George A. Coe, "Shall We Indoctrinate?" *Progressive Education* 10 (March, 1933), pp. 140–143.

[30] Horace M. Kallen, "Can We Be Saved by Indoctrination?" *Progressive Education* 11 (January–February, 1934), pp. 55–62.

[31] James Truslow Adams, "Can Teachers Bring About a New Society?" *Progressive Education* 10 (October, 1933), pp. 310–314.

[32] Henry W. Holmes, "Ultimate Values in Education," *Progressive Education* 12 (February, 1935), pp. 114–116.

[33] The two most explicit statements of the Communist view of progressive education were Howard Langford, *Education and the Social Conflict* (New York, 1936) and Zalmen Slesinger, *Education and the Class Struggle* (New York, 1937). Langford's manuscript had been a winner, along with Will French's *Education and Social Dividends* (New York, 1935), of a

believed that a full-scale revolution was the inevitable precursor of changes such as those Counts envisioned. Johanson I. Zilberfarb, a Soviet educator who was head of the pedagogical section of the Ukrainian Society for Cultural Relations with Foreign Countries predicted with some show of logic that Counts' method would lead to fascism rather than socialism or communism.[34] Leading American Communists, including Earl Browder, commented skeptically on Counts' speech, although not in the pages of *Progressive Education*. Browder had strong doubts about "any program of social change which relies upon the school system as an important instrument in bringing that change about."[35]

Thus the chief criticisms of Counts' position boiled down to the claim that indoctrination was wrong as a method and that teachers were incapable of leading the vanguard of national social reform. Few of the critics had a good word for the current social and economic system. But many of the educators who backed off from Counts had themselves little to offer by way of alternative proposals on the school's role in effecting social change. Most of them retreated into pedagogical isolation by way of curriculum revision or some other nonpolitical channel of reform.

There were exceptions. William Heard Kilpatrick announced that progressive education did need a social philosophy although not Counts' particular brand. Kilpatrick edged forward his "social philosophy of progressive education," an amorphous theory that strove to include both his earlier interest in the "whole child" and a still unclarified con-

---

Kappa Delta Pi essay contest on the question, "What Educational Program Will Best Meet the Needs of Our Developing Social and Economic Situation?" Langford used the Marxist-Leninist epithet "consistently idealistic" to describe the Experimentalist position (p. 65).

Slesinger's book had been prepared as a doctoral thesis at Teachers College, and William Heard Kilpatrick wrote an introduction to the volume noting his complete disagreement with Slesinger's point of view. Slesinger's study was an analysis of the social philosophy of various "liberal educators," ranging from Counts to Bode. Slesinger's use of the term "liberal" as applied to these educators illustrated the confusion surrounding the term. The Van Doren-Adler-Barr group of educators espoused "liberal education" and conceived it quite differently from the progressives.

[34] Johanson I. Zilberfarb, "The Soviets Survey an Educator," *Progressive Education* 10 (February, 1933), pp. 71–73.

[35] Quoted by Robert W. Iversen, *The Communists and the Schools* (New York, 1959), p. 60.

cern with society.[36] John L. Childs, student and later colleague of Dewey, Kilpatrick, and Counts, was sharply critical of the PEA's "overly general statements about the present situation."[37] He, too, urged that the PEA enunciate a social philosophy, although he did not favor such a drastic manifesto as Counts had promulgated four years earlier.[38] Childs specifically noted the presence in the Association of representatives of private schools, assumed to be wealthy, and suggested that so long as they were active in the Association, no strong statement of educational or social reconstruction could properly be issued by the PEA. J. R. P. French, headmaster of the Cambridge School, met part of Childs' argument by noting that of the twelve members of the PEA Board of Directors only he (French) represented a private school. It was true, however, that one-fourth of the PEA membership was still affiliated with independent schools.[39]

Reconstruction as Curriculum Reform

There were many members of the Association whose concept of "progressive education" was confined in the main to curriculum reform. These people constituted the most effective restraint on the enthusiasm of the social indoctrination advocates. The curriculum revisionists wanted changes both in the content of the curriculum and in the methods of instruction. Few of the original PEA partisans remained active through the thirties. The curriculum reformers generally came from the ranks of newer members, many of whom joined the Association after having read *Progressive Education,* which both in the twenties and through much of the thirties leaned heavily on new approaches to subject matter.

Testimony to the PEA's continued interest in curriculum reform can be found in the establishment of three major commissions of the

---

[36] William Heard Kilpatrick, "The Social Philosophy of Progressive Education," *Progressive Education* 12 (May, 1935), pp. 289–293. This same interest of Kilpatrick's is revealed in his chapter, "Professional Education from the Social Point of View," in *The Educational Frontier, op. cit.,* pp. 257–286.

[37] John L. Childs, "Whither Progressive Education?" *Progressive Education* 13 (December, 1936), pp. 583–589.

[38] Childs' milder statement may well be explained by the fact that he made it five years later than Counts' first major speech.

[39] "News, Notes and Reviews," *Progressive Education* 14 (February, 1937), pp. 129–130.

thirties: Wilford M. Aikin's Commission on School and College, V. T. Thayer's Commission on the Secondary School Curriculum, and Alice V. Keliher's Commission on Human Relations. Aikin's group was particularly interested in easing college entrance restrictions, so that students from progressive schools with nontraditional preparation might be allowed to enter college. Thayer's associates studied the familiar subject matter areas taught in the elementary and secondary schools with a view toward adapting "progressive methods" to them. Miss Keliher's group focused its attention on developing a curriculum based on the psychological needs of youngsters. These three commissions received the greater part of the General Education Board's grant to the PEA of one and one-half million dollars, and the research carried on by them may well rank as the Association's most nearly permanent achievement. Not one of the three commissions was interested in using the school for social reform.

PEA's interest in the "child-centered school" continued to show itself in the pages of *Progressive Education* even though much of the old spiritual zeal was missing. In 1932, as president of the Association, Burton P. Fowler wrote that schools

> . . . are not progressive unless in the actual classroom procedure, in the face-to-face relationships of teacher and pupil and among the pupils, there is evidence that an actively self-directed learning process in a more or less natural situation is the goal of the teacher's leadership.[40]

Fowler's statement appeared in the same year as Counts' "Dares." Some contributors looked back with nostalgia to the old PEA Credo, although by 1931 even the Association itself no longer officially subscribed to it. Defining a "progressive school" in that year, Arthur C. Perry argued that such a school was one whose administration and classroom procedures conformed to the Seven Principles of the Progressive Education Association.[41] Others tried to combine curriculum reform proposals with some recognition of the school as a social force. Goodwin Watson, a staunch supporter of *The Social Frontier* and chairman of the PEA's Commission on Educational Freedom, urged the development of a new secondary school with the curriculum organized

[40] Burton P. Fowler, "Progressive Education Enters a Second Phase," *Progressive Education* 9 (January, 1932), pp. 3–6. The "second phase" Fowler saw was the extension of progressive methods beyond the private schools to public school systems.
[41] Arthur C. Perry, "What is a Progressive School?" *Progressive Education* 8 (February, 1931), p. 116.

"to meet everybody's needs and to prepare for life." To accomplish this, Watson suggested that the traditional departments be replaced by new ones: Health, Personal Relations, Vocations, Money and Goods, The Social Order, Recreation, and Interpretation of the Universe.[42]

Throughout the thirties *Progressive Education* continued to open its pages to discussions demanding more attention to the child and his educational needs.[43] Outside the Association, particularly in the National Society for the Study of Education and in the National Education Association, active members of the PEA pursued this same interest. In 1934 one of NSSE's most widely known agencies, the Committee on the Activity Movement, published a report identifying the activity movement as an important strand in the fabric of progressive education.[44] In the concept "activity movement," the committee intended to include all the methodological reforms current in education in the thirties. Members of the committee included important PEA supporters: E. M. Sipple, director of the Park School, Baltimore; Boyd Bode, professor of education at Ohio State University; Alice V. Keliher, then elementary education supervisor in the Hartford, Connecticut, public schools. Columbia PEA leaders Dewey, Kilpatrick, and Goodwin Watson sat on the committee. In fact, there were more active members of the PEA on this committee than on any other NSSE committee of the thirties.[45] Such remarkable participation in this NSSE activity movement group was understandable, perhaps, because the

[42] Goodwin Watson, "A New Secondary School," *Progressive Education* 8 (April, 1931), pp. 303–310.

[43] Among the most coherent articles appearing in *Progressive Education* dealing with the emphasis on curriculum reform were Alice V. Keliher, "Where are the Progressives Going?" 10 (May, 1933), pp. 277–280; R. Bruce Raup, " 'Realistic' Education," 11 (January–February, 1934), pp. 40–44; Hilda Taba, "Progressive Education—What Now?" 11 (March, 1934), pp. 162–168; William H. Kilpatrick, Orville G. Brim, et. al., "Report on the NSSE 33rd Yearbook on the Activity Movement," 11 (October, 1934), pp. 327–359; Laura Zirbes, "What is Freedom in the Classroom?" 11 (November, 1934), pp. 383–385; Irvin C. Poley, "Must We Have the Hickory Stick?" 12 (January, 1935), pp. 45–47; and Eduard C. Lindeman, 13 (January, 1936), pp. 13–14.

[44] *The Activity Movement*, 33rd NSSE Yearbook, Part II (Bloomington, Illinois, 1934).

[45] Among the other topics the NSSE discussed in the thirties were the teaching of arithmetic (1930), the status of rural education (1931), changes and experiments in liberal arts education (1932), the teaching of geography (1933), the planning and construction of school buildings (1934), educational diagnosis (1935), the teaching of reading (1937), and the scientific movement in education (1938).

activity concept was in line with PEA's traditional interests. But it is also evidence of the dichotomy between the spoken policy statements of the PEA, a number of which expressed concern with the social order, and the actual interests of many of its members.[46] The National Education Association's Department of Superintendence also shared the PEA's interest in curriculum reform. Between 1924 and 1928, five of its yearbooks had dealt with various questions concerning the curriculum. In 1936 an entire NEA yearbook was devoted to the social studies curriculum.[47]

Curriculum reform represented the confluence of the major streams of the progressive education movement in the thirties. Although many PEA leaders believed that it was the individual child who would be primarily affected by curriculum change, others, such as Dewey, recognized the social implications of the proposals then current. Commenting on the report of the social studies group, Harold Laski wrote, "At bottom and stripped of its carefully neutral phrases, the report is an educational program for a socialist America."[48] Most PEA conservatives, however, gave little indication that they recognized these wider ramifications of the "Social Studies" curriculum reform, although nearly all of them uncritically supported it.

By 1938 John Dewey, whose patience with "overzealous and underbright" disciples seemed limitless, felt it necessary to restate his educational theory so as to clarify his position regarding the new "progressive"

---

[46] Orville G. Brim, "Basic Realities and the Activity Movement," *Progressive Education* 11 (October, 1934), pp. 328–333, and William H. Kilpatrick, "The Essentials of the Activity Movement," *Progressive Education* 11 (October, 1934), pp. 346–359. Brim, a professor of education at Ohio State University, attacked the report, and Kilpatrick defended it.

[47] The Department of Superintendence of the NEA established its Commission on Curriculum Reform in 1923 under the chairmanship of Edwin C. Broome, Superintendent of Schools, Philadelphia, Pennsylvania. The Commission produced four reports: "Research in Constructing the Elementary School Curriculum" (1925); "The Nation at Work on the Public School Curriculum" (1926); "The Development of the Junior High School Curriculum" (1927); and "The Development of the High School Curriculum" (1928). The members of the Commission were all public school administrators, a group not attracted to the PEA in the mid-twenties, but many of the participants at the meetings were active members of the Association. For example, the speakers at the "Creative Education" session in 1927 were Carleton Washburne, Burton P. Fowler, Hughes Mearns, and Flora J. Cooke.

[48] Harold J. Laski, "A New Education for a New America," *New Republic* 87 (July 29, 1936), p. 343.

methods. By the late thirties, the informed American public, as well as the PEA itself, recognized Dewey as the philosopher and father of progressive education. Although in its initial stages the PEA had believed itself to be more directly descended from Francis Parker or even from European educational reformers like Johann Pestalozzi, the Association had made early and wide use of Dewey's name and works in support of its activities. Dewey now criticized the extremes to which some progressive schools had gone in their disregard of organized subject matter in favor of active experiences. "The belief that all genuine education comes about through experience," Dewey wrote, "does not mean that all experiences are genuinely or equally educative. Experience and education cannot be directly equated to each other."[49] Dewey foresaw the attacks of the forties and fifties on progressivism: "Unless the problems of intellectual organization can be worked out on the ground of experience," the philosopher warned, "reaction is sure to occur toward externally imposed methods of organization. There are signs of this reaction already in evidence."[50]

Dewey's criticism was made of tendencies within an educational movement still significantly child-oriented. Although the old evangelical fire concerning "child-centeredness" had cooled, the PEA in the thirties sustained its early interest in the child and the environment in which he might most fruitfully learn. The emphasis remained on the learner himself and the learning situation; advocates of curriculum reform gave less attention to what the child should learn, more to the conditions under which he should learn it.

The Attempt at Synthesis

In the thirties the PEA managed to include under its doctrinal mantle most of the extant varieties of progressive education. With such an eclectic philosophy, however, the organization did not often win prime loyalty from the more outspoken apologists of the various positions. The most ardent supporters of the school as a social force, such as George Hartmann, spent much of their energies writing for *The Social Frontier* or taking active part in the American Federation of Teachers.[51] Extremists in curriculum reform, like Caroline Pratt, main-

---

[49] John Dewey, *Experience and Education* (New York, 1938), p. 13.
[50] *Ibid.*, p. 107.
[51] See George Hartmann, "A New Definition of the Educated Man," *Progressive Education* 10 (December, 1933), pp. 444–447. Hartmann was also editor of *The Social Frontier* in 1938.

tained a measured interest in the PEA, but they gave their full allegiance to the Society for Experimental Education, whose interests were more specific and limited than those of the PEA. The Association now had a large membership of midwestern public school teachers, and psychologically oriented progressive educators, such as Margaret Naumburg, found that they gave too conservative a tone to the PEA. The devotees of psychology, however, founded no major alternative educational organization. Many, like Miss Naumburg, became increasingly absorbed in psychiatry and psychoanalysis. Those educators who were mainly interested in testing and in a "scientific" approach to education generally tended to find the Educational Records Bureau more congenial than the PEA.

Lack of stated principles made it easy for the PEA to fall into middle-of-the-road progressivism. By the late thirties, the Association talked far more about what it opposed than what it stood for. The limits of its daring during these years can be hinted at by recording a 1937 statement in which the PEA disassociated itself from its alleged obsession with moveable classroom furniture:

> . . . progressive education is not dependent on furniture and fixtures. . . .
> The necessary atmosphere for modern education can be created in a
> room in which all the furniture is ranged in rows and firmly screwed
> to the floor; conversely there may be an atmosphere of tension in the
> most informally arranged classrooms.[52]

Absence of carefully delineated ideology allowed the PEA to drift in the thirties into that very dualism between thought and action that Dewey had so consistently and vigorously decried. Despite their ostensible support of Dewey's philosophy, many of the PEA leaders of the thirties were philosophically uninformed to the point of naiveté. Others were so absorbed by their interests in practical school matters that they had little time for theorizing about them. The two main educational problems that held the attention of the PEA in the thirties illustrate this dualism: the role of the school in the social order and the need for a total reform of the school curriculum. In the first instance, there was much talk about the responsibilities of the school vis-à-vis the social order, but little action on it. In the Association's board meetings and

[52] "News Notes and Reviews," *Progressive Education* 14 (February, 1937), p. 128. This statement was in marked contrast to an early article by Florence E. Bamberger, "Progressive Education and Character Building," Progressive Education Association, Bulletin No. 4 (February, 1921), which stressed flexible furnishings as a prerequisite of the progressive classroom.

policy conferences, the leaders heatedly debated the PEA's projected stand on "indoctrination" in the school and the degree of leadership that the schools should take in effecting changes in society. The school's involvement in social change was the fundamental philosophical issue of the thirties, but it was one on which the Association rigidly refused to take significant action. Such action as the Association permitted itself in the thirties was derived in theory from the amorphous basis of the Seven Principles of Progressive Education that the Association had officially put aside in 1929. All the Association's commissions, except the short-lived Commission on Educational Freedom, justified themselves theoretically on the innocuous ideology represented by these axioms.

It is true that a good deal of *ad hoc* theorizing went on at PEA meetings in the thirties and some of this activity added prestige to the Association and contributed to its image as a vital, alert organization. So long as the theorizing was not disruptively radical, publicity gained from such benevolent philosophizing would not hinder those PEA members who sought funds from foundations for Association projects. By the late thirties, however, signs were visible of a serious attempt at the merger of the two major doctrinal loyalties of the PEA. It was discovered that under the rubric of "schools for a democracy," both Counts' interest in social reform and V. T. Thayer's concern with curriculum revision could be synthesized, if in somewhat diluted form. Indeed, the concept of the special needs of schools in a democracy seemed a rather happy solution to the Association's doctrinal perplexities.

There was precedent for the invocation of the concept of democracy. Leaders of the Association might justifiably have recalled Jefferson's demand for an educated citizenry in a democracy to support their claim for the social responsibilities of the school. But the PEA leaders were often wary of historical precedent. They believed that the traditional curriculum and all its evils had survived largely because of an uncritical faith in historical precedent, and they were eager to replace these outmoded courses with new ones specifically tailored to what they took to be the needs of the present age. This anti-historical bias contributed to the growth of the woolly "social studies" projects, the ingenuous courses in marriage and family living that helped to give the progressive movement a dubious reputation. Many of these group- and family-oriented curricula had already appeared before the discovery of "democracy" as an inclusive rationale for social reform. In the twenties they were justified on the basis of their alleged contribution to the fullest and most creative development of the individual. In the thirties, it was found that the "group" was easily assimilated to the more inclusive and socially oriented concept of "democracy," and with this further justification, "group" arrangements and "democratic" projects cheerfully proliferated themselves through the educational world.[53]

The "schools for a democracy" theme also soothed the radical wing of the Association, whose leader was George S. Counts. By the late thirties, Counts and many of his colleagues who had energetically backed collectivist experiments in the late twenties and thirties had now revised their estimates. The increased knowledge of Stalinism and its excesses, the publicity given to the great Soviet purges, dampened the collectivist ardor of the social reconstructionists.[54] Now their attention had shifted to the American democracy of the late thirties, which after some years of President Roosevelt's leadership, had moved out from the context of *laissez faire* industrial capitalism of which they had been so critical. The social reconstructionists, too, were willing to work under the banner of "schools for a democracy."

The same slogan also satisfied the advocates of an international outlook on education like Harold Rugg, who looked abroad with apprehension on the rapidly rising specters of fascism in Germany, Italy, and Spain. The international-outlook element in the PEA believed now that the American schools provided an excellent place in which to inculcate (the term was more tactful than Counts' "imposition" or "indoctrination") in the young the values of the democratic system.

Finally, the public schools' increased adoption of progressive education and their interest in the Association also contributed to the ac-

---

[53] Edgar Wesley reports the enormous increase in the number of school subjects in *NEA: The First Hundred Years* (New York, 1957), p. 111. "The number of required subjects in the elementary schools increased from decade to decade. By 1900 . . . a dozen. By 1930 the typical school in cities offered eighteen and by 1950 the number had grown to about thirty. An even more rapid growth of subjects occurred in the high school. A committee report of 1891 lists about thirty subjects . . . In 1923 a superintendent reported that one large city high school listed 168 subjects . . . By the 1950s the offerings were about as broad as human knowledge." Wesley concluded, "It was recognized that the curriculum was a reflection of social progress."

[54] John Dewey was chairman of an independent group, the Commission of Enquiry into Charges Made Against Leon Trotsky in the Moscow Trials, that investigated the purges and particularly the trial of Leon Trotsky. Its report, *Not Guilty* (New York, 1938), identified John Dewey as "Founder of Progressive Education in the United States" (p. v).

ceptance of the "schools for democracy" concept.[55] These schools had now come to believe that the mass appeal of the new "democratic" approach was much more consistent with their own educational activities than the intensely individualistic appeal of the early progressives. Further, the public schools tended to take a rather cool view of the country day schools that had dominated the Association in the Twenties. "Democracy" was hardly a distinguishing feature of these havens for the privileged.

The PEA first openly recognized its commitment to the "schools for a democracy" slogan in the report of the Resolutions Committee presented at the Association's 1938 national conference. An acute observer of the PEA might easily have predicted this development on the basis of a look through *Progressive Education* in the two or three preceding years. Numerous articles pointed the way to convergence on the democratic concept. At the conference of 1938 formal tribute was paid to the early leaders and goals of the Association, after which the committee quickly launched a statement of the present needs of the organization. Asserting that educational goals are indigenous to each culture, the committee noted that the American democratic society was undergoing certain stresses, particularly economic ones, and concluded,

> The common schools and teacher education institutions have not made adequate provisions for those learning experiences effective in developing insight, attitudes, and skills essential to directing the evolution of our democratic culture.[56]

The report then listed six specific ways in which the Association might assist in the desired cultural direction: aid experiments seeking methods

[55] Although it is extremely difficult to measure exactly how educational methods changed in individual public schools, the increasing membership of the Association, the publication of books in which progressive education was regarded as an established fact (for example, Mary Ross Hall, *Children Can See Life Whole* [New York, 1940]), and the beginnings of criticism of progressive education in the popular press (for example, a special issue of *Survey Graphic* devoted to "Schools: The Challenge of Democracy to Education," 27 [October, 1939], pp. 569–630) all testify to the increased acceptance of progressive education by the public schools. The increasing representation of public school personnel on the PEA Board of Directors is discussed in Chapter VI.

[56] "Report of the Resolutions Committee," *Progressive Education* 15 (April, 1938), p. 282.

of conserving and expanding democratic values; support the American Council on Education's new teacher-training project; cooperate with other groups demanding adequate financial support, including federal aid, for education; join other organizations urging the improvement of social security through the use of democratic instruments for controlling change; protest the growth of authoritarianism and dictatorship in this country; and promote the "basic unity of mankind."[57]

But at the annual meeting the Association failed to support the resolutions committee's report. Instead it was decided by vote to spend the next year studying the questions raised in it. In the next issue of *Progressive Education* both Jesse Newlon, then chairman of the Department of Social and Philosophical Foundations of Education at Teachers College, and Eugene Randolph Smith commented on the report. Newlon regretted that it had not earned the unqualified support of the Association, and Smith lamented the Association's increasingly apparent tendency to extend its interests beyond educational matters.[58]

Newlon and Smith symbolized the conflicts within the Association during the two previous decades. Smith was one of the founders of the PEA, headmaster during his lifetime of two different independent schools, the Park School in Baltimore and Beaver Country Day School in suburban Boston. Smith alone, of the early private school leaders of the Association, had remained active in the PEA throughout the thirties. Newlon, once a public school teacher and superintendent of schools in Denver, was a faculty member of Teachers College and had recently become chairman of the department at the College that most ardently sought educational reform. His colleagues in the department were Counts, Childs, Rugg, and (until his retirement in 1938) Kilpatrick. Newlon's path was the one the Association would follow in the subsequent years.

[57] *Ibid.*, pp. 282–283.
[58] Jesse Newlon, "Discussion of the Report of the Resolutions Committee," *Progressive Education* 15 (May, 1938), p. 414, and Eugene Randolph Smith, "Democracy, the Progressive Education Association and the Proposed Resolutions," *Progressive Education* 15 (May, 1938), pp. 415–419.

CHAPTER V

Progressivism in Flower

Originally the PEA had thought of itself chiefly as a clearing house for information about progressive education. It had eschewed all political activity, had even avoided seeking foundation grants for fear of "limiting its spontaneity." Spontaneity might also be limited by commitment to systematic research, and so the early PEA was often more content to describe and eulogize rather than to initiate educational experiments. The thirties brought new things, changes the retired Stanwood Cobb regretted (he was particularly bitter about PEA's turning to the foundations), but he was comforted by another old-timer, Queene Ferry Coonley, who assured him that the Association as they had conceived it had served its purpose to awaken the public to the ideas of progressive education.[1]

Mrs. Coonley was right; the nation had recognized the existence of progressive education. But there was the road ahead. Although by 1930 progressive education had been introduced to many segments of the American public, widespread endorsement of the movement was still lacking. Such endorsement became the goal of the Association during the thirties. The early PEA had used both its magazine *Progressive Education* and its annual convention to gain converts. Now the Association expanded these and other activities.

Spreading the Word

In 1930 *Progressive Education,* which had been a quarterly publication since its inception in 1924, became a monthly. In the same year

[1] Interview with Stanwood Cobb, October 29, 1962.

Gertrude Hartman, Mrs. Coonley's choice as editor, finally resigned.[2] Out with Miss Hartman went the policy of devoting each issue of the magazine to a single theme, and later issues of the periodical included much greater variety of articles. Well along in the thirties the practice of centering an issue on a single topic was occasionally revived. But generally in this decade the magazine offered articles on a number of topics in each issue; apparently the Board of Directors believed that greater variety would attract more readers, and, through them, more subscribers and members. Ann Shumaker succeeded Miss Hartman as editor and remained in this post until a year before her death in December, 1935. She was succeeded by Frances M. Foster, editor from 1934 to 1937. In 1937 Elsie Ripley Clapp became editor. Miss Clapp's selection gave support to those Association members who urged the organization to limit its principal activities to those directly connected with education and the schools. Along with Carleton Washburne, Miss Clapp had been opposed to unqualified endorsement of the report of Counts' Committee on Social and Economic Problems. Miss Clapp was well known for her work with rural schools in Kentucky and her advocacy of the school as a community center. Her 1952 book, *The Use of Resources in Education,* would contain as its introduction John Dewey's last public statement on education. Miss Clapp also served briefly as chairman of the PEA's Committee on Home and School Relations.

Although it had lost its early artistic elegance, *Progressive Education* was an important mouthpiece of the educational profession throughout the thirties. The journal contained articles by all the leading progressive educators, and these educators, the leaders in that decade, included Dewey and Kilpatrick both of whom contributed frequently. Portions of some of the decade's more important books in education appeared first in *Progressive Education;* these included Howard K. Beale's *A History of the Freedom of Teaching in the United States,* Boyd Bode's *Progressive Education at the Crossroads,* and Merle Curti's *The Social Ideas of American Education.*[3]

---

[2] Throughout the middle and late twenties the Executive Board Minutes recorded Miss Hartman's threatened resignations. Apparently, in addition to genuine editorial differences between Miss Hartman and the incoming university-dominated Executive Board, she wanted to devote a greater portion of her time to her own writing.

[3] Howard K. Beale, "Dare Society Deny its Teachers Freedom?" *Progressive Education* 11 (January–February, 1934), pp. 13–25; Boyd H. Bode, "Education at the Crossroads," *Progressive Education* 8 (November, 1931), pp. 543–549; Merle Curti, "The Social Ideas of American Educators," *Progressive Education* 11 (January–February, 1934), pp. 26–31.

Sponsorship of conferences was another method PEA used to popularize progressive education in the thirties. As the decade progressed, the Association planned and carried on summer institutes, regional and subregional conferences, local meetings, "work-study" conventions, and group discussions. Every year since its founding the PEA had sponsored an annual convention. Gradually these occasions drew larger and larger numbers; in 1936 over 4,500 persons attended the annual meeting.[4] The PEA had frequently arranged its annual convention date to coincide in time and place with the NEA's meeting, but by the late thirties PEA no longer needed the pull of the older organization's convention. The 1936 banner crowd assembled at the PEA gathering in Chicago while the NEA held its convention in Portland, Oregon.

In addition to the annual conference, the PEA sponsored a number of regional meetings. In the early thirties these were largely in the eastern United States, but by the mid-thirties, mainly on the initiative of Executive Secretary Frederick L. Redefer, the Association organized conferences throughout the nation. In 1936 nearly two dozen gatherings took place in such scattered locations as Portland, Oklahoma City, Montevallo (Alabama), Toledo, and Hartford.[5] The proliferation of conference centers continued, and in 1938 nearly fifty such meetings occurred. Besides the metropolitan centers many smaller towns were hosts for PEA-sponsored conferences. In 1938 these included Morgantown, West Virginia; Winona, Minnesota; Findlay, Ohio; Santa Barbara, California; and LaCrosse, Wisconsin.[6] Clearly the PEA had moved from its former isolation among private schools into the arena of public education.

Many of these regional meetings attracted nationally known speakers. At one New York City meeting in 1933, speakers included Eleanor Roosevelt, Norman Thomas, Louis Howe, Harry Overstreet, Sidney Hook, and William Heard Kilpatrick.[7] The indefatigable Kilpatrick, as well as Boyd Bode and Burton P. Fowler, frequently traveled about the country stumping for progressive education.

For some time the Association had shrewdly recognized the importance of courting teachers attending college and university summer sessions and had sent its executive secretary on lecture tours to various centers of higher education. Beginning in 1929, the Association spon-

---

[4] "News Notes and Reviews," *Progressive Education* 13 (April, 1936), p. 300.
[5] *Loc. cit.*
[6] *Loc. cit.*
[7] "News of the Association," *Progressive Education* 10 (November, 1933), p. 435.

sored a series of annual summer campus programs. The first was at Pennsylvania State University, and 145 persons attended the three-week session. Next summer 75 turned up for a six-week institute at Vassar College that the PEA sponsored in conjunction with the college's Euthenics Institute.[8] For the next two years Syracuse University campus was the home of the PEA summer institutes, and in 1932 the Association sponsored an additional institute at Alabama College. The year 1933 saw the Association cooperating with summer institutes on progressive education at Syracuse, New York State Teachers College at Buffalo, Alabama College, and College of Charleston. There was also a PEA summer conference in the Virgin Islands.[9]

The peak of the summer programs was in 1933. After that the PEA characteristically shifted its attention to other activities, although summer programs were held at Sarah Lawrence College in Bronxville, New York, in both 1937 and 1938. The Association published a number of booklets containing the major addresses at the annual conferences; these began in 1937 and were titled *Progressive Education Booklets*. Another brief venture was a series of radio talks that the PEA sponsored in 1930 and 1931, and again in 1938. Speakers engaged for the first talks admirably illustrated the diversity of the movement. Kilpatrick and Counts of Teachers College; Caroline Pratt, principal of the highly individualistic City and Country School; Robert Leigh, president of Bennington College; Florence Cane, art instructor at her sister's psychologically oriented Walden School; and Howard W. Nudd, director of the Public Education Association of New York City.[10]

[8] "News of the Association," *Progressive Education* 8 (February, 1931), p. 156.

[9] "News and Comments," *Progressive Education* 10 (May, 1933), pp. 288–289. The extent of the spread of progressive education even in 1933 was revealed by the number of summer workshops dealing with progressive education sponsored by various colleges: Ohio State University; Teachers College, Columbia University; University of Cincinnati; Yale University; University of Chicago; Winnetka Summer School for Teachers; National College of Education; Northwestern University; University of California at Los Angeles; Vassar College; University of Iowa; University of Wisconsin; Duke University; Peabody College for Teachers; Vanderbilt University; Colorado State Teachers College; Cornell University; Western Reserve University; New York University; University of Pittsburgh; and the University of Michigan. Many of these summer programs were staffed with leaders of the PEA.

[10] "News and Comments," *Progressive Education* 7 (November, 1930), pp. 359–360. Another series of radio programs sponsored by the Commission on Human Relations of the PEA began in January, 1938. "Notes and News," *Progressive Education* 14 (November, 1937), p. 566.

Research in the Thirties

Until 1930 the PEA's activities were largely limited to publicizing progressive education; no educational research projects were backed by any arm of the Association. But early in that year, after a long meeting, the Executive and Advisory Boards of the Association issued a statement: "It was the general feeling that in addition to our routine pursuits, we should give assistance in the solution of a few immediate problems. . . ." Specifically, a committee was appointed to enter into a thorough study of college entrance requirements and examinations, and of the whole relationship between schools and colleges.[11] This was the beginning of the PEA's sponsorship of research in education.

The decision to embark upon educational research was one result of the influx into the Association of several young educators aglow with their new profession's faith in science. They had joined the PEA in the belief that this enlightened organization would sponsor projects that the staid and established NEA would avoid. Notable among them were Lois Hayden Meek, director of the Child Development Institute at Teachers College, and Harold Rugg, who had recently joined the Teachers College faculty and was working with the Lincoln school. Miss Meek, Rugg, and their followers impressed many PEA members as showing considerably more interest in the projects themselves than in the Association.

The PEA's first excursion into research required forming the Committee on the Relation of School and College, which was directed by Wilford M. Aikin. Aikin was at that time headmaster of the John Burroughs School, Clayton, Missouri; after his work with the PEA, he joined the faculty of the School of Education at Ohio State University. Aikin's group began its study on a total contribution of $800 from four interested private schools: Lincoln, Tower Hill, Francis W. Parker, and John Burroughs.[12] The first substantial grant came from the Carnegie Corporation's Foundation for the Advancement of Teaching, which

[11] Editorial, *Progressive Education* 7 (June, 1930), p. 252.

[12] "Report of the Commission on the Relation of School and College," *Progressive Education* 9 (April, 1932), p. 292. The headmasters of the four schools that made the initial grant were all active in the PEA: Otis Caldwell, a speaker at the Association's first conference, at the Lincoln School; Burton P. Fowler, then president of the PEA, at the Tower Hill School; Flora J. Cooke, a member of the Advisory Board and a frequent contributor to *Progressive Education,* at the Francis W. Parker School; and Wilford M. Aikin, chairman of the new commission, at the John Burroughs School.

had just sponsored a similar study in Pennsylvania; later, the General Education Board supported the project.

Although originally formed as a "committee," the school and college group became a "commission" in 1934; the change was a symbol of increasing prestige. Among educators, however, the group was familiarly known as sponsors of the "Eight-Year Study." From a number of leading colleges the commission gained the assurance that they would accept for admission certain graduates of the thirty schools participating in the experiment without regard to distribution of the students' high school credits. The commission then compared the progress in college of the students from traditional college preparatory programs and those from the "thirty schools," which had been allowed free rein in their high school curriculum. Selection of the schools, students, and colleges all took place during the thirties, but the extensive evaluation of the experiment and the publication of the commission's reports were not completed until 1942.

Aikin's commission, the first of PEA's research projects, received much early publicity.[13] Partly because of its success, other committees began to sprout in the Association throughout the thirties. Most of them wanted to make rather specific investigations of educational problems. Apart from Aikin's commission, the two other most successful research groups—success being measured in terms of longevity and results produced—were V. T. Thayer's Commission on the Secondary School Curriculum, organized in 1933, and Alice V. Keliher's Commission on Human Relations, formed in 1935. The Thayer commission was constituted on the recommendation of the Aikin group, which had noted the lack of adequate guides to a "progressive" curriculum.

V. T. Thayer, who led the Secondary School Curriculum Commission, was Educational Director of the Ethical Culture Schools in New York City. Apparently the PEA was anxious to maintain a professional balance on the commission's first executive committee, for it was composed of a university professor of education, Boyd Bode; the headmistress of a private school, Katherine Whiteside Taylor; and a superintendent of schools, Willard W. Beatty. The commission rejected

---

[13] Among the best of these early articles were "Committee on School and College Relations," *The School Review* 40 (April, 1932), pp. 241–245; Raymond Walters and Wilford M. Aikin, "Coordination of School and College Work," *School and Society* 35 (June 18, 1932), pp. 841–845; "Experimental College Entrance Units," *North Central Association Quarterly* 9 (January, 1935), pp. 345–363; and "The Schools Dominating the Colleges," *Bulletin of the Association of American Colleges* 21 (May, 1935), pp. 264–295.

minor revisions of subject matter and limited adjustments of teaching methods as a totally unsatisfactory means of curriculum reform. It reported that it conceived instead "the chief task of secondary education to be that of helping adolescents to secure for themselves values, emotional unity, skill, understanding, and purposefulness for the life in which they find themselves involved." [14] The commission soon recognized that its knowledge of adolescents was woefully inadequate, and one of its first acts therefore was to engage Caroline B. Zachry, a New York City psychologist who had studied for her doctorate under Kilpatrick, to head a Committee on Adolescents.[15] Throughout the thirties Miss Zachry conducted an extensive study of adolescent behavior, which she published in 1940 as *Emotion and Conduct in Adolescence*.[16] Although the commission appointed other committees (one under Herbert W. Smith looked into intellectual development), the Zachry committee remained the most effective arm of the Commission on the Secondary School Curriculum.

Out of Thayer's and Aikin's commissions arose a separate body, the Commission on Human Relations, headed by Alice V. Keliher, formerly Elementary Supervisor of the Hartford public schools. Miss Keliher's group was a favorite of the General Education Board that suggested several projects—one was on the educational value of radio and motion pictures—for the commission to study. The establishment of this energetic platoon, which rapidly expanded to include a number of research assistants working on diverse projects, was a significant factor influencing the Association's decision to move to its four-story brownstone headquarters on West 90th Street in New York City in 1935.[17]

Other committees seemed to arise in response to particular interests

[14] "News of the Association," *Progressive Education* 12 (February, 1935), pp. 118–119.

[15] Benjamin Spock has described Miss Zachry as a "pillar of strength and wisdom in the Progressive Education Association" in his article "How My Ideas Have Changed," *Redbook*, October, 1963, p. 122. See also my biographical article of Miss Zachry in the forthcoming *Dictionary of Notable American Women*.

[16] Only two publications of the Commission on the Secondary School Curriculum appeared between 1930 and 1938: Lawrence Henry Conrad, *Teaching Creative Writing* (New York, 1937) and a committee report, *Science in General Education* (New York, 1938).

[17] Among the publications of the Commission on Human Relations between 1930 and 1938 were Alice V. Keliher, *Life and Growth* (New York, 1938); Louise Rosenblatt, *Literature as Exploration* (New York, 1938); Bernhard J. Stern, *The Family: Past and Present* (New York, 1938); and Katharine W. Taylor, *Do Adolescents Need Parents?* (New York, 1938).

of various members. Examples of these were Allan Hulsizer's Committee on Summer Institutes, W. Carson Ryan Jr.'s American Committee on International Education, Harold Rugg's Committee on Adult Education, Paul R. Mort's Committee on Federal Support to Education, and Emma Schweppe's Committee on Cultural Relations. Each of these had a short life, generally ranging from one to three years. Frequently they were organized in the light of the chairmen's fond hopes that by presenting themselves to a foundation, they might be the recipients of a grant from that foundation. The Thayer and Keliher commissions are examples of the successful application of this tactic; the Committee on the Training of Teachers for Progressive Schools is an illuminating illustration of its failure. Variously termed the Committee on the "Training," "Preparation," and, finally, "Education" of Teachers, that group was first headed by Willard W. Beatty in 1933. Later in the year Beatty was succeeded by Laura Zirbes, professor of elementary education and head of the demonstration school at Ohio State University. The group sought a large grant from the General Education Board in order to make a comprehensive survey of teacher education in the United States with particular emphasis upon the new requirements for teachers in progressive schools. The General Education Board, which had already invested nearly half a million dollars in PEA projects, decided to let the American Council on Education administer the teacher-training survey. The disappointed PEA committee finally disbanded in 1937.[18]

The Committee on Rural Schools, later called the Committee on Progressive Education in Rural Schools, was another group that reflected the particular interests of a small section of the PEA's total membership. First headed in 1932 by Allan Hulsizer, who was then director of the rural demonstration school in Georgetown, Delaware, the committee tried to gather information about isolated rural schools in an effort to adapt progressive methods to them. More than any other section of the PEA, this group showed a continuity of interests with the pre-World War I progressives. The concerns of the rural school committee were strikingly similar to those of Mrs. Porter Harvey of Kirksville, Missouri, the incarnation of 1915 rural progressivism.[19]

---

[18] The ACE's Commission on Teacher Education was formally established in 1938 under the over-all direction of Karl W. Bigelow. The commission published eight reports in the 1940s.

[19] Mrs. Harvey was the heroine of Evelyn Dewey's New Schools for Old (New York, 1919).

Appropriately, the committee collaborated with the Vermont Country Life Commission on its first project, a pamphlet entitled "Rural Vermont." Marcia A. Everett, a Helping Teacher in Warren County, New Jersey, succeeded Hulsizer as chairman in 1935. Erwin Sassman of the Francis W. Parker School, Chicago, followed her as chairman in 1936.

Two other committees concentrating on similar problems were Lois Hayden Meek's Committee on Home and School Relations and the Committee on School and Community Relations, first headed by Elsie Ripley Clapp, and later by Edmund DeS. Brunner as the Committee on Community Relations. Both were organized in 1933. In the thirties, the work of Dr. Meek's committee was closely tied in with projects at Teachers College's Child Development Institute, of which she was director. Both these committees saw the school as an institution of great potential influence in all aspects of community life. The Meek committee stressed the subjective influences of school life upon the home while the Clapp-Brunner group was principally concerned with the use of the school as a community center. In its early years under Miss Clapp, the committee focused on rural schools, and its interests tended to duplicate those of the older Committee on Progressive Education in Rural Schools.

Two other committees complete the total of sixteen established between 1930 and 1938. John R. P. French, headmaster of the Cambridge (Massachusetts) School, founded the Committee on Experimental Schools in 1936. A job of this group was to receive and transmit information on educational experiments. It is interesting to note that fifteen years after the PEA had been established "to act as a clearing house for experiments in education," it had moved so far from its original goal that a special committee had to be organized for this purpose. The French committee, however, did not prosper as did its parent organization. Unlike the experimental schools in the twenties, their counterparts in the following decade stressed not the child but his parents and their participation in the school life. They also showed great interest in the relation between the school and the community. In 1937 French's committee published a booklet describing these developments under the title *What the Schools are Doing*. The Commission on Intercultural Education, organized in 1937, was the last group founded during this period. Headed by Fritz Borgeson of New York University, it was an outgrowth of Mrs. Rachel Davis DuBois' work on the Commission on Human Relations.

Political Interests of the Association

In addition to measures taken to popularize progressive education and to investigate educational problems, the PEA also attempted in the thirties to influence public policy on educational and, sometimes, even directly political issues. The Association usually employed the editorial page of *Progressive Education* to propound its views, although in at least one case a special group, the Commission on Educational Freedom, was set up to promulgate the PEA line. Generally the Association limited itself to statements or brief exposés on questions that interested it; rarely did it take any action on these issues.

Those political views that the Association manifested were generally similar to the ones advanced by the most liberal wing of New Deal supporters. This was particularly evident in the later thirties when the editorials of *Progressive Education* and the resolutions at the annual business meetings often extended beyond conventionally educational topics into questions of public moment. They were not overly ambitious, however. In 1936 the Association scolded the Supreme Court for its ruling on the Agricultural Adjustment Act, questioned the American Legion's insistence of flag ceremonies, and cheered Franklin Roosevelt's re-election.[20]

Two major interests of the Association were academic freedom and the role of the federal government in education. Through the activities of the Commission on Educational Freedom and in the pages of *Progressive Education,* the Association gave publicity to infringements of academic freedom. The PEA had originally sought the aid of the American Association of University Professors' committee that was investigating violations of teachers' rights. According to Executive Secretary Redefer, however, the AAUP informed the PEA that it handled only cases on the college level, for in the high schools the teachers "just taught facts." [21] In 1934 the PEA sent Boyd Bode of Ohio State University and Frank Baker of Milwaukee State Teachers College to join representatives of a number of organizations to discuss problems

---

[20] Editorials in *Progressive Education* 13 (February, 1936), pp. 77–78; 13 (April, 1936), pp. 225–226; 13 (December, 1936), pp. 581–582. These views obviously did not represent the total membership but rather, and more significantly for this study, the position of the Association itself. The editorials were frequently followed by the initials of the president of the Association, or the editor of *Progressive Education,* or by a chairman of a commission.

[21] Interview with Frederick L. Redefer, November 1, 1962.

of academic freedom. The groups represented were: the American Association of University Women, the American Council on Education, the American Civil Liberties Union, the American Federation of Teachers, the National Congress of Parents and Teachers, the National Education Association, the National Council on Religion in Higher Education, and Phi Delta Kappa.[22] On the basis of this meeting and the earlier rebuff by the AAUP, the PEA formed its own Commission on Educational Freedom in 1935.[23] Although it had emphasized its interest in the academic freedom of the elementary and secondary school teacher, the PEA actually devoted a considerable fraction of its time to the problems of college faculty. The Commission on Educational Freedom was the only one formed by the PEA to have regional chapters; during the late thirties these local groups carried on a number of investigations, although their work did not receive substantial publicity.[24]

The Association also criticized the prohibition of union member-

---

[22] "News of the Association," *Progressive Education* 12 (February, 1935), pp. 122–129; and "News Notes and Comments," *Progressive Education* 12 (March, 1935), p. 209.

[23] In interviews on November 1, 1962, with Frederick L. Redefer and on February 4, 1960, with Goodwin Watson, each contended that the PEA's Commission on Educational Freedom had inspired the formation of the NEA's Defense Committee. Both Watson and H. Gordon Hullfish served as chairmen of the commission. Other members included John McChesney, Hotchkiss School; Beryl Parker, New York University; Ellen Donohue, American Civil Liberties Union; Alonzo Meyers, New York University; Harold Hand, Stanford University; Roma Gans, Teachers College; and George Axtelle, Northwestern University. (The institutional affiliations listed are those at time of the person's service on the commission.)

[24] The principal published reports were: Editorial, *Progressive Education* 13 (December, 1936), pp. 581–582; and the sharply critical letter of the PEA's report of the Davis affair from the president of Yale University, James R. Angell, which appeared in *Progressive Education* 14 (January, 1937), p. 61; and "Resolutions at the Annual Business Meeting," *Progressive Education* 14 (April, 1937), p. 285. Under the principal of freedom of speech, the Association also supported the right of existence of Commonwealth College, Meno, Arkansas, an avowedly socialist institution. Editorial, *Progressive Education* 12 (April, 1935), p. 218.

Reports of cases in the University of Illinois archives include the following investigations: Adams Case; Alma College; Frank August; Cooks Case; Corunna, Mich.; Jerome Davis; Eby Case; Elmhurst Case; Edgemont School; Flint, Mich.; Victor Jewett; Kansas City, Mo.; Highland Park, Mich.; Lark Haven, Manistee, Mich.; Milford, Ohio; Muskegon, Mich.; Payne Case; Oklahoma City; Shields Case; Shigley-Kent School; Syracuse; Valhalla; and Wisconsin Rapids.

ship to St. Louis teachers and the requirements of the Massachusetts State Loyalty Oath.[25] The protests had little effect. The Association was more successful in its campaign to rid the Civilian Conservation Corps manual of its restrictions on discussions of controversial issues. The educational director of the CCC notified the PEA that as a result of the editorial in *Progressive Education* calling the offensive paragraphs to his attention, he was ordering their deletion from subsequent editions of the manual.[26]

A second major political interest of the PEA took the form of its consistent support of the federal government's role in education.[27] In addition to urging federal monetary aid to education, the PEA also encouraged the national government to become more directly involved in educational matters. As early as 1930, PEA had urged the appointment of a Secretary of Education with cabinet rank.[28] In 1937 the Association called for the establishment of a federal department of education.[29] But the Association expressed its disappointment with the National Youth Administration and its fear that the CCC might become a military unit.[30] On the positive side, the Association actively supported the proposed child labor amendment to the Constitution.[31]

On a few deplorable occasions the Association allowed its psychological extremists to turn essentially political or legal problems into psychological or limitedly educational questions. An unhappy instance of this category-switching happened in 1934. That year, the December issue of *Progressive Education* was devoted to mental health. In the "News Notes and Comments" section appeared a letter from a widowed school teacher who had just read Howard K. Beale's article in the January–February number, "Dare Society Deny its Teachers Freedom?" On the basis of that article and the PEA's avowed advocacy of academic freedom, the teacher wrote to *Progressive Education* poignantly

---

[25] Editorial, *Progressive Education* 12 (November, 1935), pp. 433–434.

[26] Editorial, *Progressive Education* 13 (January, 1936), pp. 5–6.

[27] Editorials in *Progressive Education* 10 (December, 1933), pp. 439–440; 11 (March, 1934), p. 154; 12 (January, 1935), pp. 3–4; 12 (March, 1935), p. 211; 12 (May, 1935), p. 287; 12 (October, 1935), pp. 369–370; 12 (December, 1935), pp. 499–500; 15 (April, 1938), p. 273.

[28] Editorial, *Progressive Education* 7 (April, 1930), pp. 145–146.

[29] Editorial, *Progressive Education* 14 (February, 1937), pp. 77-78.

[30] "News Notes and Reviews," *Progressive Education* 13 (April, 1936), pp. 300–303.

[31] Editorials in *Progressive Education* 14 (February, 1937), p. 77; 14 (April, 1937), p. 230; 13 (March, 1936), pp. 149–150; 12 (February, 1935), p. 74; 11 (November, 1934), p. 382.

describing her two-week imprisonment in a Georgia jail while awaiting trial on a charge of inciting an insurrection. According to her letter, she had been arrested while a group met at her home to discuss war, and her home had been searched for Communist literature. She had been released when the grand jury dismissed her case, but she was then fired from her teaching position. The editorial note preceding the letter observed that "many questions" were raised by this communication, but the two that seemed to strike *Progressive Education* of paramount importance were, "What is the effect of repression of ideas upon mental health?" and "What effect has the fear of similar experiences upon the mental health of other teachers?" [32] Such an abysmal misunderstanding of the issues in question could hardly have increased liberals' confidence in the political sophistication of the PEA's leaders. Another comparable example of political naiveté appeared in 1936 in an editorial initialed "F. M. F." (probably the editor, Frances M. Foster) attacking German Nazi policy chiefly for its *"educational harm"* to Jewish boys and girls.[33] These instances show the limited political understanding of some of the PEA leaders responsible for *Progressive Education* and may explain why many persons of academic sophistication hesitated to affiliate with the Association.

Affiliation with the New Education Fellowship

A different activity of the PEA in the thirties grew out of formal affiliation with the British-based international New Educational Fellowship in 1932. The PEA had tenaciously refused to make any formal agreement with the NEF in the twenties, but the new leaders of the Association (particularly, Harold Rugg) did not share Cobb's fear of Beatrice Ensor, NEF's chief evangelist in the United States.[34] In the thirties there was much less need for the Association to be apprehensive about NEF's possible dominance of the PEA than there had been in the previous decade, for by 1932 the PEA had become a strong, independent organization with assertive leaders. Financial difficulties had been an obstacle to merger in the twenties, but even these were not now so pressing. Despite the fact that the Association was often badly in debt in the thirties, its commissions were receiving substantial grants from the foundations.

[32] *Progressive Education* 11 (December, 1934), p. 491.
[33] Editorial, *Progressive Education* 13 (May, 1936), p. 324.
[34] Both Cobb, in an interview on October 29, 1962, and Redefer, in a November 1, 1962 interview, reported Cobb's distrust of Mrs. Ensor.

The NEF held its sixth international conference at Nice in 1932. Harold Rugg, a member of the American Committee on International Education that represented the PEA at the conference, was elected to the governing board of the NEF. Rugg, who for some time had been enthusiastic about international cooperation in education, returned to the United States to present a glowing report on the Nice conference and the NEF to the PEA Board of Directors of which he was a member. On October 1, 1932, the Board voted to make the PEA the American branch of the NEF.[35] At an earlier meeting, the Board had rejected Mrs. Ensor's suggestion that the PEA change its name to the American section of the NEF. At this time all other NEF branches were known as national sections of the parent organization.[36]

Throughout the thirties the PEA kept its relationship with the NEF civil, if not ardent. American representatives of the Association attended the seventh international conference of NEF in Cheltenham, England, in 1936.[37] Following the English meeting, W. Carson Ryan returned to scold the Americans for their "complete lack of an international outlook." [38] The PEA also sent delegations to the regional conferences of the NEF in South Africa in 1934, Mexico in 1935, Canada in 1937, Australia and New Zealand in 1937, and Hawaii in 1938. But the Association's link to the NEF in the thirties was pretty much the result of Harold Rugg's and W. Carson Ryan's insistence. PEA's affairs were prospering in most other areas, and the Association allowed these leaders to carry on their international educational interests under PEA auspices. While the Association officially supported the NEF tie, as a whole it showed less enthusiasm for this project than for its home-grown activities. Perhaps one reason for PEA's lack of interest in the international body was NEF's apparent failure to discriminate in matters of greater or less importance in the activities of its member countries. For many Americans in the thirties, the Soviet Union was the center of their extra-national interests, but the NEF showed no greater interest in Russian education than it did in that of any other nation.

[35] Board of Director Minutes, October 1, 1932.
[36] Board of Director Minutes, December 12, 1931.
[37] The NEF held seven world conferences between 1921 and 1936: Calais, 1921; Montreux, 1923; Heidelberg, 1925; Locarno, 1927; Elsinore, 1929; Nice, 1932; and Cheltenham, 1936. PEA representatives attended all but the 1923 one at Montreux.
[38] Board of Directors Minutes, September 26–27, 1936.

Money and Membership

A perennial interest of the PEA was solvency and the problem immediately related to its solution, membership. As usual, the PEA was short of funds in the early thirties. The substantial individual gift list and the expanding membership, which had improved the Association's fiscal health in 1929 and 1930, both dropped suddenly with the onslaught of the Depression. The period of greatest crisis was 1932 when in a single year the Association accumulated a deficit of over $9,000. Printers' bills accounted for most of this.[39] During that year both Executive Secretary Redefer and Editor Shumaker took leaves of absence without pay. By early 1933, however, the situation had improved. The annual conference brought in a net profit of $2,500, and the membership increased by 1,600 to a total of 7,000.[40] The greatest assistance, however, was a grant of $5,000 in May, 1933, from the General Education Board for "general support and central planning." [41] Although most of GEB's grants to the PEA were to the Association's three major commissions, the Association itself received a $15,000 general grant in 1934 [42] and $2,500 in 1936 "to improve the magazine." [43] Over the years the PEA's commissions received a total of more than $1,500,000 from the GEB. These commission grants helped to publicize the Association itself and thus stimulated increase in membership. Membership growth always lagged two or three years behind the grants to the commissions.

In 1937, *Progressive Education* reported, "It can now be definitely stated that the Association has weathered the economic storm." [44] In the preceding three years the Association had doubled its membership and had secured grants of three quarters of a million dollars for research; at the same time publication and rental costs had doubled.[45] Although pleased with its improvement in fiscal status, the Association recognized that it had reached a "ceiling" in its foundation grants and would in the future have to provide its own sources of support. At that

---

[39] Board of Directors Minutes, March 4, 1933.
[40] *Loc. cit.*
[41] Board of Directors Minutes, May 19–21, 1933.
[42] Board of Directors Minutes, May 13, 1934.
[43] Board of Directors Minutes, February 27–29, 1936.
[44] "News Notes and Reviews," *Progressive Education* 14 (February, 1937), p. 127.
[45] *Loc. cit.*

time only the General Education Board was providing financial assistance to the PEA. The Carnegie Corporation had given the Aikin commission a total of $10,000 between 1931 and 1935. But William Learned, a member of the Carnegie staff who had conducted an educational survey for Carnegie similar to Aikin's for the PEA, seemed not altogether pleased with the work of Aikin's group. Too little attention, it appeared, was paid to objective testing as a means of evaluation. As a result, Carnegie made no further grants to the PEA or to any of its commissions.[46]

In the mid-thirties the Association conducted another campaign for life memberships. This was feasible since most of the persons who had bought life memberships in the twenties were no longer active in the Association, and an entirely new group of prospects was there to be tapped. Some success was achieved in this project, and, with the funds collected, the Association acquired a little "venture capital" that it could use either for emergencies or for projects of particular interest.

After some fluctuation in the early thirties, the Association membership steadily increased, reaching a peak of over 10,000 in 1938. As the decade wore on, drastic qualitative changes in PEA membership occurred. In 1939, only 30 per cent of the Association members were in public school work. By 1937 public school representation had jumped to 70 per cent, leaving only one-fourth of the membership connected with private schools. Parents and other laymen then made up only a very small fraction of the membership.[47]

The PEA was at the height of its flowering in 1938. In its "schools for democracy" theme the Association believed it had found a principle under which its frequently random activities could be unified. Its three major commissions were working on their sundry research projects, comfortably financed by grants from the General Education Board. Members of the various executive committees of the PEA traveled about the nation and even abroad, lecturing and leading group discussions on progressive education. Other educational organizations were seeking the PEA's advice and cooperation on various projects.

Popular acceptance followed professional recognition. *Time* magazine's cover story of October 31, 1938, featured the Progressive Education Association, a color portrait of PEA Executive Secretary Frederick L. Redefer gracing the cover. *Time* assured its readers that Redefer's

---

[46] Letter from Florence Anderson, Secretary of the Carnegie Corporation of New York, October 29, 1962.

[47] Editorial, *Progressive Education* 7 (June, 1930), p. 252, and "News Notes and Reviews," *Progressive Education* 14 (February, 1937), pp. 126–130.

claim, "We are no longer a rebel group," was indeed accurate and seconded the estimate of William C. Bagley, professor of education at Teachers College and one of the PEA's most outspoken critics, that the Association then wielded "a dominant influence in U.S. education." [48] *Time* shrewdly observed, however, that the progressives were justifiably worried that their program was spreading too quickly and too thin. "Most bandwagon-jumping schools have swallowed chunks of Progressive methods, little Progressive philosophy," it noted.[49] In its conclusion *Time* accurately predicted the difficulty that was to haunt the Association during the remaining years of its existence, "For the first principle and the religion of Progressive Educators is Democracy, and their biggest question, how to achieve it." [50]

[48] "Progressive's Progress," *Time* 32 (October 31, 1938), p. 31.
[49] *Loc. cit.*
[50] *Ibid.,* p. 37.

CHAPTER VI

Confusions of Purpose

⊰⊱

Time magazine's 1938 celebration of the Progressive Education Association was flattering and marked genuine national recognition of the PEA. But the feature story did not mean that American educators and laymen were anywhere near unanimity in supporting either progressive education in general or the PEA in particular. Less than fifteen months after Executive Secretary Redefer's picture had appeared on *Time's* cover, *The Saturday Evening Post* published an article titled "Lollipops vs. Learning," an antiprogressive polemic. The author, Ann L. Crockett, who had taught for ten years in a progressive high school, contended that progressive teaching methods, as she had observed them, were neither philosophically nor practically sound. Her criticism of methodology swung wide enough to include the entire progressive movement, but she leveled her attack on progressive education's inadequate philosophy squarely at the PEA:

> Progressivism is not a system at all; it is, rather, an attitude. No comprehensive statement that could pass as its philosophy has ever been issued by the P.E.A., and there is probably no one inclusive statement of it to which all members would agree. Like most Reformers, the Progressivists jumped on too many horses and rode off in too many directions. In twenty years of experience they have never settled on where they should go, or how fast. Out of the welter of definitions and counter-definitions of policy coming from the P.E.A., serious students can glean only two consistent points: First, to fit the school to the individual child; and second, to guard the child against strain in the learning process.[1]

[1] March 16, 1940, p. 29. (Reprinted by permission of *The Saturday Evening Post.* Copyright 1940, The Curtis Publishing Company.) In May, *Pro-*

Although Miss Crockett's criticisms may have been more sweeping than the situation warranted, she was right on one point at least. The Association had no statement of philosophy or purpose. Since its disavowal of the original Seven Principles of Progressive Education in 1929, the Association had sought philosophical harmony, although not always with the same degree of concern. The search for an ideology reached a peak of intensity in 1938 when Paul R. Hanna, professor of education at Stanford University, presented his committee's report on a proposed philosophy to the Association. That statement received only partial support, but it served as the basis upon which a new committee began deliberations. During the year 1938–1939, four conferences were held, and in 1939 a new proposal was presented to the Association at the annual business meeting. The committee solicited comments on the report from the members, and more than sixty individuals or groups replied. The bulk of the work on what became the Association's principal doctrinal statement was completed between 1939 and May 1941.[2] Orville G. Brim, a professor of education at Ohio State University with a particular interest in rural education, served as chairman of the committee during its first year, and his colleague in the School of Education at Ohio State, Harold Alberty, succeeded Brim as chairman. H. Gordon Hullfish, another member of the School of Education faculty at Ohio State, was general editor of the statement. Two other members of the committee, Laura Zirbes and Ruth Streitz, were also on the faculty of Ohio State's School of Education.[3]

Doubtless, convenience dictated the composition of the committee, but the selection of so many Ohio State University faculty members showed that the hold of the eastern professional educators on the leadership of the Association was gradually weakening. In the first decade of its existence, eastern private school leaders had dominated the Association; in the second decade, the period of its greatest power and prestige, eastern professional educators, particularly certain pro-

---

gressive Education contained counterattacks on Miss Crockett's article to which she replied placatingly, "I went to considerable pains to point out that I had no quarrel with the best of the methods of progressive education. I was, clearly, as stated, dealing with schools where the ideals of Progressivism have been carried to stupid and dangerous extremes." *Progressive Education* 17 (May, 1940), p. 299.

[2] The report appeared as a separate supplement to the May, 1941, issue of *Progressive Education* and was entitled, *Progressive Education: Its Philosophy and Challenge* (New York, 1941).

[3] The remaining members of the committee were Alice V. Keliher, Daniel Prescott, Louis Raths, Paul B. Sears, and Paul Witty.

fessors at Teachers College, had led the PEA. In the third decade, one marked by the Association's decline, control shifted to professional educators at midwestern state universities such as Ohio State and Illinois. Only during the first ten years were the PEA leaders chiefly elementary or secondary school teachers or administrators—and, of course, most of these represented private schools. After 1930 the most powerful group in the Association was composed of faculty members of schools of education. A few school superintendents remained important, such as Carleton Washburne and Harold Shane at Winnetka, but in the end they too would leave their superintendencies for university positions (Washburne to Brooklyn College and Shane to Northwestern and then to Indiana University). The membership of the Committee on Philosophy provided the first concrete example of this new trend; another example was the election in 1940 of Carleton Washburne as national president of the PEA, the first since 1930 from west of the Alleghenies. After 1940 nearly all the presidents of the PEA represented midwestern universities.[4]

Toward the end of the thirties, Boyd H. Bode had become sharply critical of the progressive movement's failure to achieve a sense of social responsibility and a coherent philosophy.[5] Although Bode was the most prominent member of the education faculty of Ohio State, he was not appointed to the PEA committee on philosophy. He represented the "old school" progressives. Like Dewey he had been in the vanguard of the movement, first advocating greater freedom for the child and a curriculum less determined by tradition, and later urging the schools to accept their responsibilities. Of the senior national leaders in educational philosophy, Dewey, Bode, and to a lesser degree

[4] Washburne's successors were Vinal Tibbetts and Virgil Rogers, both public school administrators, the former from Long Island, New York, and the latter from suburban Chicago. Tibbetts and Rogers shared the presidency of the Association during parts of 1943 and 1944. They were succeeded by Frank E. Baker, president of Milwaukee State Teachers College, 1944–1946; John J. DeBoer, professor of education at Roosevelt University and later (1947) University of Illinois, 1946–1948; Kenneth Benne, then professor of education at the University of Illinois, 1949–1951; H. Gordon Hullfish, professor of education, Ohio State University, 1951–1955.

[5] Bode's *Progressive Education at the Crossroads* (New York, 1938) criticized the movement's failure to achieve a sense of social responsibility and a coherent philosophy; and that—as well as his age and imminent retirement—effectively separated him from the younger and often more woolly-headed enthusiasts of progressive education.

Kilpatrick made their chief contributions to pedagogy prior to 1940.[6] All three of these older educators, as well as other veterans like Counts and Rugg, continued to write during and after World War II, but of all the pre-World War II leaders of the PEA only the perennial Rugg continued his active role after the war when American pedagogy was dominated by younger men. After 1945 new educational organizations such as Association for Supervision and Curriculum Development (ASCD) and National Council for Accreditation of Teacher Education (NCATE) moved into the national spotlight, and many of the leaders of these groups were more concerned with practical curricular problems than with educational theories. Although the ideology of the progressive education movement did not shift as noticeably as it had before and after the First World War, the leadership of the Association underwent nearly as complete a reorganization as the leadership of the movement had between 1915 and 1920. Much of the enthusiasm that had marked the organization in the thirties was gone in 1945. The remedies offered by the Association in 1933 during the anxiety of the Depression seemed inappropriate to a nation caught up in a wave of new economic prosperity. Criticisms of capitalism had become distinctly less popular.

Failure of the 1941 Statement

Recognizing the variety of views that had characterized the progressive education movement during the past twenty years, the Committee on Philosophy observed in its report that:

> It is entirely normal that within the membership of the Progressive Education Association there should be wide differences of position and conviction. It is of the essence of the progressive attitude that differences be carefully protected, even fostered. A statement of common philosophy is, therefore, difficult to make. Yet events and convictions force the effort. . . . It is now entirely clear that education, if it is not to remain at the mercy of uncriticized tradition or become the victim of relentless social forces, must dedicate itself to the clarification and achievement of those values to which our best thinking now points. Here, at last, we find a common ground.[7]

[6] Theodore Brameld has noted William Heard Kilpatrick's interest and activity in the various changes in PEA policy in the postwar years, but Kilpatrick's position seems to have been that of a respected elder rather than a crusading leader.

[7] *Progressive Education: Its Philosophy and Challenge, op. cit.,* p. 3.

The report was divided into five sections: Basic Democratic Values, Requisites for Individual Development, The Effects of a Confused Culture, Evaluating Educational Results, and Implications for the Educational Profession. Only the fifth dealt with education, and under this heading the committee discussed ten "implications."

I. The school should be the exemplification of democratic living at its best.

II. There should be greater recognition of and cooperation with other social agencies on the part of educators.

III. If the school is to be an integral part of its community, it must be organized in terms of such responsibilities. Too often the mechanics of school organization interfere with its real purpose and function.

IV. When educators believe that the democratic way is the best way of working together, they will re-make their professional values in these terms.

V. Education should deal directly with the values individuals hold as they enter educative experiences.

VI. Educators should be interested in the history of the growth and development of each individual.

VII. The significance of the view herein developed of the individual as a dynamic and unitary organism is far-reaching. At no point is this more evident than in those expressive attitudes we normally associate with aesthetic interests.

VIII. The educator should recognize more clearly that his efforts will create active patterns of behavior.

IX. The educator has the responsibility to help individuals select values and purposes in terms of what may properly be called "their surrounding reality."

X. If we are to entertain real hope for the progressive advancement of the democratic values, our present practices in the education of teachers must be reconceived and reconstructed.[8]

Understandably this attempt to state a systematic philosophy for the Association failed to rally the organization or to be taken seriously as the credo of the progressive education movement. The most obvious

[8] The first sentence of each section is included except in two instances in which two sentences are included to clarify the committee's report. *Progressive Education: Its Philosophy and Challenge, op. cit.*, pp. 23–28.

explanation for this failure was the language of the statement, platitudinous to the point of vacuity. Another example of turgid prose may be drawn from the committee's effort to summarize its assumptions:

> In a word, the Committee will attempt to set a *direction* for education, the gradual realization of which may become the value by which education defines itself as progressive. It believes that men *become intelligent* in social action, and that they may *become devoted* to the view that that which makes human association *human* is the responsible use of intelligence on the part of all in the interests of all.[9]

Dewey's *Democracy and Education* certainly did not establish standards of stylistic clarity, but at least the ideas in that work were discernible. The committee's prose style so thoroughly obscured any concepts that it might have wished to clarify that one could glean little from the report but the earnestness of the writers and their benevolent intentions.

The foggy language hid a more fundamental difficulty—the committee's attempt to base an educational policy on two contradictory premises. Spirited denials to the contrary notwithstanding, the committee's effort was substantially an attempt to compromise the two previous extremes of progressive education—the child-centered enthusiasm of the twenties and the society-centered evangelism of the thirties. At the beginning of its report, the committee asserted that it was "not interested in battling for either position. Apart from a reconstruction that would make each extreme unrecognizable, it is doubtful that a reconciliation of these two positions is possible." [10] The committee was quite right; reconciliation was impossible. Nevertheless the committee attempted it. The early child-centered thesis of progressive education was re-labeled "Requisites for Individual Development," and its antithesis was recognized as "The Effects of a Confused Culture." Hopefully, the committee strove for reconciliation and advance in terms of the all-embracing concept of "Basic Democratic Values." But unlike Hegel's "synthesis on the higher level," the committee's attempt to liquidate the polarity between child-centeredness and society-consciousness in the solvent of "democracy" failed to satisfy the philosophical demands of the situation. The "reconstruction," which the PEA recognized as necessary, was not achieved. Claims about "basic democratic values" remained imprecise; they neither

[9] *Ibid.*, p. 4.
[10] *Loc. cit.*

established an idea nor delineated a line of action. The most that could be said for them was that they set a tone of moral uplift.

By its invocation of "democracy" the committee strove to move the Association away from narrowly defined educational interests into some sort of social purposefulness. In an effort to relate its comments on "Basic Democratic Values" to education, the committee set down in the italics it used with prodigality, *"The Committee holds the dominant ideals of our democratic culture, consciously reinterpreted and refined, provide this central direction for education."* [11] The statement made clear that all educational activities must be judged on the degree to which they were consistent with "the dominant ideals of our democratic culture." Application of the criterion of "democracy" to measure value of educational activities in schools throughout the United States resulted in what many early progressives considered disastrous consequences in the forties and early fifties. In any case, "democracy" had been extended from the area of political philosophy to educational policy and had replaced learning and even "growth" as the official meaning of education.

Dissension in the War Years

Pervasive dissatisfaction, a chronic symptom of the PEA in the late thirties, continued unabated following publication of the report of the Committee on Philosophy. The unity that the Association had hoped would result from the report did not ensue. The ineffective language of the document was read under the glare of a war that was soon to become global. Americans were moving from their customary peacetime occupations to governmental and military activities. After Pearl Harbor, the PEA began to lose its leaders to military service. By 1943 a number of leaders of the Association were in uniform; Carleton Washburne, president of the PEA, and Frederick L. Redefer, its devoted director, offered their talents to the Army. Both Washburne's and Redefer's reminiscences of this period suggest that they left the Association and its myriad problems without real regret.

In many ways Washburne's record of leadership in the Association matched Harold Rugg's for durability, if not for variety and changeability of interests. Washburne had been introduced to progressive education when he was a student at the Chicago school named for the man Dewey called "the father of the progressive education movement," Francis W. Parker. Washburne went on to study at San Francisco

[11] *Ibid.*, p. 5 (italics mine).

Normal School under Frederick Burk, a protege of G. Stanley Hall. Imbued with the ideas of Parker and Hall, as translated by their followers, Cooke and Burk, Washburne moved to the upper-income Chicago suburb of Winnetka in 1919, the same year the PEA was founded. There he introduced to the public elementary schools his method of individualizing instruction, which became renowned in America as the "Winnetka Plan."

Washburne joined the Association in the twenties, and although he later recalled that he found Stanwood Cobb and his colleagues "misty-eyed," [12] his own eyes, in fact, were not entirely dry. He too claimed that the school's job was the development of children's creativity. As did many of the early leaders of PEA, Washburne represented the elementary school, and although his was publically supported and most of theirs were privately financed, the difference in clientele in this particular case was minimal.[13] Washburne shared some of the early PEA leaders' interests in international education, and in the twenties he toured Europe visiting various "progressive" schools.[14] He remained active in the Association throughout the thirties, although during that decade his political and social conservatism stood at considerable variance with the views of the leaders of the Association. He was particularly opposed to Counts' demands for social indoctrination in the schools.[15] By the late thirties Washburne's pedagogical bent came back into favor under the rubric of "education for democracy." In 1940 he was at last elected president of the Association for a three-year term. On his return to the United States after World War II, Washburne followed the path of many school superintendents by joining the faculty of a school of education (Brooklyn College). He remained active in the PEA, again trying to scale down radical proposals at PEA meetings in the late forties, and continued his interests in foreign education as an American representative of the NEF.

After both Washburne and Redefer left for war service, the actual management of the Association fell to Vinal Tibbetts and Virgil Rogers, the former, superintendent of schools in River Forest, Illinois, and the

---

[12] Interview with Carleton Washburne, May 19, 1960.

[13] Martin Mayer quotes Francis Keppel, then Dean of the Harvard Graduate School of Education, as calling such wealthy suburban school systems "private schools run on public funds." *The Schools* (New York, 1961), p. 43.

[14] Washburne published his impressions of this trip in *New Schools in the Old World* (New York, 1926).

[15] Washburne's opinions on this subject were recorded in the minutes of the annual business meeting of the Association, March 4, 1933.

latter having been associated with the schools of Manhasset, New York. During the difficult war years these relative newcomers to PEA affairs were beset by problems on every side. The philosophy committee's 1941 report had been received rather glumly. The General Education Board's last major grant to the Association had expired in 1941, and by 1943 the Association was nearly insolvent. The important commissions of the Association had disbanded, and the reports of the much-heralded "Eight-Year Study," the work of Aikin's commission, appeared in 1942 in virtual obscurity. Of the old PEA leaders, only Rugg, Kilpatrick, and Childs remained active. Rugg assumed the editorship of the final issues of *Frontiers of Democracy* in the fall of 1943; Kilpatrick, then nearly seventy years of age, was chairman of the Board of Editors. Rugg finally became thoroughly disgusted with the Association when, in the midst of one of its most agonizing financial crises, it refused him $300 for editorial expenses in the October–December, 1943, issues of the magazine.[16] Those were the final issues of the once vital journal.

By the time of the fall board meeting in 1943, the old organization was nearly dead. Rogers was chosen to fill Tibbett's remaining term as president of the Association, and Tibbetts moved to Redefer's old position as director.[17] Of the seventeen persons at the meeting only three, Theodore Brameld, B. Othanel Smith, and Roma Gans, were leaders in the postwar Association.[18] At the meeting new names for the Association were considered. The decision to change the name of the Association was based on the group's conviction that the term "progressive education" unnecessarily narrowed the scope of its activities, and the Association, which was fundamentally a "pioneering group," must be free to "recognize new jobs in new times." Specifically, the group now saw the Association's task to be a "move to a larger basis of operation than was previously true." Brameld, one of the few nationally known educators who remained active in the PEA throughout the turbulent decade of the forties, opposed the shift in name. Progressive education, Brameld contended, was known as a definite philosophy of education, and, as a result, by the decision to eliminate the old name

---

[16] Rugg recounted this incident with some bitterness in his *Foundations for American Education* (Yonkers-on-Hudson, 1947), p. 581.

[17] Tibbetts left the Manhasset schools after a serious disagreement with the school board. His abrupt departure from Manhasset made possible his acceptance of the directorship of the PEA following Redefer's resignation in 1943. See Carleton Washburne's letter to officers and members of the Board of Directors of the PEA, August 17, 1943, in the Archives at the University of Illinois.

[18] Minutes of the Board of Directors Meeting, October 15–17, 1943.

"[we] may be accused of being ashamed of our work, of giving up the fight." [19] Even in 1944, Brameld was not a man who shunned unpopular causes or who avoided a fight.[20]

Considerable discussion over the proposed re-christening followed, and a variety of names was proposed: Community Education Association, National Association for Democratic Living, Association for International Cooperation, American Educational Union, and American Education Fellowship. The last seemed best, although there was some feeling that the word "education" should be omitted from the new name to facilitate a broadening of the Association's activities; the final choice was "American Education Fellowship." The secretary of the meeting noted that "The name American Education Fellowship was most favored by the committee for the following reasons: (1) the linking connotation with the New Education Fellowship, (2) the word 'fellowship' is symbolic of our general aim and purpose." [21]

Thus again, as it had done once before in a period of crisis twenty years before, the Association turned to its European pedagogical counterparts to reaffirm membership in a common movement.[22] It was no accident that the Association's official interest in the NEF was greatest in the twenties and in the forties, periods of crisis for both groups. In the thirties when the PEA had been relatively prosperous, it had a minimal amount of contact with the NEF.

Inevitably the decision to drop "Progressive Education Association" necessitated finding a new title for the journal that had so long and faithfully reflected the organization's old name. Among the new titles

[19] *Loc. cit.*
[20] Brameld's career, begun in the years of the Depression, has embodied a number of controversies, largely stemming from a political ideology that favored a more rational distribution of national wealth than he found under American capitalism. A discussion of this principle in his *Design for America* (New York, 1945), a publication sponsored by the Association, evoked much criticism.
[21] Minutes of October 15–17, 1943. The members voted on the name change in a mail ballot, the results of which were announced as favoring the new name "by a vote of ten to one." "American Education Fellowship," *Progressive Education* 21 (May, 1944), p. 201. Unfortunately, but perhaps understandably, the total number of ballots cast was not given. One might suspect, however, that it was very low, for in a period of greater activity and on a more heated issue, the 1947 policy statement, Harold G. Shane, then superintendent of the Winnetka schools, recalled that only 68 votes were cast. Interview, July 25, 1960.
[22] Despite the change to American Education Fellowship from 1944 to 1953, "Progressive Education Association" will be used throughout this book to identify the organization.

proposed for the magazine were "Current Education," "Educational Adventures," "Learning to Live," and "Education Today." The unanimous choice was "Education Today," the change to be effected immediately.[23] A month later the board had to look for another title, since "Education Today" turned out to be the name of an existing periodical. "American Education" was then selected and voted into immediate use,[24] only to be dropped at the next meeting; it appeared that this title too was pre-empted by a current periodical. A third time the board met and strove; the fruit of its exertions this time was "Education for Democracy." [25] But as luck would have it, this admirable title was also unavailable for use. The Association abandoned its search and continued to publish the journal as *Progressive Education.*

To add to the problems of the journal in the war years, its editor, Toni Taylor, left during the summer of 1944 to join the staff of *Look* magazine. In January, 1944, the price of the journal had dropped from fifty to thirty-five cents a copy, and even at the lower price it was not a bargain. In the twenties *Progressive Education* had high standards of format and art work, and in the thirties it had considerably improved its editorial content. Its list of contributors in the thirties included most of the leading figures in American elementary and secondary education, as well as those in professional schools of education. A quota of those prominent in higher education were contributors as well.[26] The contributions of the forties, understandably enough, were not of the same quality. The war alone could not explain the serious decline of the magazine, although it may have hastened its deterioration. As a group, American educators of the forties were not concerned about the questions of creative expression or social indoctrination that had absorbed their predecessors in the two previous decades. In the absence of the old issues, the Association seemed becalmed, unwilling or unable to conceive viable alternative questions.

The lack of clear purpose, contributing to the increasing paralysis of the Association, was shown in the Board of Director's statement of May, 1944, justifying the organization's new name and policies:

> Education must not only participate in community affairs, it must join with all types of people who wish to build "schools of the people."

[23] Minutes of the Board of Directors Meeting, October 15–17, 1963.
[24] Minutes of the Executive Committee, November 1, 1943.
[25] Minutes of the Executive Committee, April 3–4, 1944.
[26] Among the contributors of the thirties were historians James Truslow Adams, Howard K. Beale, and Merle Curti; educators John L. Childs, George Counts, John Dewey, William Heard Kilpatrick, Robert Leigh, and Alexander Meiklejohn.

It must cope with community problems and help to determine what the future of every community is to be like. The period which we are now entering should be marked by a more intimate relationship with parents, interest groups, adult education—in short, with all aspects of the community which surround the child and curriculum and which largely determine whether the schools are or are not to function as people's schools.[27]

The absence of dynamism and professional interest in this vague populism was apparent. Education's social responsibilities were declared boundless; its academic responsibilities were not mentioned.

In the fall of 1944, *Progressive Education* announced "A New Program for New Times." The statement of purpose of this manifesto called attention to the need "to define good education; and then to enlist and direct fighting interest of its membership to achieve it." Some methods of achieving "good education" were set down as well as an additional list of eight suggestions as to how the Association might assist in executing these reforms.[28] Neither the stated purpose nor the various general and specific methods of effecting it revealed anything but a superficial approach to a highly complex philosophical question. To define good education is a problem that has been the concern of philosophers since Plato. The writers of "New Program for New Times" dodged the problem of definition (they had raised it themselves) and hurried on to claims that "good education" could be achieved by "applying democratic principles to the educative process," by "integrating the school more completely into the life of the community," and, finally, by "utilizing school equipment more efficiently."[29] The Association was in fact applying a shotgun approach to many problems in the apparent hope that at least a few of these proposed courses of action would solve some problems. Even scare tactics were dragged in to discredit educational celebrities suspected of recommending conservative reforms.[30] Thus it became clear even to those sympathetic to

[27] "American Education Fellowship," *Progressive Education* 21 (May, 1944), p. 201.

[28] *Loc. cit.*

[29] *Loc. cit.*

[30] Typical of the barrage that the Association issued was a letter sent January 7, 1944, over the signature of Vinal Tibbetts, then director. He enclosed a press release announcing a series of radio talks sponsored by Educator for Freedom, Inc., an organization committed to assisting American education to produce "better informed, more responsible, and more thoughtful citizens." Among the twelve speakers on the series were Walter Lippmann, Robert Hutchins, Stringfellow Barr, Scott Buchanan, Mortimer Adler, Pitirim A. Sorokin, John Erskine, Mark Van Doren, and

progressive education that such an unsystematic ideological approach had little chance of success. The Association's ultimate failure was final evidence that its ills were not curable by haphazard treatment.[31]

The deterioration of the Association that had begun in the late thirties accelerated during the war years. Leaders of the progressive education movement itself increasingly disassociated themselves from the organization. Although Dewey remained honorary president until his death in 1952, his last major statement to the Association was during a speech in 1937.[32] Boyd H. Bode, never as closely connected with the PEA as some of the other leaders of the progressive movement, made his last general statement in *Progressive Education* in 1940. This was his highly critical review of V. T. Thayer's *Reorganizing Secondary*

Alexander Meiklejohn. Tibbett's letter referred to "the sinister aspects of the new movement" and noted that Sorokin's recent book, *The Crisis of Our Age* (New York, 1941), was "enough to give the creeps to any progressive." Tibbetts concluded, "All of these men at one time or another have shown their reactionary hand as individuals. Now they are ganging up, obviously to frighten the American people into taking education back to the middle ages. . . . I suggest that you and all the progressives you know listen carefully to these broadcasts which are being put on apparently with plenty of money behind them and do whatever you can to arouse progressives to this very definite threat." At least two of the speakers, Lippmann and Meiklejohn, had befriended progressive education in earlier years. Ohio State University Archives.

[31] Surviving correspondence in the Illinois archives gives a sample of members' opinions of the change of name and the new program. Among those writing the organization in support of the statement were A. R. Mead, University of Florida; Fred Calkins, of the Marshall School, Albuquerque, New Mexico; Grace Langdon, Federal Works Agency; and Ruth Streitz, Ohio State University. Writing to Tibbetts on January 17, 1944, H. Gordon Hullfish, however, sharply criticized the name change, "I find myself more than a little disturbed by the suggestions of the Board to change the name of the Association. I have no objection to what is implied in the particular recommendation, American Education Fellowship. Many people are certain to regard such a change as a retreat under sharp fire and I'll be damned if I want to play into the hands of our critics." Writing to Hullfish on December 5, 1952, Frederick L. Redefer noted that he had supported the change in name in 1944 in the hope that it would stimulate the organization's international activities. Since he believed the name change was construed as a "retreat," he favored a return to Progressive Education Association.

[32] John Dewey, "The Challenge of Democracy to Education," *Progressive Education* 14 (February, 1937), pp. 129–130. Dewey published one additional article in the journal, "Implications of S. 2499, The Education Act of 1947," 24 (April, 1947), pp. 206–207.

Education, the summary report of the Association's Commission on the Secondary School Curriculum. While admitting progressive education's responsibility for the development of democracy, Bode concluded, "But if the program for reorganization offered in this book is a fair sample of what progressive education has to contribute, it will be superseded and it will deserve to be." [33] The Thayer program, while similar to the notions the Association lauded in subsequent policy pronouncements like the "New Program for New Times," was perhaps more systematic than any of them. Bode's prophecy was accurate, but not immediately fulfilled.

Attempt at Resurgence

Although the Association's situation had been precarious throughout the war, it did manage to rally briefly in the immediate postwar years. This temporary revitalization resulted largely from the efforts of a group of professors of education at midwestern state universities, particularly the University of Illinois. The renewed activity began shortly after John J. DeBoer was elected president of the Association in 1946.[34] DeBoer, then a professor of education at Roosevelt University, Chicago, was a native Chicagoan, receiving his Ph.D. from the University of Chicago in 1938. He was known to educators as the unsuccessful candidate who opposed George S. Counts for the presidency of the American Federation of Teachers in 1940. By 1940 Counts had moved considerably from his position of the early thirties, and he campaigned at the convention in opposition to Stalinism, accusing Stalinists of the recent murder of Leon Trotsky in Mexico City. DeBoer, though certainly not a spokesman of the Stalinists, nevertheless was the candidate of the more radical faction at the AFT convention.[35]

In 1947 the Association moved its headquarters from New York

---

[33] Boyd H. Bode, "Needs and the Curriculum," *Progressive Education* 18 (December, 1940), pp. 532–537. Bode did contribute an article in the Dewey commemorative issue, "John Dewey: Philosopher of Science and Democracy," *Progressive Education* 30 (October, 1952), pp. 2–4.

[34] DeBoer had run against Forrest Long of New York University. Tibbetts wrote Long on February 19, 1946, telling him that DeBoer had won, and adding, "Personally I am very sorry about this. . . . Apparently the Mid-West boys and girls stand firm where a native son is involved." Archives at the University of Illinois.

[35] Robert Iversen has an excellent discussion of the 1940 Buffalo AFT convention in *The Communists and the Schools* (New York, 1959), pp. 117–118.

City, its home since 1935, to Chicago. DeBoer urged the move as an economy measure so that Tibbetts, who was drawing an annual salary of $6,000 but, according to DeBoer, appeared to be doing little for the Association, could be relieved of his duties.[36] The financial resources of the Association had been so depleted that it was unable to pay the $278 freight bill for shipment of its files, records, and other office equipment.[37] Despite these difficulties, DeBoer succeeded in bringing out a new, low-budget version of *Progressive Education* in October, 1947; the issue contained an announcement of the first postwar national convention of the Association. The national conference, wrote the optimistic DeBoer,

> . . . symbolizes the revival of a vigorous progressive spirit in American education. Progressive education has been wishfully "buried," with appropriate obsequies, so many times during the last five years that one wonders what fantastic definitions its enemies are giving to the term. Certainly the concepts popularized by the Progressive Education Association are not dead.

DeBoer cited the wide acceptance of the principles that the Association had argued for in the twenties and thirties, then rallied the faithful with a new slogan—progressive education in a progressive society! With this call to action, a new program was launched that gave the life of the Association its final short-term lease. DeBoer stated:

> One idea implicit in progressive thinking has . . . suffered eclipse in American education, especially since the close of World War II. It is the view that in the long run no education system can be better than the society in which it operates, and that therefore progressive education demands a "progressive society."[38]

[36] Tibbetts went from his position as director of the Association to the headmastership of one of the progressive schools whose faculty had identified itself in the twenties with the PEA, Hessian Hills School, Croton-on-Hudson, New York.

[37] Interview with Harold Shane, July 25, 1960. An example of the organization's frantic search for funds was Fred Barnes's August 7, 1946, letter to DeBoer. Barnes then worked in the central office in New York, and he wrote to DeBoer suggesting that the organization accept financial aid from a liquor organization in turn for publishing a pamphlet on alcohol education. DeBoer reported in an interview, June 26, 1964, that he considered the notion preposterous. The Barnes letter is in the Archives at the University of Illinois.

[38] "Forward, Progressive!" *Progressive Education* 26 (October, 1947), p. 225.

On this clearly radical note, DeBoer assumed leadership of the Association, although he did not by any means have the unanimous support of his vice presidents and Board of Directors. Among the most outspoken of DeBoer's critics were superintendents of schools from two of the most economically privileged Chicago suburbs, Harold Shane of Winnetka (now in Carleton Washburne's old job) and Lester Ball of Highland Park. Others on the board were more sympathetic to DeBoer's views, notable among them Theodore Brameld, then a professor of philosophy of education at New York University.

The argument between these two principal factions of the Association reached its peak at the 1947 convention. DeBoer and other leaders had hoped that the meeting would attract 3,000 persons, a figure reached by some of the annual PEA conventions in the thirties. Only one-third that number came.[39] Among the convention's principal speakers were David Lilienthal, Langston Hughes, and W. E. B. DuBois. None had been active previously in the progressive education movement, but each had been identified frequently with liberal or radical social and political causes.[40] Their presence at this annual convention highlighted the Association's turning away from specific pedagogical concerns to wider social, political, and philosophical issues.[41] Most of

[39] The low attendance has been variously attributed to the Thanksgiving holidays, competing meetings, bad weather, and overcrowded trains. Interviews: Harold Shane, July 25, 1960; Theodore Brameld, January 3, 1963; and John J. DeBoer and Archibald W. Anderson, March 11, 1963. John F. Bowman, then business manager of the organization, reported in a January 7, 1948, letter to DeBoer that 1,124 persons had attended the meeting and that registration receipts had been $1,314.86.

[40] The appearance of Hughes and others at the 1947 convention gave the American Legion what it considered cause for concern. On December 10, 1947, it circulated a mimeographed sheet attacking the 1947 conference and the organization, which it asserted "is made up mainly of the followers of the socialistic philosophies of Professor John Dewey, Teachers College, Columbia University." Among those on the program specifically attacked were Harold Rugg, Eduard C. Lindeman, Frank W. McCulloch, Theodore Brameld, and W. Carson Ryan. DeBoer replied to Frederick L. Pond, Supervising Curriculum Consultant, Department of Public Instruction, Commonwealth of Pennsylvania, who had sent him a copy of the Legion's statement, on April 15, 1948, that the organization was "firmly devoted to the ideals of American democracy" and that "not one of them named in the indictment is a Communist." Archives at Ohio State University.

[41] The Association's obvious attempt at this meeting to attract persons outside the group of professional educators underscores DeBoer's cognizance of the importance of widespread political support. The Association's inability to

the topics for the various sessions of the 1947 convention stressed the need for improving human relationships. A somewhat radical equivalent of "brotherly love" was in the air, and the presence on the program of such well-known Negroes as Hughes and DuBois reinforced this impression. (During this period *Progressive Education* was carrying many articles on intercultural understanding.)

The convention began on Thanksgiving Day, but because of a protracted discussion that was by no means harmonious, the new policy statement was not ready until the following Saturday.[42] Originally this report was to have been prepared by Dean Ernest O. Melby of the School of Education, New York University, and chairman of the Association's policy committee at that time.[43] The statement was even referred to occasionally as the Melby Report. But it is a fact that the report was actually prepared by Theodore Brameld.[44]

---

gain such adherents is discussed on a wider scale by Cremin in *The Transformation of the School*, pp. 269–270. Archibald W. Anderson, a participant in the failure Cremin analyzes, has disagreed with Cremin's view (Interview, March 12, 1963) but has not offered a more reasonable explanation.

[42] The minutes of the Board of Directors' daily meetings throughout the conference and the general membership session on Saturday (which the secretary concluded with the word "Amen"!) reveal the extent of disagreement that existed within the organization. Archives at Ohio State University.

[43] Melby even failed to come to the Chicago convention. DeBoer wrote him on November 18, 1947, imploring him to attend and serve as moderator during what he foresaw as the "bitter debate" over the report. In a letter dated November 25, 1947, the day before the conference opened, Melby replied that he was "too busy" to attend.

[44] The committee appointed by DeBoer to prepare the statement included Ernest O. Melby, New York University, chairman; F. G. Macomber, Drake University; Harold Benjamin, U.S. Office of Education; Harold Taylor, Sarah Lawrence College; Theodore Brameld, University of Minnesota; and Eduard C. Lindeman, New York School of Social Work. Archives at the University of Illinois.

Correspondence between Brameld and DeBoer at the University of Illinois indicates that Brameld actually drafted the report although Robert K. Speer of New York University had prepared an alternate draft, presumably at Melby's suggestion. Brameld apparently wrote the report at Minnesota in late 1946 and was to present his draft to a committee meeting in New York in January, 1947. Because of bad weather, Brameld missed the meeting, but the report reached New York where Vinal Tibbetts sent it to Melby with a note on January 23, 1947, "I did send a copy over to Spear [sic] so that he could incorporate the best of Brameld's thinking into his statement. A letter from Ted would indicate that he feels that his own statement is better and less complicated than the one sent

Brameld had studied philosophy at the University of Chicago under T. V. Smith, and the latter had written an introduction to Brameld's doctoral dissertation, "A Philosophic Approach to Communism," when the University of Chicago Press published it in 1933. After some years at the University of Minnesota, Brameld left in 1946 following the publication by the PEA of *Design for America.* Ostensibly this was a cooperative document, but unfriendly critics contended that the radicalism espoused in the book was all Brameld's. After several years at New York University, Brameld joined the faculty of Boston University, together with Kenneth Benne, who was to be DeBoer's successor as president of the Association. Among Brameld's most controversial articles was "Karl Marx and the American Teacher," which appeared in the October, 1935, number of *The Social Frontier.*

The original of Brameld's statement prepared for the convention appeared in the November, 1947, issue of *Progressive Education,* but the Board of Directors believed that the published version needed considerable modification. Chief criticisms of the report were that it minimized the educational interests that had formed the keystone of the Association's policy since 1919, that it committed the American Education Fellowship to advocacy of a socialistic economy, and that it failed to indicate the organization's support of democracy.[45] According to Archibald W. Anderson, a colleague of DeBoer's at the University of

---

him by Spear [sic]. Personally I do not agree because I think Brameld has put too much emphasis on international education." Melby replied January 30, 1947, that he and Speer had gone over Brameld's material and thought they should "try to touch up the Brameld statement somewhat." This correspondence is in the Archives at the University of Illinois.

One of the members of the committee, F. G. Macomber, wrote DeBoer on October 10, 1947, saying that although he was a member of the committee, he had not been consulted about a statement of policy for the entire organization. Furthermore, his inquiries to Melby had not even been acknowledged. Archives at Ohio State University.

[45] Archibald W. Anderson, "A Report on the National Conference," *Progressive Education* 25 (January, 1948), p. 9. Brameld included the following handwritten note to DeBoer on a copy of the report presented to the members at Chicago, "Dear John, The question marks mean that my corrections are *suggestive* only. I think you have done a fine job of condensing and of translating my version into English. It is not easy for me to tell, but I have the feeling your version lacks a little of the 'righteous indignation' of the original due to your desire to simplify. I think you might ask Melby and Speer how they react to each. Remember, I'm not sure about this. I just want to be sure the public statement has fire and packs a wallop. I don't think the original did that enough either. Ted" Archives at the University of Illinois.

Illinois, the revised version did something to repair the faults of omission in the original statement.[46]

President DeBoer and Brameld reported that the revised policy statement was passed unanimously at the final Saturday morning session. The minutes reveal only that the members agreed "to leave the decisions as to the implementation of the new policy as delineated in the Brameld report (revised) to the Board of Directors and officers of the Fellowship." [47] Brameld admitted, however, that in order to gain unanimous support of the proposal, some members—perhaps Lester Ball, Harold Shane, H. Gordon Hullfish, Harold Alberty, or V. T. Thayer—simply did not vote.[48] Carleton Washburne, who also opposed Brameld's position, has suggested that the report was pushed through the business session at a time when few members were present.[49] Brameld, however, recalled that the meeting room, which they estimated would hold between three and five hundred persons, was filled. DeBoer confirmed his recollection.[50] In any case, the officers of the organization decided to allow the members to vote on the new policy through a mail ballot. One was eventually prepared and sent to the membership, but unlike the late thirties when over two thousand ballots were returned in an election, only sixty-eight members voted. On this small count the new policy won by approximately two to one.[51]

[46] Interview with Anderson, March 11, 1963. For a different view see H. Gordon Hullfish's letter to B. O. Smith, April 20, 1948, at the Archives at the University of Illinois.

[47] Board of Directors Minutes, November 29, 1947, Archives at Ohio State University.

[48] Interview with DeBoer, March 11, 1963, and Brameld, January 3, 1963. A letter from DeBoer to W. Carson Ryan, December 10, 1947, reported, "The Saturday business meeting went off very well indeed. There was spirited debate over the new program, but at the end the Brameld Policy Statement, with certain revisions were [sic] accepted unanimously." Archives at Ohio State University. See also letter from F. S. Rosecrance to DeBoer, November 22, 1947, in which he outlined the positions of various members on the Brameld policy.

[49] Interview with Washburne, May 19, 1960.

[50] Interviews with Brameld, January 3, 1963, and DeBoer, March 11, 1963. The entire 1947 meeting is still an exceedingly controversial issue, capable of arousing much heated discussion among such principals as DeBoer and Washburne. Describing the 1947 statement in 1963 DeBoer said, "Really the controversy [was] a result of the cold war psychology and the paranoia that went with it."

[51] Interview with Shane, July 25, 1960, and a statement in *Progressive Education*, "Balloting on the AEF policy, published in the February number was regrettably small. But the vote ran well over two to one in favor of

The opponents of Brameld's views, led by Lester Ball and Harold Shane, did not remain silent. The "conservatives" prepared a minority report, which was subsequently published without publicity in a later issue of *Progressive Education.*[52] Shortly after their announced opposition to Brameld's proposal, Harold Rugg, who supported the new policy statement, dubbed the opposition "ball and chain," an emblem of what he considered their constricting influence upon genuine progressive development.

Final Decline: 1949–1955

The statements of the Association in the late forties illustrated accurately its effort to transform itself from a group with a primarily educational commitment to one with an essential political orientation. Brameld admitted that the new statement undoubtedly drove some conservative school superintendents from the organization, but such departures were inevitable if his goal of the Association as a barricade of "progressive—the conservatives would call it "radical" or even "socialistic"—leadership were to be achieved." [53] Actually Brameld re-

---

the new policy." *Progressive Education* 26 (October, 1948), p. 26. Hullfish wrote B. O. Smith, editor of *Progressive Education,* on April 20, 1948, "I am enclosing my vote against the adoption of the new policy. In the first place, I am in considerable doubt as to what the policy really means. Its internal confusion was illustrated when it was discussed at the Chicago meeting. Since the statement in no way reflects the discussion at Chicago, the matter is just where it was. It is right here that I have my second objection. The Board was instructed by motion to change the statement in accordance with the discussion on the floor at Chicago. This point really disturbs me." Archives at the University of Illinois.

[52] Ball and Shane centered their criticism of the policy on its "dogmatism" —economically, socially, and educationally. They urged a return to the permissive educational philosophy characteristic of the Association in prior years and emphasis upon getting these principles enacted as practices in the schools. Lester B. Ball and Harold G. Shane, "The New A.E.F. Policy in Review," *Progressive Education* 25 (April, 1948), pp. 110–112. Shane wrote DeBoer on April 16, 1948, identifying the article as "Lester's" and saying that he "acquiesced to Lester's request that I permit the use of my name as associate author." A month earlier (March 20, 1948) Shane had written DeBoer that he was resigning as vice-president of the organization. Archives at Ohio State University.

[53] Among those whose letters of resignation following the 1947 statement are preserved are Paul J. Misner, superintendent of schools, Glencoe, Illinois, February 2, 1948; Edward G. Olsen, director of school and community relations, state of Washington, June 9, 1948; Kenneth E. Oberholtzer,

gretted that the entire conservative opposition did not desert the Association; for then, at least, a small unified nucleus might have taken some effective action.[54] Although many "conservatives" left the Association, enough remained, such as Ball, Shane, and Hullfish, to force the Association to modify and therefore to weaken its stands in the late forties. Proposed revisions of the organization's official position appeared nearly as regularly as the journal itself.[55] These modifications forced the organization to confront its familiar dilemma: was it concerned primarily with the educational development of children or was it principally interested in using the schools and teachers as agents of social change? The same lines were drawn although devotees of "life adjustment education" replaced the child-centered enthusiasts of the twenties, and advocates of international cooperation or intercultural understanding substituted for the social critics of the thirties.

In the twenties and thirties these arguments, under the heading "progressive education," had stimulated considerable excitement, but

superintendent of Denver public schools, January 2, 1951; Emily V. Baker, Arizona State College, October 18, 1950; and R. H. Classon, principal, Southwest High School, Minneapolis. Archives at Ohio State University. The author is indebted to Walter Shott, Ohio State University, for assistance in locating these letters.

[54] Interview with Brameld, January 3, 1963. Among those writing in support of the new policy were Frederick L. Redefer, New York University, December 18, 1949; Grace Rotzel, The School in Rose Valley, Maylan, Pennsylvania, January 4, 1947(?); J. S. Schultz, Bluffton College, Bluffton, Ohio; and Corinne Seeds, University of California, January 11, 1948.

[55] John J. DeBoer, "The Role of Progressives in Education," *Progressive Education* 27 (October, 1949), pp. 26–27; "Looking Forward with A.E.F.," *Progressive Education* 27 (May, 1950), pp. 212–213; "Plans for Revising A.E.F. Policy Statement," *Progressive Education* 29 (October, 1951), p. 29; Kenneth Benne, "Do We Need a New Policy Statement for A.E.F.?" *Progressive Education* 29 (January, 1952), pp. 124–125; Roma Gans, "A New Policy for These Times is Needed," *Progressive Education* 29 (January, 1952), pp. 125–126; Carleton Washburne, " 'A New Policy'—Some Needed Revisions," *Progressive Education* 29 (January, 1952), pp. 126–128; H. Gordon Hullfish, "A Word from the President of this Fellowship," *Progressive Education* 30 (October, 1952), p. 21; "What Should be the New Policy of the A.E.F.?" *Progressive Education* 30 (January, 1953), pp. 57–84; Harold Rugg, "A Proposed Statement of Policy for Progressive Education," *Progressive Education* 31 (November, 1953), pp. 33–40, 43; Archibald W. Anderson, "There is Something in a Name," *Progressive Education* 31 (November, 1953), pp. 46–50; "A.E.F. Policy Rescinded," *Progressive Education* 31 (November, 1953), pp. 57–58; and "A Proposed Statement of Policy for the Progressive Education Association," *Progressive Education* 31 (January, 1954), pp. 85–86.

in the postwar years they caught little attention. The most popular educational questions of the late forties and early fifties dealt with the training of returning servicemen and with attacks upon the lack of intellectual content in the American schools. Neither of these problem areas interested the Association, although in the early years of the war it had established a commission on postwar educational questions.[56] The Association itself became the target of much of the anti-quackery criticism of the late forties and early fifties; these critics believed the schools, in their excessive concern for well-rounded social development, were neglecting their responsibility to train youngsters' intellects.

The Brameld–DeBoer attitudes were even less popular in these years that were overshadowed by the House Un-American Activities Committee and the McCarthy Committee hearings. In this era of guilt by association, few were eager to join radical causes. The national political apathy of the immediate postwar period acted as a general damper upon the recruitment possibilities of the social reform wing of the Association. Elementary and secondary school teachers in the United States have never composed a fertile source of support for radical causes. The exceptions have largely been in metropolitan areas, such as New York City where Local 5 of the American Federation of Teachers was dominated by Communists through the thirties. American teachers have generally come from middle or lower middle class social origins. As a group they have been less intellectually able than those in other professions.[57] The regional teachers colleges, in which many of these teachers had been trained, do not have outstanding records of challenges offered to views often stiflingly conventional and conservative. Such teachers made up a substantial portion of PEA membership even in the late forties. As a whole they were not receptive to radical calls.

By the end of the decade of the forties, the Association was com-

---

[56] A commission was set up in 1941 variously called the Commission on Education's Role in Reconstruction and the Commission on Post-War Reconstruction and was headed by Grayson Kefauver of Stanford University. In 1943 a National Commission on Educational Reconstruction was proposed, and the project was discussed at Board of Directors' meetings. Minutes, April 27–29, 1941; October 10–12, 1941; February 21–22, 1943. Despite all the talk nothing concrete emerged, and the discussions fell victim to the general disintegration of the Association in the mid-forties.

[57] Harold E. Mitzel, Lester Dubnick, "The Relative Scholastic Ability of Prospective Teachers," *Journal of Teacher Education* 12 (March, 1961), pp. 73–80.

pleting another philosophical swing around two quadrants of its ideological circle. President DeBoer's final message to the members, which appeared in October, 1949, admitted the failure of the Association's postwar radicalism. DeBoer stated:

> The American Education Fellowship has declared itself in favor of a program of action. As its retiring president, I shall be the first to confess that it has thus far been unsuccessful in initiating the kind of action it proposed.[58]

With DeBoer's retirement, the Association ended its period of most emphatic radicalism and also of greatest social concern. Although the new president, Kenneth Benne, was identified by Brameld as one of his chief supporters, the principal interests of the Association rapidly shifted from wide-ranging questions of equality—social, political, and educational—back to much more narrowly defined questions of curriculum. Benne signaled this shift in his second major statement to the Association in January, 1950, when he argued for a "new" emphasis upon child study in the Association.[59] Two months later Benne urged that greater attention be devoted to the problems of elementary education.[60] Both these areas were major interests of the Association in its earliest years, but in those years the need for reform in the traditional methods of education was considerably clearer than it was in 1950.

Presumably the recommended new attention to child study and elementary schooling would entail criticism and reconstruction of the old progressive ways of the twenties. But the fact remained that child study and elementary education appeared neither as controversial nor as interesting in 1950 as the previous issues the Association had debated. Further evidence of the Association's efforts to return to the same topics that had brought it success in the past was Benne's proposal in November, 1950, that an "eight-year study for the 1950's" be instituted.[61] Aikin's investigation of the thirties had been the Association's single most successful project, bringing the Association its largest individual grants and probably its greatest prestige.

By February, 1951, the questioning mood of some prominent

[58] John J. DeBoer, "The Role of Progressivism in Education," *op. cit.*, p. 26.
[59] Kenneth Benne, "Establishing the Conditions of Educational Progress II," *Progressive Education* 27 (January, 1950), p. 90.
[60] Kenneth Benne, "A Question About Progress in Elementary Education," *Progressive Education* 27 (March, 1950), pp. 138–139.
[61] Kenneth Benne, " 'Eight-Year Study' for the 1950's," *Progressive Education* 28 (November, 1950), p. 36.

members of the Association had become general enough so that, at its annual meeting, the members adopted a resolution calling for "a re-examination of the purposes to which the American Education Fellowship is committed." [62] Roma Gans and Carleton Washburne, both of whom had opposed the most radical policies of the DeBoer–Brameld faction, were appointed to prepare statements embodying their views of the Association's policies. After asking for general contributions, Benne assured the readers of *Progressive Education* that "Notions distinctly different from those previously published will be included in the magazine." [63] Both Gans and Washburne were critical of the old policy, Miss Gans because it failed to integrate satisfactorily its objectives of concern for international education and of understanding of personality development and the behavior of groups.[64] Washburne was considerably more specific in his statement, which, in effect, urged the Association leadership to return to the good old days when school superintendents and other administrators, not "university professors on tenure," were custodians of the interests of the Association. Washburne, who had been a superintendent in Winnetka, an area notably lacking socialistic sentiments, observed that as a result of the 1947 statement a number of public schoolmen who had formerly been active in the Association had either left the organization or neglected to take an active part in its affairs.[65] Washburne's essential criticism of the 1947 policy was that it was too dogmatic. It offered solutions when it should have raised problems, and it made the organization one principally devoted to social action, not to pedagogical reform.[66]

It was fitting that the last president of the Association should have been H. Gordon Hullfish. A student of Boyd Bode at Ohio State University, Hullfish had written a doctoral dissertation criticizing Edward L. Thorndike's refutation of the theory of transfer of training. As a

[62] Kenneth Benne, "Plan for Revising A.E.F. Policy," *Progressive Education* 29 (February, 1951), p. 29.
[63] *Loc. cit.*
[64] Roma Gans, "A New Policy for These Times is Needed," *op. cit.*
[65] Carleton Washburne, " 'A New Policy'—Some Needed Revisions," *op. cit.*
[66] The subsequent letters that the editor selected to print in the journal supported the Gans–Washburne position, although one writer, William F. Bruce, raised a familiar query to the membership: Should the organization disband in the knowledge that its original objectives, largely in pedagogical method, had been achieved? This view, of course, was an implicit denial of the Brameld–DeBoer position, for clearly their objectives of a politically and socially active professional organization within a socialized state had not been achieved.

young man, he had joined Kilpatrick, Dewey, and Bode in contributing to *The Educational Frontier*, a key statement of the socially conscious progressive educators of the thirties. Subsequently a member of the faculty of the School of Education at Ohio State University, Hullfish became the symbol for Brameld and his radical followers of the old-line progressivism of the twenties and thirties, the sort that eschewed social reconstructionism and the politically "progressive" stands of the social reformers of the forties. At first Hullfish had vigorously opposed Brameld's proposed statement of policy in 1947. But his friend Archibald W. Anderson said that eventually he came round to support the statement.[67] Hullfish had strongly encouraged the Committee on Revision of Policy, which had been appointed during Benne's term as president.

With Hullfish's elevation to the presidency came the organization's final shift of headquarters, from the College of Education at the University of Illinois to the College of Education at Ohio State University. One of Hullfish's first acts as president was the preparation of a statement sent to the membership asking them to vote on changing the name of the organization from "American Education Fellowship" back to "Progressive Education Association." [68] Three months later the entire issue of *Progressive Education* was devoted to discussions of policy for the organization. The contributors were a varied lot, including Hullfish, Brameld, Washburne, Isaac B. Berkson, Alain Locke, and the indestructible Kilpatrick.[69]

The last statement of policy, which appeared in November, 1953, was chiefly the work of Harold Rugg, the loyal PEA supporter who ten years earlier had edited the final issues of the Association's ill-fated journal, *Frontiers of Democracy*.[70] Brameld saw Rugg as one of his supporters in the effort to achieve a broader outlook in the PEA, and certainly Rugg's work on *Frontiers of Democracy* qualified him as a

[67] Interview with Anderson, March 11, 1963. Anderson said that this was Hullfish's view in the mid-fifties.
[68] H. Gordon Hullfish, "A Word from the President of this Fellowship," *Progressive Education* 30 (October, 1952), p. 21.
[69] "What Should be the New Policy of the A.E.F.?" *op. cit.* Despite the plethora of articles on the philosophy of the Association or perhaps because of it, the topic did not seem to be one of interest to the readers. Editor Anderson reported that he had fewer requests for extra issues of the issue devoted solely to policy questions (January, 1953) than for any other issue that he edited. Interview, March 11, 1963.
[70] Harold Rugg, "A Proposed Statement of Policy for Progressive Education," *op. cit.*

member of the Brameld faction. Rugg, however, was always a bit eclectic, as his book written with Ann Shumaker in the twenties, *The Child-Centered School,* shows clearly.[71] Rugg revealed the mettle of his eclectic philosophy of education in the 1953 statement by confounding both the partisans of social reconstructionism (such as Brameld and DeBoer) and the advocates of a "life adjustment curriculum" when he called for a "civilization-centered" school as well as an "education-centered" community.[72] Presumably these formidably reorganized agencies would reconcile the conflicts of all past disputants. But such a reconciliation was not in the cards; by the mid-fifties the Association membership included more institutions than individual persons—the institutions had begun subscribing to *Progressive Education* in the twenties. Thus, in the end the membership of the Association was largely determined by disinterested institutional librarians; the interested educators and laymen had nearly all left. So, Hullfish concluded in 1955, the PEA was really in fact dead, although the journal *Progressive Education* with its subscription list of about 1,900 would continue to appear for two more years under the aegis of the John Dewey Society.[73]

[71] Rugg's last book, published posthumously, exemplified his ability to write on topics of current interest. It dealt with the problem of creativity: *Imagination* (New York, 1963).

[72] Harold Rugg, "A Proposed Statement of Policy for Progressive Education," *op. cit.*

[73] Interview with Archibald W. Anderson, March 11, 1963.

CHAPTER VII

Final Projects

⚸

Although *Progressive Education* managed to publish two more years under the sponsorship of the John Dewey Society, most of the Association's other activities came to a halt long before 1955, the year the Association died. Acceptance of the John Dewey Society as a Commission of the Association in 1939 was followed by the takeover of the moribund periodical *The Social Frontier*, which then appeared as an organ of the PEA under the title *Frontiers of Democracy* until its demise in 1943. The so-called Eight-Year Study, the work of the Commission on the Relation of School and College, was published in 1942–1943. V. T. Thayer's Commission on the Secondary School Curriculum printed its findings in 1939. Alice V. Keliher's Commission on Human Relations saw to the publication of six major books before it disbanded in 1942. These were the last major commission activities of the Association.

The Social Frontier *and* Frontiers of Democracy

A chronicle of the vicissitudes endured by the magazine *The Social Frontier*, re-christened *Frontiers of Democracy* in 1939, reveals in microcosm many of the problems of the Association and of the progressive education movement as a whole. The reader will recall that *The Social Frontier* appeared in the mid-thirties under the editorship of George S. Counts as a vehicle of ideas of those educators and others who represented the radical position on social reconstructionism. *The Social Frontier* and *Progressive Education* had a number of executive board members in common and a sizeable community of interest existed among the contributors to both periodicals. After the good years of 1934 and 1935, marked by distinguished contributors and a healthy subscription list, *The Social Frontier* quickly lost its vitality.[1] In 1939, Counts, whose educational and social philosophy the journal had espoused more than any other man's, resigned as editor. With him went Norman Woelfel and Mordecai Grossman. Counts' own views were shifting, doubtless under the impact of the Moscow trials, and he turned much of his extracurricular energy to work in reducing the influence of the Communist-dominated Local 5 of the American Federation of Teachers. On Counts' departure, the chairmanship of the Board of Editors fell to William Heard Kilpatrick, and the new editor was George Hartmann.

The Kilpatrick–Hartmann partnership guided the magazine from the fall of 1937 until the fall of 1939, two lean years marked by decreasing circulation and mounting deficits. The editors of *The Social Frontier* had approached the PEA in 1937 to discuss the possibility of closer cooperation and even a possible merger.[2] By the spring of 1939, *The Social Frontier's* financial situation had become quite desperate. Under Kilpatrick's leadership, the journal's editorial policies had lost whatever fire had survived from the febrile years of the mid-thirties. A new plea for merger was inevitable.

The outlook of *The Social Frontier* was certainly less radical in 1939 than it was in 1934. Nevertheless the Association hesitated to commit itself to sponsor the journal. At the February, 1939, meeting of the Board of Directors, W. Carson Ryan, Jr., chairman of the meeting, twice cast the deciding vote: first, supporting a motion placing the Board of Directors on record as "favoring the unity of forces that are seeking to advance the frontier of social philosophy and educational practice," and, second, opposing a motion that recommended declining the proposals of the John Dewey Society and *The Social Frontier* for merger with the Association.[3] Among the sponsors of the first motion was Laura Zirbes, professor of education at Ohio State University and one of the members of the PEA's Committee on Philosophy, which was then preparing the 1941 policy statement. The second motion, urging complete rejection of the merger, was proposed by Williard W. Beatty, an early leader of the PEA, and was seconded by Vinal H. Tibbetts, then school superintendent in Manhasset. The compromise motion, which squeaked by with Ryan's support, affirmed that the PEA was in

[1] For an earlier discussion of *The Social Frontier,* see Chapter IV, pp. 71–73.
[2] Minutes of the Board of Directors, February 25, 1937.
[3] Minutes of the Board of Directors, February 21, 1939.

sympathy with the unification of the Association, the John Dewey Society, and *The Social Frontier*, but that no practical means of achieving this was yet apparent.

Two months later the "practical means" evidently became apparent, and the Association accepted the John Dewey Society as a commission of the Association. The Society was expected to work closely with the existing PEA Commission on Educational Freedom, but there is no record of subsequent cooperation. After considerable debate, the PEA Board decided to publish *The Social Frontier* as well as continuing publication of *Progressive Education;* the former would emphasize philosophy, the latter, method. This artificial separation between theory and practice had the immediate effect of further weakening both periodicals. *Progressive Education* deteriorated into an educational cookbook, a compendium of mechanistic teaching hints. *The Social Frontier*, on the other hand, had less and less theory to go on. The journal had lost many of its contributors who had genuine philosophical concerns. Moreover, after the Soviet purges of the late thirties and the Hitler–Stalin pact of 1939, the course to social reconstruction, so clearly in sight only a few years before, was now hopelessly obscured. Both journals were sinking fast, and any hope for their ultimate salvation rested on their combining their resources.[4] PEA's decision to publish the journals separately further enfeebled their precarious hold on existence, and the Association's official sponsorship under these terms was just another drain on its own rapidly emptying treasury.

One of the conditions of the Association's sponsorship of *The Social Frontier* was that its name be changed to *Frontiers of Democracy*. The old name had too many radical connotations, and the new one fitted well into the Association's current fixation on all things "democratic." Another of the Association's requirements was that James L. Hymes, Jr., then managing editor of *Progressive Education*, serve as managing editor of *Frontiers of Democracy*. Hymes' own interests symbolized his completion of the transformation of the journal. His predecessors had been such politically oriented men as Counts, Woelfel, Grossman, and George Hartmann; Hymes was a specialist in elementary education who subsequently wrote regularly in professional education journals on child development. The wheel had come round again, and for nearly the last time. In May, 1940, Hymes was appointed editor of *Progressive Education*, and he continued as managing editor of both publications until October, 1943, when Harold Rugg replaced

[4] *Frontiers of Democracy* brought only 1,078 new subscribers to the Association. Minutes of the Executive Committee, December 16, 1939.

him on *Frontiers of Democracy* and Toni Taylor succeeded him on *Progressive Education*. A brilliant man with adequate financial resources might have been able to juggle the two journals to produce simultaneous and effective results, but this combination did not occur, and both journals suffered accordingly.

The first year of *Frontiers of Democracy* was illusively encouraging. In September, 1940, the journal could report to its new sponsor that circulation was up to 3,800. This was not bad, though nothing to compare with the 6,000 figure of the mid-thirties.[5] *Progressive Education,* however, failed to share its companion publication's modest success. The older journal was suffering as a result of its belated emphasis on practical teaching points. Here it competed with all the journals published by the state teachers' associations, and most impecunious teachers did not feel it necessary to buy *Progressive Education* when their frequently mandatory state membership provided the other journal free. Nor did articles featuring helpful hints for teachers arouse much interest in those parents and concerned citizens who at one time had formed a substantial part of the membership. Apparently advertisers noted the decline in subscribers, and revenue from this important source fell alarmingly. The downward turn in *Progressive Education's* fortunes did little to endear *Frontiers of Democracy* to the old guard of the PEA who had opposed the merger in the first place. By 1940 a recurrent topic at meetings of the PEA Board of Directors was the possible ending of publication of *Frontiers of Democracy*.

By the fall of 1943 the general disintegration to which the PEA had fallen victim reached *Frontiers of Democracy*. In the 1943 fall issue, Harold Rugg attempted to revitalize the journal with an infusion of radicalism, much as DeBoer would do in his attempt to get some life back into the Association itself in 1946. Rugg sought support for his controversial number at the October, 1943, Board of Directors meeting. Brameld's remarks and those of the new president Virgil Rogers were favorable, but these are the only comments recorded in the minutes.[6] Two weeks later—ten days after the journal had reached subscribers— a meeting of the Executive Committee of the Association was held in New York City at a place not far from Rugg's office. In a bitter refer-

[5] Minutes of the Board of Directors, September 27, 1940.
[6] The minutes of the October 15–17, 1943, Board of Directors meeting clearly indicate Brameld's and Rogers' support. "Mr. Brameld indicated that he would go along with the editorial policy [as Rugg described it in the Fall, 1943, issue]. Mr. Rogers felt that unless the magazine is militant and aggressive it will become like thousands of other journals that deal gently with these problems."

ence to this "secret meeting," Rugg reported that he was not invited to attend.[7] Prominent on the agenda of the meeting was a discussion of the future of *Frontiers of Democracy.* Roma Gans, a colleague of Rugg's at Teachers College, moved that *Frontiers of Democracy* be discontinued as a publication of the Association. The motion passed unanimously. Those present and voting were Virgil Rogers, who had vigorously supported the journal in Rugg's presence two weeks earlier, Arthur Keesler, Marion Carswell, Vinal Tibbetts, and Toni Taylor. Four reasons were given for discontinuing the journal: it was a financial liability; it served no purpose in the proposed community-oriented program of the Association; it was competing with the liberal weeklies *Nation* and *New Republic;* and under present conditions the Association could not support two journals.[8]

Thus the decision to abandon *Frontiers of Democracy* in 1943 was based on both financial and ideological considerations.[9] It is interesting to note that not one of the members of the Executive Committee who sat in judgment on the fate of the periodical in 1943 had been active in the Association five years before. Nor was anyone, with the exception of Miss Gans, active in the Association five years later. Moreover, the

[7] Harold Rugg, *Foundations for American Education* (Yonkers-on-Hudson, 1947), p. 581. Rugg's departure from *Frontiers of Democracy* caused a considerable flurry. Apparently Rugg prepared a statement of his grievances that embarrassed the leaders of the Association. See Vinal H. Tibbett's February 8, 1944, letter to Virgil M. Rogers. Several months later (June 12, 1944), Frank E. Baker, the new president of the Association, sent a letter to the members of the Board of Directors reporting, "Since last November he [Rugg] has engaged in the publication and distribution of statements that have been harmful to the interests of the American Education Fellowship. According to the records, Harold Rugg is not a member of the American Education Fellowship, nor was he a member of its predecessor, the Progressive Education Association, at any time during the last five years except for the year 1942." Baker then asked the Board to vote on whether to retain Rugg as the New Education Fellowship representative. The decision was by a majority of two to one not to retain him. Archives at the University of Illinois.

[8] Minutes of the Executive Committee, November 1, 1943.

[9] In the only extended study of *The Social Frontier* Chester A. Bowers has contended, "the journal represented a frequently insolvent but determined effort to evangelize educators to accept what was in reality only part of Dewey's educational theory. The result helped to discredit progressive education in the eyes of the public and to split the progressive education movement into factions that dissipated its strength in internecine fighting." Chester Alfred Bowers, "The Educational and Social Philosophy of *The Social Frontier:* 1934–1943," unpublished doctoral dissertation, University of California, Berkeley, 1962.

Association's "community-oriented program," whose purposes were judged to be ill served by the journal, had also completely disappeared by the immediate postwar period. The financial problems, however, remained, and remained insoluble.

Closing Activities of the Commissions and the Eight-Year Study

Analysis of the Association's commissions shows parallels to the history of *The Social Frontier*'s decline. Prominent in the mid-thirties when they were doing their principal research, the three major commissions that were supported by large grants from independent foundations expired quietly in the early forties. Just as the Association had attempted to breathe new life into *The Social Frontier* by changing its name and by attempting to find a vigorous social program for it at the last moment, so the Association feverishly devised new commissions and committees with research proposals to present to foundations in the hope that some project would catch favorable attention and thus give to the Association some reason to continue its existence. The parallel with *The Social Frontier* may be extended further: despite one or two valiant efforts to establish a national commission with the prestige of the prewar Commission on the Relation of School and College, all the Association's commissions and committees were gone by the end of the war.

Certainly the Commission on the Relation of School and College, established under the leadership of Wilford Aikin in 1934, was the Association's most widely known project. The findings of this commission's research project, variously known as the "Eight-Year Study" and the "Thirty Schools Project," were published during the most crucial period of World War II in a series of five volumes under the over-all title *Adventures in American Education*.[10] The books were received with varying degrees of enthusiasm. The first volume, which described the study, sold 6,400 copies; the last, explaining the ways in which the schools altered their programs, less than 1,000.[11]

[10] The five volumes were Wilford M. Aikin, *The Story of the Eight-Year Study* (New York, 1942); H. H. Giles, S. P. McCutchen, A. N. Zechiel, *Exploring the Curriculum* (New York, 1942); Eugene R. Smith and Ralph Tyler, *Appraising and Recording Student Progress* (New York, 1942); Dean Chamberlin, *et. al.*, *Did They Succeed in College?* (New York, 1942); *Thirty Schools Tell Their Story* (New York, 1943).

[11] Frederick L. Redefer, "The Eight-Year Study . . . After Eight Years," *Progressive Education* 28 (November, 1950), p. 35. See earlier discussion of Aikin group, pp. 89–90.

Evaluation of the study, and interpretation of its results, varied widely among proponents of progressive education. Eugene R. Smith, whose principal interest in the mid-forties was quantification of educational data, judged the work of Ralph Tyler's Committee on Evaluation and Testing to be of primary significance.[12] Frederick L. Redefer reported that "the most important residue of the Eight-Year Study was the cooperative method of work that developed during the eight years. Teachers became active participants in education." Such a "cooperative method" had been an ideal of Redefer's since the late thirties when he introduced panel discussions as the typical program format at PEA conventions.[13] A more direct assessment of the Eight-Year Study was made some years later by William Brickman, who, unlike the other commentators on the importance of the project's result, had no direct connection with the project itself. In an introduction to a review of current trends in secondary education in 1950 Brickman wrote, "The prevailing principles and practices of secondary education derive their inspiration, it would seem, from the results of the Eight-Year Study." [14] Brickman, for many years editor of *School and Society*, professor of education at New York University and later at the University of Pennsylvania, may have overestimated the impact of the project, but even the most skeptical observer today must acknowledge the pervasive influence of this study. In fact, the widespread adoption and expansion of the central tenet of the study, that the traditional academic curriculum offered in the high school is not the only satisfactory method of college preparation, led to much of the criticism of the American high school in the late fifties and early sixties.

Although some of its apologists claimed a good deal more for it, the study did indicate conclusively that students without the traditional college preparatory curriculum could succeed in college. Much heated

[12] Eugene Randolph Smith, "Results of the Eight-Year Study," *Progressive Education* 22 (October, 1944), pp. 30–32.

[13] Redefer, "The Eight-Year Study . . . After Eight Years," *op. cit.*, p. 35. In his doctoral dissertation, however, "The Eight-Year Study—Eight Years Later: A Study of Experimentation in the Thirty Schools" (unpublished study, Teachers College, Columbia University, 1952, p. 42) Redefer stressed the significance of the Tyler book. The importance of the Eight-Year Study seemed to depend on the vantage point of the observer. If he were a testing enthusiast, Tyler's work seemed most important. If he believed, as Redefer commented that he did in an interview November 1, 1962, that panel discussions were a major pedagogic innovation, then "cooperative method" was of great significance.

[14] William W. Brickman, "The Secondary School," *School and Society* 72 (August 5, 1950), p. 90.

debate occurred over how significant was the unorthodox preparation of some students in their ultimate college success, and the severest critics suggested that even four years spent on a farm would not necessarily prevent a student from succeeding in college.[15] In any case, the results of the study supplied ammunition to those critics who sought curricula geared to the total life of the student rather than simply to entrance in college.

Curiously enough, the logical extension of the study was not made: an examination of a curriculum designed upon "life needs" for the student who did *not* go to college.[16] With the exception of one short-lived commission, the Association focused its interest upon the college-bound student rather than upon the large majority of young people who did not enter college. Undoubtedly the commission performed a useful service in demonstrating to even the most tradition-minded that a traditional high school course was not necessary for success in a traditional college. To extrapolate from that conclusion—as some did who admired the report—that other ways of trying to prepare for college or for life were equally good, or even preferable, was risky and had the effect of discouraging support of the commission's findings among many uncommitted educators.

Commission on the Secondary School Curriculum

Just as the Commission on the Relation of School and College conducted most of its research during the mid-thirties, so also did its offspring, V. T. Thayer's Commission on the Secondary School Curriculum. Thayer and his associates, Caroline B. Zachry and Ruth Kotinsky, published their summary of the commission's activities in 1939 under the title *Reorganizing Secondary Education*. Certain critics did not consider the report remarkable for its new ideas.[17] Written in the rhetoric characteristic of the period, the document put forward two

[15] Helmer G. Johnson, "Some Comments on the Eight-Year Study," *School and Society* 72 (November, 25, 1950), pp. 337–339, and Paul B. Diederich, "The Eight-Year Study: More Comments," *School and Society* 73 (January 20, 1951), pp. 41–43. These two articles were reprinted under the same titles in *Progressive Education* 28 (March, 1951), pp. 161–164.

[16] Wilford M. Aikin later noted this as one of the changes he would make in the study if he were to do it again, "The Eight-Year Study: If We Were to do it Again," *Progressive Education* 31 (October, 1953), pp. 11–14.

[17] See W. Carson Ryan, Jr., "Secondary Education and Youth," *Progressive Education* 16 (October, 1939), pp. 394–395.

major claims: democracy should be inseparable from school life; and "needs"—social, economic, and personal—of young people should determine the content of the curriculum.

The Thayer commission's underscoring of the unique responsibility of schools in a democracy, an emphasis common in the late thirties and the early forties, reminded some educators of the social concern of the progressives of the early thirties. At least three principal features, however, distinguish the two views. First, the social reconstructionist educator of the thirties looked initially to the society and, being dissatisfied with it, turned to the school as an agency for correcting the more general malaise. The socially conscious theorist of the late thirties and early forties, on the other hand, focused his attention upon the school, not the society. His interests lay chiefly in curricular changes that he believed would link the school more directly with society. Second, socially oriented educators of the Depression era viewed society, and understandably so, as desperately in need of correction. The system was in trouble, and it was up to the schools to take the lead in making the necessary alterations. The post-Depression educators had much greater faith—some would say naiveté—regarding their society and earnestly wished to do nothing more than teach youngsters an appreciation of certain sets of values, called democratic, that they really believed to exist in the society. Such a view reflected the post-Depression society unified by the external threat of fascism and the reality of war.

Finally, the educators of the early thirties, recognizing the need for drastic action, boldly endorsed "imposition" or "indoctrination" as an educational means of achieving their desired goals. But their successors, not desiring such specific forms, urged less direct ways of inculcating belief. In an era of national unity created by catastrophic world events, anything but commitment to democratic values was unthinkable; but this unity was to be achieved by higher means than the World War I "victory cabbage" campaigns or the anticapitalist polemics of the early thirties.

Caroline B. Zachry's *Emotion and Conduct in Adolescence,* published in 1940 by the Association and Appleton-Century-Crofts, was probably the Association's best-seller.[18]   Miss Zachry's book was the

---

[18] Frederick L. Redefer reported that it sold about 12,000 copies, nearly twice the number of volumes of the summary report of the commission. V. T. Thayer, Caroline B. Zachry, and Ruth Kotinsky, *Reorganizing Secondary Education* (New York, 1939). "The Eight-Year Study . . . After Eight Years," *op. cit.,* p. 35.

outgrowth of work conducted by her Committee on Adolescents, which functioned as part of Thayer's commission.[19] Caroline Zachry was one of the most psychologically oriented progressive educators. Although she graduated at the bottom of her class at Chapin School, New York City, a status that prompted her headmistress to forecast that she would not be able to finish college, Miss Zachry received in due course a Ph.D. from Columbia University.[20] Doubtless with her own adolescent experiences in mind, Miss Zachry was emphatic about the responsibility of the secondary school to determine the nature of the various problems facing youngsters in school, and to shape the curriculum accordingly.

Miss Zachry's work was notable for some of its psychological insights, and her book remains one of the most comprehensive discussions of adolescence. It is a question, however, as to whether its excellence as psychology warranted its frequent subsequent use as a pedagogical guide. Quite often educators assumed that, having established the "needs" of adolescents, it followed that their schools should meet them. Not very often did progressive educators of the late thirties and early forties concern themselves about the school's responsibility for acquainting the student with his cultural heritage or even for meeting his specifically intellectual "needs." A certain anti-intellectualism, by no means always intended, became the inevitable concomitant of the successful pursuit of the goal of psychological and social adjustment.

Another major activity of V. T. Thayer's Commission on the Secondary School Curriculum was the work of a group of committees that examined ways in which traditional subject matter areas could be adapted to meet the twin demands of democracy and psychological needs established by the commission. These published studies were potentially among the most interesting reports the Association sponsored, each considering a subject area (science, mathematics, language, social studies, art) in the context of general education.[21] Each volume was written by a committee and no individual authors were identified.

[19] The other major report of the Committee on Adolescents was Peter Blos, *The Adolescent Personality: A Study of Individual Behavior* (New York, 1941).

[20] Interview with Greer Zachry, brother of Caroline Zachry, December 9, 1960. See also my biographical note on Miss Zachry in the forthcoming *Dictionary of Notable American Women*.

[21] The major reports were *Science in General Education* (New York, 1939), *Mathematics in General Education* (New York, 1940), *The Social Studies in General Education* (New York, 1940), and *The Visual Arts in General Education* (New York, 1940).

Perhaps because they appeared as war threatened, or again because committee authorship prevented full synthesis of the material, the books failed to receive much attention.

Commission on Human Relations

The third major commission of the Association was Alice V. Keliher's Commission on Human Relations. Aikin's committee on the relation of school and college had started with the school and attempted to diagnose its problems and to suggest alternative solutions. The chief problem, the Aikin group believed, was a high school curriculum that was too narrow and formal. In response to this critique of the traditional high school curriculum, Thayer's commission on the secondary school curriculum was established. Thayer's group specified ways in which the curriculum should be revised. Thayer's group made clear (Caroline B. Zachry was particularly emphatic) that the curriculum should be adjusted to the youngsters' social and psychological requirements. In order to implement Miss Zachry's findings, it was necessary to procure new teaching materials geared to "the psychological needs of youth rather than around the logical stricture of the academic disciplines." [22] The Keliher commission's chief task was the preparation of these materials. Supported by funds from the General Education Board through 1940, the Commission on Human Relations sponsored publication of six volumes.[23] The best known of these books was Katharine Whiteside Taylor's *Do Adolescents Need Parents?* in which the author responded to her interrogative title with an energetic "yes." Miss Taylor, director for many years of one of the oldest and best progressive schools, the Shady Hill School in Cambridge, Massachusetts, stressed the need for a relationship between parents and children based upon the parents' understanding and acceptance of the youngsters' psychological characteristics. According to Miss Taylor, parents were needed as "reference points" for their offspring's progress to maturity. Another of the six published studies, Louise M. Rosenblatt's *Literature as Exploration,* argued that literature had untapped possi-

[22] Alice V. Keliher, "Commission on Human Relations," *Progressive Education* 12 (October, 1935), p. 425.
[23] Katherine W. Taylor, *Do Adolescents Need Parents?* (New York, 1938); Louise M. Rosenblatt, *Literature as Exploration* (New York, 1938); Bernhard Joseph Stern, *The Family, Past and Present* (New York, 1938); Alice V. Keliher, *Life and Growth* (New York, 1938); W. Robert Wunsch and Edna Albers, eds., *Thicker Than Water* (New York, 1939); and Walter C. Langer, *Psychology and Human Living* (New York, 1943).

bilities as a storehouse of wisdom on human relationships. Miss Rosen-blatt, then a member of the English department at Barnard College, concluded that the "semantic" values of literature had been stressed long enough, and that it was time to stress literature's richness as sociology and psychology.

Miss Keliher's commission met the same fate as Aikin's and Thayer's: after publication of its studies, the research for which had been financed by foundation grants, the commissions ceased. The Keliher group searched vigorously for funds during 1940, but by the fall of 1941 it was clear that no further subsidy could be hoped for. The commission formally disbanded in May, 1942.[24]

Each of these three major commissions of the Association—Aikin's on school and college, Thayer's on the secondary school cur-riculum, and Miss Keliher's on "human relations"—had tackled educa-tional problems requiring serious attention. Their efforts at systematic research were among the first in areas where research projects have since proliferated formidably. Sizeable volumes, some of substantial interest, were published as the direct result of the work of these com-missions. The questions raised by each of these Association groups were not satisfactorily answered by them, nor has agreement been reached on them yet. The significance of the commissions lay primarily in their exploratory ventures down avenues which have since seen heavy traffic. It is not necessarily to these commissions' discredit that their utterances, like many pronouncements by the Association as a whole, became educational clichés in their own lifetime.

Finances: End of the Funds

In the early forties the Association repeatedly devised projects and established commissions with imposing titles (example, the Commis-sion on National Educational Planning) and sent them off to secure grants that, it was hoped, would allow them to conduct research on a handsome scale, bringing credit and returning prominence to the Association. Among the more ambitious of these ventures was the Commission on Educational Reconstruction whose chairman, Grayson Kefauver of Stanford University, estimated at the PEA's annual meet-

---

[24] Minutes of the Board of Directors, May 5–7, 1940; October 10, 1941; May 16–18, 1942. Although the commission officially disbanded in 1942, Alice V. Keliher, Lawrence Frank, and Mark May continued as an Execu-tive Committee in the event that a project and/or funds would be dis-covered.

ing in 1943 that the budget for the first year would be $72,000. Kefauver identified the commission's chief problem as lack of funds.

Kefauver's difficulties in obtaining cash proved typical of the Association's efforts in the forties. A few grants were secured: $5,000 from the Rackham Foundation for the New Education Fellowship International Conference to be held at Ann Arbor, Michigan, in 1941; $1,000 from the Carnegie Corporation for Frederick L. Redefer to prepare a history of progressive education; $4,500 from the U.S. Office of the Coordinator of Inter-American Affairs for continued work with Latin American educators; $750 from the Marshall [Field] Fund to prepare a booklet, "New Bill of Rights"; and $900 from the General Education Board to cover general expenses during Redefer's absence in England.[25]

These few grants represented but a fraction of the requests that the Association made to foundations in the forties. Between 1940 and 1945 the Association solicited funds unsuccessfully at least fifteen times. Among these efforts was a proposal to the Marshall Field Foundation in 1944 for $30,000 annually for four years "to implement the American Education Fellowship program" and one to the General Education Board at the same time to pay the expenses for a spring Board of Directors meeting.[26]

Repeated failures to secure funds clearly demonstrated that the organization would have to devise some other scheme to conquer its financial problems. A logical alternative was to increase the membership, but with no funds to publicize it, no research to gain public attention, and no regular publications beside a magazine of steadily declining quality, the Association understandably did not attract new members. In fact, barely 50 per cent of those who were members renewed their subscriptions in 1941.[27]

In 1938 the General Education Board had given the PEA $70,000 for workshops, nearly $70,000 for its Commission on Human Relations, and almost $35,000 for field services.[28] During that same year, over

---

[25] Minutes of the Board of Directors, February 20, 1940; October 10–12, 1941; March 29, 1942; Fall, 1942; February 20–23, 1943.

[26] Minutes of the Board of Directors, April 3–4, 1944.

[27] Minutes of the Board of Directors, February 19, 1941. Actually a 50 per cent figure is a somewhat inflated estimate of the journal's popularity among individual members. Undoubtedly a significant portion of the 50 per cent who did renew were actually libraries that wanted to maintain a complete set of the journal.

[28] Minutes of the Board of Directors, November 19–20, 1938, and April 22–23, 1938.

2,200 mail ballots were returned to the Association's annual election of officers.[29] Two years later only 150 ballots were returned in a similar election. Less than nine years later an auditor declared the Association insolvent.[30]

The Association's annual budget in 1939–1940 was over $50,000, and in 1941 it claimed assets of over $16,000, of which the largest single item was the Life Membership Fund.[31] A year later the assets had dwindled to what was left of the Life Membership Fund, just over $3,000.[32] Four years later annual expenses were estimated at $21,000 with an anticipated net loss for the year of $3,000.[33] The following year the Association was forced to look into means of obtaining a $5,000 loan to pay its indebtedness and to gain a small financial backlog.[34] As the money drained away, memberships dropped correspondingly.[35]

World War II certainly aggravated the financial troubles of the Association, but the war alone cannot be held responsible for the decline. The end in 1941 of the large grants from such foundations as the Carnegie Corporation and the General Education Board forced the Association to curtail the activities of its commissions, at that time its most vital activity. Each of the three major commissions, Aikin's, Thayer's, and Miss Keliher's, had finished its research by 1941. The Service Center continued to publish a few pamphlets, but its activities also had declined sharply by 1941.

A final note on the causal factors responsible for the Association's declining fortunes may be put in terms of competition. In its early years the PEA had been, with the NEA, the Child Study Association, and the National Society for the Study of Education, one of the few organizations committed to the "new education." Now the PEA was feeling the effects of competition from a number of other educational

[29] Minutes of the Board of Directors, February 24, 1940.

[30] Minutes of the Board of Directors, October 4, 1946, and Interview with Harold G. Shane, July 25, 1960.

[31] Minutes of the Board of Directors, March 23, 1940, and April 27–28, 1941.

[32] Minutes of the Board of Directors, March 23, 1940, and April 27–28, 1941.

[33] Minutes of the Board of Directors, October 15–17, 1943.

[34] Minutes of the Board of Directors, October 15–16, 1944.

[35] From the fall of 1938 to February, 1941, the membership figure dropped from approximately 10,000 to 8,349. This latter figure included the approximately 1,500 new members who had come into the Association when it had assumed publication of *The Social Frontier.* Minutes of the Board of Directors, February 19, 1941.

organizations committed to many of the same principles the PEA had introduced.[36] Proliferation of national, state, and local groups pushing for "modern education" deprived the Association of much of its uniqueness. Its own members could now turn to other groups, many of them with far more lively programs, for information about current activities in education.[37] The Association was no longer seeking educational reform, but rather was interested in preservation of a status quo, a much less exciting activity.

Closing Down

In April, 1955, H. Gordon Hullfish, the last president of The Progressive Education Association, reviewed the dwindling membership list of his organization. He noted that over 2,000 of the 2,600 "members" were, in fact, college and university libraries that began subscribing to the magazine *Progressive Education* in the twenties or thirties when it was one of the most interesting and vital publications on the educational scene.[38] Librarians, wishing to maintain a complete set of a serial, continued their subscriptions; but their renewals certainly did not reflect a commitment to the PEA or its goals. Unlike the Association's founder, Stanwood Cobb, Hullfish was not single-mind-

[36] In the postwar years particularly, many new educational organizations were formed that competed with the PEA for members. The one most frequently cited as a competitor (by Shane, Brameld, and Hullfish) was the Association for Supervision and Curriculum Development.

[37] Writing to John J. DeBoer on May 13, 1948, Ruth Streitz, long an active and vocal member of the Association from Ohio State University, contended, "All of us interested in education believe in its social aspects, but unless we serve the teachers, principals and superintendents, we have no real reason to exist. While the Progressive Education Association has remained stationary or gone somewhat downward, other professional organizations are attracting the people who should be in the Progressive camp. I refer particularly to the organization now known as the Department of Supervision and Curriculum Development and the other group known as the Association for Childhood Education." Archives at Ohio State University.

[38] Memorandum in Archives at Ohio State University from Hullfish to Benjamin Fine, prepared for Fine's article on dissolution of PEA in the June 21, 1955, *New York Times*. A letter written September 29, 1955, from Lawrence E. Metcalf, editor of *Progressive Education*, to Robert Jewett reported the membership and subscriptions during the past year had been 2,100, of which 1,800 had been libraries in schools, colleges, and universities. Archives at the University of Illinois. Whichever figure one accepts, the preponderance of library subscriptions is clear.

edly devoted to continuing the organization and its journal at all costs. Hullfish was a man of many obligations and varied commitments. Seeing that interest in the organization had seriously declined, he proposed to his colleagues on the executive board of the John Dewey Society that the Society, which had a long history of close connection with the PEA, take over publication of the journal and that the Association itself disband. This was approved.

On June 25, 1955, the Progressive Education Society was officially dissolved at a meeting in Urbana, Illinois, the state in which the organization was then chartered. A month later the membership endorsed the decision with only six dissenting votes.[39]

For two years the John Dewey Society continued to publish *Progressive Education.*[40] Faced with increased printing costs, the Society decided in 1957 to discontinue the journal. Its former editor, Archibald W. Anderson, has insisted that *Progressive Education* could have been continued at its circulation rate of that time (1,900) if some subsidy had been available during the late fifties.[41] But even those loyal to the periodical admitted that by the mid-fifties the journal was making little scholarly or professional contribution.[42] *Progressive Education* had lost its unique role, that of popularizing new experiments in education. But however disheartened its supporters may have felt about the demise of the journal and of its parent organization, many agreed with Hullfish's statement in the final issue, "It [*Progressive Education*] departs . . . with a realization that it has been a responsible

[39] For obituaries of the Association, see Frederick L. Redefer, "A Blow for Education," *Nation* 189 (October 8, 1955), pp. 303–304; and brief notations in *Newsweek* 46 (August 1, 1955), p. 76; and *Time* 66 (July 4, 1955), p. 34. *Time* inadvertently called the organization the "Public Education Association." This mistake drew a letter from the director of the still-active Public Education Association in New York City.

[40] Robert Jewett emphasized the informal nature of the John Dewey Society's decision to publish *Progressive Education* in an interview at Columbus, Ohio, August 3, 1964. Jewett was active both on the Editorial Board of *Progressive Education* in its last years and in the John Dewey Society.

[41] Interview with Archibald W. Anderson, March 11, 1963.

[42] Editor Metcalf recognized the magazine's problems and circulated a letter on September 29, 1955, to Maurice Hunt, F. I. Shoemaker, Miles Cary, Ralph Pounds, John Goodlad, Vynce Hines, Morris Lewenstein, George Axtelle, and Robert Jewett in which he said, "Many of the manuscripts published last year were not good, and would not have been published by this magazine had alternative manuscripts been available." Archives at the University of Illinois.

participant in some of the more constructive thinking that has changed American education for the better." [43] Although arguments might abound over just what aspects of this "constructive thinking" had done most to improve American education, no informed critic of American education in 1957 could honestly wish for a return to the general educational practices of 1919. Improvements had occurred, and the Progressive Education Association could take considerable credit for them.

[43] H. Gordon Hullfish, "Hail and Farewell," *Progressive Education* 34 (July, 1957), p. 119.

CHAPTER VIII

End of an Era

☙❧

Sometime between 1919 and 1955 the phrase "progressive education" shifted from a term of praise to one of opprobrium. To the American public of 1919, progressive education meant all that was good in education; thirty-five years later nearly all the ills in American education were blamed on it. It was only natural that, to a large section of the enlightened public, the association whose name included the fateful term stood as the embodiment of progressivism in education. That is, after the First World War, the Progressive Education Association was taken to be the official and organized expression of that general trend in American education known as the progressive movement. This was pretty much the case. Despite the public's imprecise knowledge about the Association itself, the widespread assumption that during its lifetime the PEA represented the progressive movement as a whole is a valid one. Progressive education's sins of commission and omission were also the Association's, and common to both the general movement and the specific organization was responsibility for much of the improvement in American education between 1919 and 1955.

The Association and the progressive education movement as a whole shared common ground in at least five important areas: commitment to child-centeredness in education; belief in the responsibility of the school in society; conviction of the need to evolve a philosophy of progressive education; orientation toward research; a trend to homogeneity in the character of supporters and consequent increasing isolation from the American mainstream. Certainly other educational organizations were affected by progressivism, but it was the PEA that institutionalized the often vague aspirations of the movement and transformed its unclarified tenets into a pedagogical canon.

The centrality of the child in the educational process was a hall-mark of progressive education in the twenties. This concept entailed the importance of individual differences and its corollary, the necessity to develop the creativity of the child. The slogans "creativity" and "individual differences" became clichés, even to progressives, but their acceptance and initial vogue marked a radical shift from the educational orthodoxy of the previous generation—mental discipline and faculty psychology. No organization campaigned more tirelessly, none more monotonously, than did the PEA in behalf of the child as the crux of the school; no other educational group matched PEA's energy in proclaiming the importance of the child's individuality, the utter necessity of the development of his unique gifts.

The school's responsibility to society, a characteristic emphasis of the progressive education movement both before and after the First World War, was never an unbroken line in the ideology of the PEA; there was always an element in the Association who were not very much interested in questions of social responsibility. But two important periods in the history of the PEA showed the organization's social potential. The school's social responsibility received its sharpest expression in George S. Counts' address to the PEA in 1932, "Dare Progressive Education be Progressive?" and his committee's report to the Association in 1933, *A Call to the Teachers of the Nation.* John J. DeBoer's editorials in *Progressive Education* in 1947, and the 1947 policy statement of the Association exhibited the views of the post-World War II radicals—"progressives" in the sense used in Henry Wallace's presidential campaign—on the relationship between the schools and the social order.

John Dewey's *Democracy and Education* of 1916 has remained the most inclusive exposition of the philosophical basis of the progressive education movement. In its later years, particularly in those after the First World War, the movement as a whole declined alarmingly from the point of view of philosophy and style. It was unfortunate that the decades of the PEA's existence coincided with this period of progressive education's ideological decline. Many critics of progressive education in the thirties and forties—forgetting Dewey's prewar classic —pointed to the PEA's ideological pronouncements, few and thin as they were, as the progressive movement's only statements of philosophy. Citing such works as Kilpatrick's *The Project Method,* Agnes DeLima's *Our Enemy the Child,* and Lester Dix's *A Charter for Progressive Education,* many progressive educators described as *philosophy* what at best were successful pedagogical devices and practical methods.

Another characteristic shared by both the Association and the progressive education movement in their later years was enthusiastic support of educational research. Beginning with the pioneering work of E. L. Thorndike in learning theory and Lewis Terman in intelligence testing, educational research gained many adherents among progressive educators in the thirties and forties, culminating in the "action research" of the fifties. In the name of "science" innumerable surveys and experiments were conducted. Among these were perceptive studies of complex phenomena in education such as the work of Ralph Tyler's Committee on Evaluation, which was part of the Commission on the Relation of School and College. Some of the other "research" sponsored by the Association was not so laudable; the PEA, like the progressive education movement in general, often failed to make the distinction between research as a means to the solution of a problem and research simply as an end in itself. The Association was further committed to research as a means of soliciting funds from foundations, a tactic used in force between 1939 and 1941. Excessive and uncritical devotion to research led, in Martin Mayer's words, to "progressivism's great disservice to education . . . its deliberate training of teachers to distrust their own observations for the sake of achieving 'science.'"[1]

Perhaps one of the least understood and (to the informed public) most irritating features of the progressive education movement was the part played by the newly self-conscious group of professional educators. Over the decades the progressive movement changed from one founded on a wide and heterogeneous base of support to one whose leaders were, near the end, almost completely limited to professors at midwestern schools of education. The center of gravity of the Association shifted concurrently. Founded by a miscellaneous group of little-known private school teachers, supported at the outset by laymen, and titularly led by the president emeritus of Harvard, the PEA was transformed as early as 1930 to an association dominated by a growing power group of professional educators. Despite DeBoer's attempt at the 1947 convention to broaden the Association's base, the PEA never again had substantial support outside the teaching profession. Neither did the movement as a whole.

These factors, then, show the elements common to the Association and the progressive education movement in the years between the wars. Mutual concern with the same pedagogical questions makes very plain the similarity of interests between the movement and the Associa-

---

[1] Martin Mayer, *The Schools* (New York, 1961), p. 66.

tion. Active participation in the PEA by most of the leading progressive educators is almost too obvious evidence of the Association's integral relationship to the general movement. But such coincidence of interests and activities should not be taken as proof that the Association and the progressive education movement were identical. The reform movement in education variously labeled the "progressive education movement" (Cremin), "the new education movement" (Hofstadter), and "modern education" (Kilpatrick), antedated the Association by at least thirty years. Nevertheless during the period 1919 to 1955, years when the PEA assumed the status of official spokesman of the movement, the progressive education movement and the Association were so close as to be nearly indistinguishable.

Progressivism, Old and New

The progressive education movement and the PEA suffered many of the same handicaps, although one cannot accurately say they suffered the same fate. Cremin's thesis that the progressive education movement was a continuous, though developing, force in American education from 1876 to 1955 must stand a little strain if we compare the state of American education in 1955 to that of 1876. The goals of the educational reformers of the 1880s and the 1890s were much more extensively and permanently achieved than were those of their successors thirty and forty years later. The Progressive Education Association mirrored the state of the progressive education movement between 1920 and 1955; it did not reflect the interests of pre-World War I progressivism. The Association's isolation from the spirit of the leaders of late nineteenth-century and early twentieth-century progressive education is one of the most revealing aspects of the Association's development.

The intensity of PEA's pedagogical enthusiasms was not matched by their duration; what lasted in progressive education were the older reforms. The emphasis on child study, on vocational education, on community-centered schools, on educational research, and on a flexible curriculum, all planks in the platform of educational reformers at the turn of the century, continued to find favor among educators and parents of schoolchildren both in the palmy days of the progressive education of the twenties and thirties, and in the brief period of retrenchment following the Second World War. If one accepts the continuity of the pre- and post-World War I progressive education movement, one can then view the PEA's fulfillment of its original primary goal, "to publicize new practices in education," as being nothing less than a complete success. Certainly the new methods were publicized and, for a decade or two, widely accepted. But the innovations of the late nineteenth and early twentieth centuries were taken up into the mainstream of American education, while many of the changes urged by the PEA's leaders and contemporaries, popular for a decade or two, soon passed from vogue. Arthur Bestor, one of the most widely read critics of progressive education, distinguishes between the permanence of the "old style" and the transiency of the "new style" progressive education in *The Restoration of Learning.* Bestor writes glowingly of the Lincoln School of Teachers College, Columbia University, "one of the most progressive schools in the country," during the 1920s. During that decade, says Bestor, the Lincoln School brought "teaching of the basic disciplines to the highest perfection possible in the light of modern pedagogy . . . by emphasizing the relevance of knowledge and intellectual skill to the problems of practical life and citizenship." [2] But already by the mid-twenties, Bestor noted, the Lincoln School's excellent program had begun to weaken under the abundance of aimless group discussions and class projects introduced by a new course, social studies. It was the same period, the mid-twenties, that saw the rise of the Progressive Education Association as a significant national educational organization. The developing social studies courses with their new pedagogical methodology were among PEA's favorite innovations.

A number of reasons can be suggested for the simultaneous decline of the PEA and the progressive education movement. The first has to do with the assault on the traditional curriculum.

Opposition to the Traditional Curriculum

It was characteristic of both the Association and the post-World War I progressive education movement that their early programs of opposition, such as their attacks on rigidity in the traditional curriculum, were much more clear and persuasive than their positive programs. Both could effectively reproach classicists for their insistence on teaching "dead languages" like Latin, but both failed to implement,

[2] Arthur Bestor, *The Restoration of Learning* (New York, 1955), pp. 140–142. Five years later in *The Process of Education* (Cambridge, Massachusetts, 1960) Jerome Bruner reported the views of a number of prominent American academicians at a conference at Woods Hole, Massachusetts, as favoring just such a return to the "structure" of the basic disciplines.

or even to suggest, solid alternatives. It was not the progressives of the twenties and thirties but the antiprogressives of the fifties and sixties who insisted on an effective program of modern language teaching in the schools.

The push away from the traditional curriculum was one of the most individual aspects of progressive education at its height, and in this the PEA was certainly a leader. Its best-known commission argued in its Eight-Year Study for just such a revolution in the college preparatory curriculum. One of its two other major commissions tackled new approaches to the traditional curriculum, which left the old one nearly unrecognizable, while the other proposed an entirely new curriculum.

Disturbed by this indifference to the traditional curriculum, the Canadian writer Hugh MacLennan observed in 1960, "they [the young] are beginning to say openly that what has cheated them more effectively than anything else has been the educational system they are offered." [3] A similar observation was made a quarter of a century earlier by historian Samuel Eliot Morison regarding President Charles W. Eliot's introduction of the elective system at Harvard: "It is a hard saying, but Mr. Eliot, more than any other man, is responsible for the greatest crime of the century against American youth—depriving him of his classical heritage." [4] A significant difference between the Harvard elective system, as it developed, and the progressive educators' unrelenting rejection of traditional subject matter was the subsequent modification of the elective system by A. Lawrence Lowell, Eliot's successor at Harvard. Lowell's arrangement permitted students to take some elective courses according to their own interests, while retaining a core of prescribed study. The progressive educators, however, always had a hard time bringing themselves to revise their own dogmas, leaving proposals for compromise to their critics, who hastened to accept much of progressivism while at the same time showering the movement with vocal abuse. Thus, few critics really wanted a return to the narrow classical curriculum of the early twentieth century;

[3] Hugh MacLennan, "The Rout of the Classical Tradition," *Horizon* 3 (November, 1960), p. 18.

[4] Morison modified his statement for Harvard by observing that most of the young men who entered Harvard had already had the beginnings of a traditional education at such schools as Exeter or classical high schools. The extension of a free or partially free choice curriculum to the secondary schools prevented such an alternative for the products of progressive schools. Samuel Eliot Morison, *Three Centuries of Harvard* (Cambridge, Massachusetts, 1936), pp. 389–390.

rather they accepted many of the general progressive movements reforms, particularly the early innovations such as manual training, home
economics, and laboratory sciences. Leaders of the PEA, however,
generally failed to recognize that the pendulum of curriculum reform
had swung too far, and they continued to press for classes designed to
meet the students' short-term needs. Such courses as marriage and the
family, communication skills or "problems of democracy" replaced the
history and English courses of the previous decades. This subversion of
traditional subject matter was most pronounced and (according to its
critics) pernicious at the secondary school level, the level at which the
PEA did nearly all its research and the one at which the foundations
were most willing to provide grants.[5]

Indifference to Crucial Problems

Failure of the Association and of the later progressive movement
to recognize the extreme and irresponsible nature of their position on
curriculum reform was a principal factor in their ultimate decline, but
their indifference to other important problems also contributed to the
fall. The educational reform movement prior to the First World War
had wide interests. Educators had been concerned about the child
both in the classroom and in the community. During the later period,
however, while progressive educators talked a great deal about "the
whole child" and his many and varied needs, their concerns seemed
taken up either by the content of the curriculum or by the problem of
the relation between school and society. These educators professed
great concern for adolescents, but they ignored some of the most
interesting experiments being carried out for youngsters in their teens.
The leaders of the movement and those of the PEA itself paid little
attention to truly revolutionary youth projects such as the National
Youth Administration or the Civilian Conservation Corps. Instead, in
the decades between the wars, the movement seemed to focus its
interest on the educational activities of college-bound youth, although
in 1940 just over 15 per cent of the eighteen to twenty-one-year-olds
were in college. Only one commission of the Association concerned
itself with the needs and interests of the majority of youngsters who

[5] Richard Hofstadter has noted in *Anti-Intellectualism in American Life*
(New York, 1963), p. 360, "This tendency [to dissolve the curriculum]
became most serious in the education of older children and especially at
the secondary level, where as the need arises to pursue a complex, organized program of studies, the question of curriculum becomes acute."

were not college bound, and this body was short-lived and without foundation aid. The Association's most successful research project, on the other hand, dealt specifically with college entrance requirements. Moreover, most of the colleges participating in the study run by the Commission on the Relation of School and College were exclusive and expensive institutions available only to a minority of even college-bound students. This study, which took place entirely during the Depression years, paid little attention to the large and relatively inexpensive state universities and municipal colleges.

Just as the Association fell short in considering the problems of the bulk of the youth whose educations were affected by the Depression years, so also did it fail to give adequate notice to other primary contemporary educational problems. During the late forties the popular magazines abounded with articles on education. The same journals that in the twenties and thirties had discussed pedagogical reforms proposed by PEA leaders now featured articles by a variety of other educators and laymen that set out the dilemmas encountered by teachers and institutions in a wide assortment of areas.[6] A 1946 article in the *New Republic* titled "The Crisis in Education" discussed twenty-one educational issues of considerable importance. Among these were the increase in enrollments, shortage of teachers, matriculation of veterans, overcrowding of colleges, inadequacy of teachers' and professors' salaries, federal aid to education, financing of school systems, problems of Negro education, and the changing role of private schools.[7] In the two previous decades the *New Republic*'s educational interests had virtually coincided with the PEA's, but by the mid-forties the Association had so limited the scope of its interests that it now had little in common with those of the renowned liberal weekly.

Progressive Education itself was noticeably silent on these pressing

---

[6] The *Ladies' Home Journal*, which under the editorship of Edward Bok at the turn of the century had published a number of Scott Nearing's articles describing and praising new educational programs, presented another series of articles in the late forties criticizing the extremes the progressive reforms had led: Christian Gauss, "Aims of Education," 65 (January, 1948), pp. 42 ff.; Richard Livingstone, "Some Tasks for Education," 64 (October, 1947), p. 11; F. T. Spaulding, "What Kind of High School Do You Want?" 65 (August, 1948), pp. 48 ff. Agnes E. Meyer pointed to some of the critical problems facing urban schools in "Are Our Public Schools Doing Their Job?" *Atlantic* 183 (February, 1949), pp. 32–36.

[7] "These Are The Facts About: The Crisis in Education," *New Republic* 115 (October 7, 1946), pp. 434–436.

questions, apparently content to fill its pages with criticisms of capi-
talistic economy, attempts to achieve formulas of philosophical unity,
and homages to the life-adjustment movement. The leaders of the PEA
during this period were almost entirely faculty members in colleges and
universities; yet the Association neglected to address its attention to the
most fundamental change faced by every college and university in the
postwar years: the veterans on the campus. Those university professors,
who in other situations were quite vocal about recognition of immediate
needs, chose in this instance to ignore the immediate situation around
them, preferring instead to seek solutions to more remote problems.
True, the Association had established a commission in the early years
of the war to evaluate the effects of the war on education, but lacking
the $70,000 deemed necessary as an operating budget for its first year,
it never became fully organized.

Perhaps the most widely read report on education of the 1940s, the
Harvard statement *General Education in a Free Society*, received little
notice in *Progressive Education*, although it dealt with many of the
questions that the Association had considered of critical importance in
the previous decade. Vinal Tibbetts, then executive director of the
Association, made some superficial critical comments on it in his
monthly column in the magazine, but, beyond this, small attention was
paid to it. The degree to which the Harvard report, so widely read
and discussed in academic circles and in the general press, was ignored
by *Progressive Education* is an accurate sign of the acute self-involve-
ment of the organization in its later years and its indifference to educational concerns outside its immediate circle.[8]

Not only did the Association fail to contend with current problems
such as the education of the youth during the Depression or of servicemen after the Second World War, but it also failed to deal seriously
with continuing problems, such as the education of immigrant children,
slum youngsters, and rural youth. Each of these groups had caught the
attention of educational reformers of the late nineteenth and early
twentieth centuries. The social settlement workers had joined forces
with the educators, notably under the leadership of Jane Addams in
Chicago, to attempt to achieve better programs for youngsters in urban
slums. The Gary schools in the second decade of the twentieth century

[8] Vinal H. Tibbetts, "Frankly Speaking," *Progressive Education* 23 (November, 1945), p. 50. Among the comments on the report were Jacques
Barzun's excellent review in the *Atlantic* 167 (October, 1945), pp. 52–56
and F. O. Matthiessen's critique, "Harvard Wants to Join America," *New
Republic* 113 (August 20, 1945), pp. 220–221.

stood as an outstanding example of an entire school system's attempt to educate both the immigrant parents and children, and, in the opinion of progressive apologist Randolph Bourne, the Gary schools were most "progressive." Mrs. Harvey's school, described by Evelyn Dewey in *New Schools for Old,* was, with all its awareness of the educational problems of poorer children, a widely cited example of progressivism before World War I. Bills providing federal funds for agricultural education and home economics training in the grade and high schools were widely supported by pre-World War I progressives. After the war, it was another matter.

Problems of immigrants, slums, and agricultural life did not disappear after the First World War, but progressive educators' concern for these problems waned noticeably. In the thirties occasional statements by Elsie Ripley Clapp (later released from her position as editor of *Progressive Education* after brief tenure) called attention to the special educational problems of youngsters in rural Kentucky and Tennessee. The influx of Spanish-speaking Puerto Ricans to the schools in metropolitan New York and other cities went unnoticed by the PEA. The enormous problems all metropolitan school systems confronted with the deterioration of the "inner city" and the resulting changes in the cultural and ethnic character of the school population also failed to gain the attention of the PEA. Nor did the baby boom of World War II, which by the late forties and early fifties resulted in enormous overcrowding of the elementary schools, awaken the PEA from its apathy. Finally, and perhaps least defensible in an organization that in the thirties and forties had preached social responsibility so strenuously, the Association ignored the movement for desegregation of the public schools, both during the years when northern cities were gradually desegregating their schools (the late forties and early fifties) and after the *Brown v. Board of Education* Supreme Court decision in 1954 that declared segregation in the public schools unconstitutional. True, the years of these events coincided with those of PEA's rapid decline, but the failure of the Association to rally under the powerful stimulus of the desegregation activity shows the extent to which the organization had lost its old awareness of social problems.

Isolation of the Leaders

The Association's insistence on an extreme position on curriculum reform and its failure to respond to some of the crucial educational problems of its time were two factors leading to its demise. The common effect of both was the increasing isolation of the PEA leadership from other educators and from American society as a whole. Founded with the support and patronage of laymen, and heir to the wide backing of the pre-World War I progressive education movement, the Association gained supporters within the emerging education profession in the twenties and thirties. It was a propitious time for fledgling educational organizations, for it was the period of the emergence of a self-aware group of professional educators. In the old days, elementary and secondary school teachers were often no more than temporary help, not career teachers at all, intent on teaching only briefly while on route to more permanent occupations. The combination of swollen enrollments, the widespread extension of secondary education, and the resulting interest of the states in licensing teachers, led irresistibly to the formation of educational organizations especially designed for the many new teachers. Newly professionalized, many of these teachers, as well as their professors of education, felt more at home in specifically education-oriented groups like the PEA than they did in discipline-centered organizations like the American Historical Association or the Modern Language Association.

The PEA in its earliest stages had substantial support from laymen and from private school teachers. In the late twenties and the thirties academic administrators also joined it. By the early thirties the majority of the leaders came from the faculties of schools or colleges of education, although one might still find the president of a liberal arts college taking an active part in the organization. By 1939, however, the criticism that "the Association was too often sponsoring meetings at liberal arts colleges and not frequently enough at teachers colleges" [9] pushed the organization more firmly still into the arms of the professional educators, and the PEA became increasingly separated from the academic life of the country, a fact openly lamented at a PEA board meeting in 1940 by Robert Leigh, president of Bennington College.[10] The trend Leigh noted continued as the leadership of the Associations moved to such citadels of professional education as the University of Illinois and Ohio State University. At the midwestern state universities then, the separation between the faculty of the liberal arts divisions and the school of education was often nearly impassible. The PEA had become entirely identified with professional education, although many of its recommendations continued to deal with the subject matter areas.

[9] Minutes of the Board of Directors, February 21, 1939.
[10] Minutes of the Board of Directors, May 5–7, 1940.

The limitation imposed on the PEA by its top-heavy professional educator component is illustrated by John J. DeBoer's effort to wake up the Association in the late forties with the radicalism of the Wallace era. DeBoer recognized that the Association urgently needed new members and fresh blood, and he valiantly tried to attract them by taking bold and decisive social positions in the journal. What DeBoer and his supporters failed to realize, however, was the extent to which professors of education, never a group distinguished by radical sentiments, had taken control of the Association. In the thirties it had been possible to commit the Association to a socially radical pronouncement; the political climate was different then, and the PEA was not yet in the hands of established professors of education at midwestern colleges of education. In the forties and fifties, this was no longer possible. The unwillingness of the Association to be aroused by post-World War II progressivism illustrated again its limiting homogeneity of membership and the increased isolation from contemporary social problems on the part of the professional educators composing the organization.

The Association's fundamental estrangement from the main-line academic and intellectual communities of the nation is also shown by its determined anti-intellectualism.[11] In its early years, the Association's avowed suspicion of intellectualism was not a hindrance, even for an organization committed to education, for in the twenties few significant elements of American society placed high value on intellectuality. The Association's espousal of "democratic education for democratic society" fitted the anti-elitist view common in the twenties and thirties. Although a vigorous American intellectual life flourished during this period, it was not highly regarded by the society as a whole nor did the intellectuals of the time consider themselves in a strategic position in the culture. In the late forties and early fifties the situation perceptibly

---

[11] A letter from Herman H. Horne, an American philosopher of education, to Stanwood Cobb on January 6, 1930, expresses one prominent progressive educator's views on the anti-intellectualism of the movement: "Intellectualism makes ideas primary and actions secondary; voluntarism makes action primary and ideas secondary. Dr. Dewey, being a voluntarist in his conclusions, is *ipso facto* an anti-intellectualist. You may be interested in a book prepared some years ago by Schinz on Anti-Intellectualism which is a criticism of the pragmatic movement in our country. . . . There is no doubt about Dr. Dewey in his results being an anti-intellectualist. His whole argument in *The Quest for Certainty* is that knowledge is a consequence of action. Logically this is a difficult proposition to prove inasmuch as the results of past action can be funded as knowledge." Archive at Teachers College Library, Columbia.

changed. Richard Hofstadter has identified the publication of the *Partisan Review*'s 1952 anthology "Our Country and Our Culture" as a symbol of the recognition of the intellectuals by themselves and by society of their newly significant position in America.[12] The election campaigns of Adlai E. Stevenson in 1952 and 1956 revealed a significant and vocal group of "eggheads" who identified themselves with Stevenson as not only their political but also their intellectual choice. Ironically, the successful Democratic candidate in 1960, whom the intellectuals endorsed much less enthusiastically, carried out the promise the defeated Stevenson was unable to fulfill; John F. Kennedy gave with his wife far more public support and recognition to American intellectuals than any of his recent predecessors.

The emergence of a self-conscious and vigorous group of intellectuals occurred seemingly without the awareness of the leaders of the PEA. Typically, the educational programs supported by the new groups were anathema to the PEA. It remained committed to its dogma of "democratic education," while the new approach to education in the fifties was moving toward a more nearly elitist philosophy of education. Such opposite positions have fused no better than the child-centered and society-centered arguments in the Association's 1941 statement on philosophy. In the case of the elitist approach, however, the Association chose in most instances to ignore the attack. When it did recognize the elitists, its criticisms of that group were lumped with those of all opponents of progressive education, and the convenient epithet "anti-democratic" was widely employed.

Not all leaders of the PEA were anti-intellectual, but the organization's corporate actions and statements could certainly be so described. These attitudes were no handicaps in the twenties and thirties when the persuasiveness of progressive education's experimentalism was overwhelming. But, in the years when the experiments were no longer fresh and important, segments of American society were arguing for intellectual competence rather than equalitarianism; the Association remained committed to both experiments and equalitarianism, thus falling short of a cardinal rule of successful reform movements: anticipate and lead public demands.

James B. Conant's 1963 book, *The Education of American Teachers,* suggests reforms that, if enacted, would lead to massive changes in the preparation of future teachers. The Conant reforms, if carried out, might well lead to the disappearance of the professional educator as a

[12] Hofstadter, *Anti-Intellectualism in American Life, op. cit.,* p. 394.

class, leaving the training of teachers to the liberal arts colleges supplemented by subject matter study in regular graduate disciplines. (It should be noted that professional educators remain the largest single group of supporters of progressive education, although few of them now care to identify themselves with the movement by name.) It is interesting to speculate that the projected disappearance of the professional educator caste would have followed the demise of the Progressive Education Association, which in its turn had fallen heir to the earlier, more vitally ideological period of the progressive movement. If such a series of events should occur, the progressive education movement; from its inception in the late nineteenth century until the final dispersal of its supporters in the late twentieth, will serve as an interesting case study of a social movement.[13]

The Disagreement over Philosophy

Another major factor leading to the Association's final decline was its inability to achieve a philosophical synthesis of the warring elements in its own commitments. In its earliest years the Association fervently insisted that it had no stated philosophy and, furthermore, did not wish to have one since any philosophical alignment might constrict its activities. Implicitly, however, the PEA was definitely committed from the first to a kind of individualism that entailed maximum freedom for the child in the classroom and maximum opportunity therein for development of his creative potential. The Depression years were not the happiest times for creative individualism and even the most enraptured and Rousseauan supporters of youthful creativity were by then tempering some of their extreme statements of the previous decade. By 1933 Counts had spoken, and the responsibility of the school in society became the educational vogue of the thirties; social reconstructionism took the lead for a while over creative individualism.

The failure of the movement or the Association to achieve a philosophical synthesis of its individualist and social components resulted from the difficulty of reconciling these two major points of view on a small stage. Even on purely intellectual grounds, creation of such a synthesis would have required unusual metaphysical hardihood.

---

[13] Jerome Davis traces the development of a social movement from its inception as a recognized need until its final stage when "bureaucracy, inflexibility and reaction become dominant." *Contemporary Social Movements* (New York, 1930), pp. 8–9. The PEA in the forties and fifties incarnated the "bureaucracy, inflexibility and reaction" of which Davis writes.

Dewey managed it partially by being ambiguous on certain key questions such as the role of traditional knowledge in the curriculum and "self-control" in the classroom; the Deweyan category of the *social* was so protean and all-comprehending that at times it nearly became a universal category. Harold Rugg and William Heard Kilpatrick tried manfully to submerge crucial differences in points of view in an effort to achieve doctrinal harmony. Even Dewey recognized his differences with friends and colleagues; in a brief article in *The Social Frontier* in 1938 the Columbia philosopher reluctantly admitted to divergence with George S. Counts and Boyd H. Bode.[14] If even such intellectually serious men as these failed to agree on the meaning of each other's statements, it is not surprising that less theoretically oriented educators would cheerfully ignore inconsistencies in theory.

Top leaders of the progressive education movement and of the Association itself, such as Dewey, Rugg, and Kilpatrick, attempted to reconcile the two extremes of the new education within their own educational philosophies. Others, who had no particular doctrine of their own, tried to cover themselves in the mantle of the 1941 report of the committee on philosophy of education. Thus the child-oriented Carleton Washburne, Caroline Pratt, Elsie Ripley Clapp, and Harold Shane could share the dais of the same organization contemporaneously with the social-minded Counts, DeBoer, Nellie Seeds, and Theodore Brameld.

Who was conservative? What was radical? Richard Hofstadter has argued:

> The new education was at bottom politically conservative, but its warm rhetoric about democracy, its philanthropic approach to the child (not to speak of its having become the object of much harassment by right-wing cranks) made it seem, at least to its advocates, "progressive," or even radical.[15]

Hofstadter is right in pointing out the dominant influence of the political conservatives in what he calls the "new education" movement, but his phrase "at bottom" is misleading; "at the end" or "ultimately" would be better. For the political radicals and genuine "progressives" exerted an important influence on the progressive education movement from its origins in the nineteenth century until its demise in the mid-twentieth.

[14] John Dewey, "Education, Democracy and Socialized Economy," *The Social Frontier* 4 (December, 1938), pp. 71–72.
[15] Hofstadter, *Anti-Intellectualism in American Life, op. cit.*, p. 356.

Radicals (called liberals in the thirties) played intermittent but crucial roles in the Association itself. Like a Pied Piper, Counts drew the whole Association after him for two years in the mid-thirties. DeBoer's efforts, genuinely radical, were the most vigorous of any in the Association after 1940. Though founded by political conservatives such as Stanwood Cobb (it was Mrs. Ensor's "socialism" that kept Cobb away from the NEF), the Association was not really "at bottom politically conservative." For one thing, a large part of the PEA membership, particularly in the happy, carefree days of child-centeredness and creativity, was as innocent as the birds of political interest of any sort. Those groups within the PEA that did represent different political philosophies, just as they represented really different educational philosophies, warred quietly within the Association for over thirty years. The conflict within the Association reflected the wider tensions within the progressive education movement as a whole. That the final Pyrrhic victory went to the less radical faction is scarcely surprising if one remembers the sombre days of Senator McCarthy and the House Un-American Activities Committee.

The Problem of Application

Another factor contributing to the failure of the Association and of the progressive education movement itself in mid-twentieth century was the problem of translation, that is, the difficulty of applying progressive methods and attitudes to pedagogical situations on a scale wider than that of the highly specialized progressive school in which these methods were more or less successfully practiced. The "progressive method," insofar as it could be determined, emphasized creativity, cooperation, initiative, and adaptability. Such a teaching approach is enormously effective when employed by a creative, cooperative, independent, and adaptable teacher. While the percentage of individual teachers possessing these traits may have been high at the laboratory and private schools where the first enthusiastic experiments in progressive education were made, persons with these rare gifts simply could not be found in any numbers to staff all the public schools of the nation that attempted "progressive" programs.

The difficulty of translating successful laboratory school experiments in progressive education into mass programs in the public schools was aggravated by the de-emphasis of the traditional curriculum. Teachers might be able to adjust to new methods, as many had who in the old days embraced Herbartianism, but to ask them to discard both their traditional methods and their subject matter was simply more of an adjustment than most could satisfactorily make. This problem is illustrated by the Gary schools. Their renowned superintendent, William Wirt, claimed that one of the keys to his program's outstanding success was his exhaustive selection procedure for his teachers. But at Gary, for all its freshened methodology and gifted teachers, those teachers were instructing in traditional subject matter areas. Other schools expecting both new methods and new subject matter, yet unable to maintain such rigorous selection procedures, understandably found it difficult to duplicate in their classrooms the exciting results of the laboratory schools. Increasingly, the informed public criticized those schools attempting "progressive education" with mediocre teachers. The alternative of traditional education with a teacher of average endowments at least left the pupil with a core of information, which, unsatisfactory as it might be, was often missing from uninspired progressive teaching.

Social Class Bias

Still another element, closely related to the problem of translation, contributed to the failure of the movement and of the Association: the limited applicability of progressive education with respect to social class. Progressive education after the First World War was strongest and most popular in schools serving middle class and upper-middle class youngsters. But it was characteristic of many of the pre-1919 experiments in progressive pedagogy that they had been conducted with children at the other end of the social spectrum.[16] The emphasis of the old-style progressive school on vocational education, urban and rural, on health education, on the school as a social center, illustrated the appeal of those schools to the underprivileged. A majority of the schools described by the Deweys in their 1915 classic *Schools of To-Morrow* were geared to the needs of such children. The familiar Dewey formula that school is life, rather than preparation for it, stood over against the traditional college preparatory emphasis of the secondary school, an emphasis that was generally most suitable for upper-middle class students.

In the transformation of progressivism between 1910 and 1920, this emphasis shifted, and the most vocal proponents of progressive education in the twenties were leaders of private schools for the

[16] See discussion in Chapter I.

prosperous in New York, Boston, Baltimore, Washington, Philadelphia, Cleveland, and Chicago. Occasionally public school systems (such as Bronxville, New York, and Winnetka, Illinois) were similarly converted to the idea of the progressive school, but the clientele of these schools closely resembled that of the well-to-do private schools. When Elisabeth Irwin tried to extend her experiments in progressive education to the children of poor immigrant Italian families (this was in the early 1920s), one Italian mother declared that she and her friends preferred that their children be sent to an old-fashioned American school where they could be Americanized in the traditional pattern. The emphasis in the progressive schools was on social adjustment, which this mother considered a luxury that could be afforded only by the children of the rich.[17]

The progressive education movement affected children in nearly all socioeconomic classes at some time between 1876 and 1955, but at no time was it simultaneously involved with the particular educational problems of each group. Before the turn of the century its attention was focused upon the educational difficulties of the lower-class children. In the second and third decades of the twentieth century the upper and upper-middle class children were the objects of the progressive education movement's greatest attention. In the thirties and forties progressive education became a pervasive force in the United States largely on the basis of revised pedagogical methods and curricular content. Although these changes were adopted in schools enrolling youngsters of all social classes, the innovations generally were much less successful in urban slum schools where other problems were more pressing.

Supporters of progressive education between the wars were usually most enthusiastic at schools such as the Ohio State University School. There youngsters came from homes where education was already highly regarded, and in such an environment teachers are more likely to be eager and able. Progressive education flourished in those atmospheres in which nearly any educational innovation, enthusiastically and intelligently presented, would have been successful. In its earliest years it was also successful in less fertile environments, but when applied as a mass educational panacea in the thirties and forties with its overemphasis on methodology and curriculum reform, its success was limited.

The Association accurately reflected the progressive education

---

[17] Caroline Ware, *Greenwich Village: 1920–1930* (New York, 1935), p. 343.

movement as a whole in its post-World War I years. At its first meetings, representatives of progressive slum schools such as Angelo Patri
of the Bronx and Persis K. Miller of a Baltimore vocational school
addressed the members, but by the mid-twenties the majority of the
Association paid little attention to Patri's school gardens or Miss
Miller's training. The indifference was mutual. Finger painting and
modern dance were not considered the most important aspects of an
immigrant youngster's American education.

Competition from Other Educational Organizations

The demise of the Progressive Education Association is partially
to be explained by the enormous increase in the number of educational
organizations during the past twenty-five years. These groups did not
have to carry the heritage of difficulties, arguments, and splintered
membership that hampered the PEA. Nor did they have to put up with
a name that became a red flag to so many in the era of revolt against
progressive education. During the affluent forties and fifties other
organizations supplanted the PEA. Many of the late leaders of the PEA
have become active supporters of the Association for Supervision and
Curriculum Development, an organization somewhat similar to the
PEA; but the ASCD does not have to drag a checkered past along
with it. It is interesting to note that NCATE, although only recently
founded, is now undergoing criticism similar to that which the PEA
experienced. The 1963 Conant report's attack on NCATE is more than
a little reminiscent of the old polemics against PEA professionalism.

Conclusion: the Legacy of the Association

The Progressive Education Assocation, as well as the movement
it represented, is still painfully fresh in the memories of many American educators. For this reason, assessments of its significance are closely
linked with personal judgements. The efforts of the Association and of
the progressive education movement as a whole remain emotionally
charged, overlaid with elements of self-justification and professional
"face." These are factors that tend to obscure the Association's contribution to American education.

Although it passed from the American scene as a separate and
distinct educational force, progressive education's most effective elements were taken up into the mainstream of American education where
they do their work in solution to this day. The PEA played an important

role as transfer agency in this respect. The second half of the PEA's history saw the control of the Association pass from the private schools and interested laymen to the hands of professional educators, most of them from the teachers colleges and education departments of American universities. These professors exerted a determining influence on a generation of future public school teachers who sat in their classes as undergraduate and graduate students. In this way, the progressive ingredient was carried over from the special precincts of the PEA to the main currents of public school education in the United States.

Although many of the curriculum experiments the Association supported are, viewed in isolation, currently in disfavor, the services performed by the PEA in demanding a re-evaluation of the structure of the traditional disciplines, were of crucial importance. The PEA's specific recommendations for the improvement of the teaching of mathematics may bear small resemblance to the current "new math" reforms, but the partisans of both faced a common problem of basic pedagogical importance: how to clarify the meaning of mathematics in the curriculum. The Association helped loosen the strictures binding the organization of academic disciplines, and although the solutions proposed by the various PEA research groups were not altogether satisfactory, the precedent for a fresh look at the way academic disciplines are put together was established.

The Association campaigned extensively and intensively for recognition of the individual differences of children. The development of the child's creative powers, as distinct from the amount of information efficiently packed into him from the outside, was a primary objective of progressive education. The Association played its part here, for contemporary interest in creative intuition, though at the moment directed more toward science than to art, is by no means discontinuous with earlier lines of interest and encouragement laid down by the PEA. An example of current interest in creativity is the effort of the College Entrance Examination Board to design a test comparable to its Scholastic Aptitude Test to measure creativity.

Finally, it will be remembered that the Association spoke frequently and with passion about the goals of education and the role of schools in society. The Association was at its best when it provided the forum for the discussion of these issues, although often at its worst when it tried to answer these questions itself. To the question, "Is progressive education obsolete?" Boyd Bode replied, "If democracy is here to stay, then the spirit of progressive education can never become obsolete. We may discard the name, and we may discontinue it as a separate organization, but we can never surrender the vision which it has tried to bring to us."[18] In its finest moments the Association embodied this vision, for it tried to arouse Americans by all the means at its disposal to a consciousness of the purposes of education. The questions raised were not finally answered—indeed, they were nearly discredited—but these questions, unlike certain of the Association's other activities, will long outlive the Association and its partisans.

[18] Boyd H. Bode, "Is Progressive Education Obsolete?" *School and Society* 66 (November 29, 1947), p. 416.

Officers of the
Progressive Education Association

❧

Year	President	Executive Secretary or Director	Editor, Progressive Education
1919			
1920	Arthur E. Morgan		
1921	Arthur E. Morgan		
1922	Arthur E. Morgan		
1923	Eugene R. Smith		
1924	Eugene R. Smith		Gertrude Hartman
1925	F. M. Froelicher		Gertrude Hartman
1926	F. M. Froelicher	Morton Snyder	Gertrude Hartman
1927	Stanwood Cobb	Morton Snyder	Gertrude Hartman
1928	Stanwood Cobb	J. Milnor Dorey	Gertrude Hartman
1929	Stanwood Cobb	J. Milnor Dorey	Gertrude Hartman
1930	Burton P. Fowler	J. Milnor Dorey	F. M. Froelicher
1931	Burton P. Fowler	J. Milnor Dorey	Ann Shumaker
1932	Burton P. Fowler	F. L. Redefer	Ann Shumaker
1933	Willard W. Beatty	F. L. Redefer	Ann Shumaker
1934	Willard W. Beatty	F. L. Redefer	Ann Shumaker
1935	Willard W. Beatty	F. L. Redefer	Frances M. Foster
1936	Willard W. Beatty	F. L. Redefer	Frances M. Foster
1937	W. Carson Ryan, Jr.	F. L. Redefer	Elsie Ripley Clapp
1938	W. Carson Ryan, Jr.	F. L. Redefer	Elsie Ripley Clapp
1939	W. Carson Ryan, Jr.	F. L. Redefer	Elsie Ripley Clapp
			W. Carson Ryan, Jr.

1940	Carleton Washburne	F. L. Redefer	James L. Hymes, Jr.
1941	Carleton Washburne	F. L. Redefer	James L. Hymes, Jr.
1942	Carleton Washburne	F. L. Redefer	James L. Hymes, Jr.
			Ruth Kotinsky
			F. L. Redefer
1943	Vinal H. Tibbetts	F. L. Redefer	Toni Taylor
1944	Frank E. Baker	Vinal H. Tibbetts	Vinal H. Tibbetts
1945	Frank E. Baker	Vinal H. Tibbetts	Vinal H. Tibbetts
1946	John J. DeBoer	Vinal H. Tibbetts	Vinal H. Tibbetts
1947	John J. DeBoer		
1948	John J. DeBoer		B. Othanel Smith
1949	Kenneth Benne		B. Othanel Smith
1950	Kenneth Benne		B. Othanel Smith
1951	Kenneth Benne		A. W. Anderson
1952	H. Gordon Hullfish		A. W. Anderson
1953	H. Gordon Hullfish		A. W. Anderson
1954	H. Gordon Hullfish		A. W. Anderson
1955	H. Gordon Hullfish		Lawrence Metcalf
1956			Lawrence Metcalf
1957			Lawrence Metcalf

Lester Dix, former principal of Lincoln School, Teachers College, also served briefly as Director during World War II.

The Progressive Education Association was incorporated on March 26, 1931, in Washington, D.C. It was later incorporated in Illinois on February 23, 1947. The organization's name was changed to American Education Fellowship in 1944 but reverted back to Progressive Education Association in 1953.

The headquarters of the Association were in Washington, D.C., from 1919 to 1935; in New York City from 1935 to 1946; in Chicago from early 1947 to late 1947; in Urbana, Illinois, from 1947 to 1952; and in Columbus, Ohio, from 1952 to 1955.

APPENDIX B

Commissions and Committees of the

Progressive Education Association

৵৵

During its lifetime the PEA organized a great many commissions and committees, some of which were very important while others scarcely functioned. Listed below is as complete a list as possible of these groups. Committees that dealt with questions affecting only the organization, such as the Committee for Coordination, are not included. The Committee on Philosophy is not included because its report was intended largely for the Association.

Information about the commissions and committees was gleaned principally from the Minutes of the Executive Committee and the Board of Directors, *Progressive Education,* and the publications of the commissions themselves. The dates given are the founding and dissolution of each commission and committee. Since records were frequently incomplete, the date the group disbanded is not always cited, although an occasional pamphlet that gained wide attention is included.

Commissions

All-Youth Commission of the Progressive Education Association (Commission on Noncollege Youth); early 1940s; Arthur Gould, Chairman.

Commission of the John Dewey Society; 1939–1944; William Heard Kilpatrick, Chairman of Executive Committee.

Commission on Educational Freedom; early 1930s to mid-forties; H. Gordon Hullfish, Chairman.

Commission on Human Relations; 1935–1942; Alice V. Keliher, Chairman.
  Publications:
  Alice V. Keliher, *Life and Growth* (New York, 1938).
  Walter C. Langer, *Psychology and Human Living* (New York, 1943).
  Louise M. Rosenblatt, *Literature as Exploration* (New York, 1938).
  Bernhard J. Stern, *The Family, Past and Present* (New York, 1938).
  Katharine W. Taylor, *Do Adolescents Need Parents?* (New York, 1938).
  W. Robert Wunsch and Edna Albers, eds., *Thicker Than Water* (New York, 1939).
Commission on Intercultural Education (Commission on Intercultural Relations); 1937–1942; W. Carson Ryan, Fritz Borgeson, Chairmen.
  Publication:
  Alain Locke and Bernhard J. Stern, *When Peoples Meet* (New York, 1942).
Commission on Education's Role in Reconstruction (Commission on Post-War Reconstruction); 1941–1943; Grayson Kefauver, Chairman.
Commission on Indian Education; 1938–early 1940s; Willard W. Beatty, Chairman.
Commission on Physical Education; early 1940s; no Chairman listed.
Commission on the Relation of School and College; 1930–1942; Wilford M. Aikin, Chairman.
  Publications:
  Wilford M. Aikin, *The Story of the Eight-Year Study* (New York, 1942).
  H. H. Giles, S. P. McCutchen, and A. N. Zechiel, *Exploring the Curriculum* (New York, 1942).
  Eugene R. Smith and Ralph Tyler, *Appraising and Recording Student Progress* (New York, 1942).
  Dean Chamberlin, *et al., Did They Succeed in College?* (New York, 1942).
  Thirty Schools Tell Their Story (New York, 1943).
Commission on Resources and Education; late 1930s–early 1940s; Paul Hanna, Chairman; joint commission of the National Education Association and the Progressive Education Association.
Commission on the Secondary School Curriculum; 1933–1940; V. T. Thayer, Chairman.
  Publications published under the Commission's authorship:
  Language in General Education (New York, 1940).
  Mathematics in General Education (New York, 1940).
  Science in General Education (New York, 1938).
  The Social Studies in General Education (New York, 1940).
  The Visual Arts in General Education (New York, 1940).
  Publications published under individual authorship:
  Peter Blos, *The Adolescent Personality: A Study of Individual Behavior* (New York, 1941).
  Lawrence Henry Conrad, *Teaching Creative Writing* (New York, 1937).

Elbert Lenrow, *Reader's Guide to Prose Fiction* (New York, 1940).

Lois Hayden Meek, *The Personal-Social Development of Boys and Girls with Implication for Secondary Education* (New York, 1940).

V. T. Thayer, Caroline B. Zachry, and Ruth Kotinsky, *Reorganizing Secondary Education* (New York, 1939).

Caroline B. Zachry, *Emotion and Conduct in Adolescence* (New York, 1940).

National Commission on Educational Reconstruction; 1942–1943; Grayson Kefauver interested but not Chairman.

National Educational Planning Commission; 1943; Virgil Rogers, Chairman.

Committees

American Committee on International Education; mid-thirties; W. Carson Ryan, Chairman.

Committee on Adult Education; mid-thirties; Harold Rugg, Chairman.

Committee on Alcoholic Consumption; late thirties; no Chairman listed.

Committee on Arts in Education; 1940; Mr. Woods, Chairman.

Committee on Camping; late thirties; Ernest Osborne, Chairman.

Committee on Child Development and Elementary Curriculum; 1938–1940; Rose Alschuler, Paul Witty, Chairmen.

Committee on Community Schools Relations; 1933–1939; Elsie Ripley Clapp, Edmund deS. Brunner, Chairmen.

Committee on Cultural Relations; mid-thirties; Emma Schweppe, Chairman.

Committee on Elementary Education; late thirties–early forties; Marion Carswell, Chairman.

Committee on the Education of Teachers for Progressive Schools; 1933–1937; Willard Beatty, Laura Zirbes, Chairmen.

Committee on the Evaluated Results of Progressive Education; 1939–1941; Derwood Baker, Chairman.

Committee on Experimental Schools; 1936–1939; John R. P. French, Chairman.
   Publication:
   What the Schools are Doing (New York, 1937).

Committee on the Role of the Federal Government in Education (Committee on Federal Government Coordination); early 1940s; no Chairman listed.

Committee on Federal Support to Education; mid-1930s; Paul R. Mort, Chairman.

Committee on Health and Safety Education (Commission on the Conservation of Human Resources); 1940–1942; Lawrence Frank, Chairman.

Committee on the History of Progressive Education; 1941; Frederick L. Redefer, Chairman.

Committee on Home-School Relations; 1933–1938; Lois Hayden Meek, Chairman.

Publication:
Sara Emily Baldwin and Ernest G. Osborne, *Home-School Relations, Philosophy and Practice* (New York, 1935).

Committee on International Cooperation; 1938–early 1940s; Harold Rugg, Chairman.

Committee on International Relations; 1941; Edna Noble-White, Chairman.

Committee on Latin American Relations; 1941–1943; no Chairman listed.

Committee on Mental Hygiene in Education; 1937–1941; Edward Liss, Chairman.

Committee on Museum-School Relations (Committee on Museums and Their Relations to Progressive Education); 1940–1944; Francis Presler, Chairman.

Committee on Parent Participation (Committee on Parent Education); 1941–1943; Ruth Streitz, Chairman.

Committee on Postwar Child Care; mid-1940s; no Chairman listed.

Committee on Progressive Rural Schools; 1932–1939; Allan Hulsizer, Marcia Everett, Erwin Sassman, Chairmen.

Committee on Radio in Education; 1937–1940; Willard W. Beatty, Chairman; Margaret Harrison, Director.

Committee on Regionalism and Education; late 1930s; Paul R. Hanna, Chairman.

Committee on Social and Economic Problems; 1932–1933; George S. Counts, Chairman.
Publication:
A Call to the Teachers of the Nation (New York, 1933).

Committee on Teacher Education; 1939–1940; Ruth Streitz, Chairman.

Committee on Teacher Placement; 1939–early 1940s; no Chairman listed.

Committee on Utilization of Research in Secondary Education; late 1930s; Willard W. Beatty, Chairman.

Committee on Workshops and Field Services; 1932–mid 1940s; Frederick L. Redefer, Chairman; Kenneth Heaton, Executive Secretary.

Bibliographic Essay

Publications of the Progressive Education Association

Undoubtedly the most important single category of sources for a history of the Progressive Education Association is the records and publications of the organization itself. The PEA sponsored an enormous number of pamphlets, reports, and books during the years of its existence, and they are not of equal value. Among the most significant are Gertrude Hartman and Ann Shumaker, eds., *Creative Expression* (New York, 1932), which accurately portrays the interests of the Association during its first decade; George S. Counts, *A Call to the Teachers of the Nation* (New York, 1933), which conveys the tone of many of the Association's statements of the 1930s; and *Progressive Education: Its Philosophy and Its Challenge* (New York, 1941), the murky report of the Committee on Philosophy. The pages of *Progressive Education* are an excellent index to the changing interests of the Association, as is *Frontiers of Democracy,* originally *The Social Frontier,* the organization's other serial publication. The booklets that preceded *Progressive Education* serve much the same purpose for the first five years of the PEA's existence. The major reports of the commissions and committees are listed in Appendix B. Generally the reports do not reveal as much about the general interests of the organization as do the smaller publications. The Yearbooks of the New Education Fellowship, which record the speeches at various annual meetings, indicate the general interests of the international progressive education movement. Periodic reports of the Executive Secretary and the Treasurer are helpful.

Unpublished Records of the Progressive Education Association

The minutes of the Executive Committee, Executive Board, and Board of Directors, as the governing body of the Association was vari-

172

ously called, are an unparalleled source of information about the PEA. The official minutes of the annual business meetings and the appended reports of various officers of the Association reveal a great deal about the problems and internal strife confronting the Association. An incomplete set of the minutes for 1924 to 1946 is available in the Teachers College Library, Columbia University. A much larger collection of materials of the PEA is available at the University of Illinois. Most of the papers there are correspondence files, records of *Progressive Education*, and financial records. A smaller collection exists at Ohio State University. The bulk of these materials deals with the years following World War II.

Interviews and Correspondence

Interviews with various persons connected with the Association and the progressive education movement were a source of varying significance. Discussions with Stanwood Cobb (Chevy Chase, Maryland, October 29, 1962), Theodore Brameld (Boston, Massachusetts, January 3, 1963), Frederick L. Redefer (New York City, November 1, 1962), Archibald W. Anderson (Urbana, Illinois, March 11, 1963), and John J. DeBoer (Urbana, Illinois, March 11, 1963, and June 26, 1964) were particularly helpful. Other conversations provided insights on specific questions: Letitia Hall Carter (Indianapolis, Indiana, December 26, 1962), Hans Froelicher, Jr. (New York City, March 3, 1960), Sidonie Matsner Gruenberg (New York City, November 21, 1962), Richard Hocking (Carlisle, Pennsylvania, September 1, 1965), William Heard Kilpatrick (New York City, January 3, 1961), Harold G. Shane (Bloomington, Indiana, July 25, 1960), Goodwin Watson (New York City, February 4, 1960), Greer Zachry (New York City, December 9, 1960), and Robert Jewett (Columbus, Ohio, August 3, 1964). Correspondence with Eugene Randolph Smith, Willard W. Beatty, and Florence Anderson was particularly fruitful.

Unpublished Manuscripts

Unpublished manuscripts of particular relevance for this study are Robert H. Beck's excellent analytical study, "American Progressive Education, 1875–1930," unpublished doctoral dissertation, Yale University, 1942; Berdine J. Bovard's descriptive paper, "A History of the Progressive Education Association, 1919–1939," unpublished doctoral dissertation, University of California, 1941; Chester A. Bowers, "The

Educational and Social Philosophy of *The Social Frontier,* 1934–1943," unpublished doctoral dissertation, University of California, 1962; Wilbur Harvey Dutton, "The Child-Study Movement from its Origin (1880) to the Organization of the Progressive Education Association (1920) [sic]," unpublished doctoral dissertation, Stanford University, 1945; Lloyd Marcus, "The Founding of American Private Progressive Schools, 1912–1921," senior thesis, Harvard College, 1948; and Frederick L. Redefer, "Between Two Wars: An Interpretation of Progressive Education in the United States of America," unpublished manuscript deposited at the Teachers College Library, Columbia University.

Unpublished manuscripts of more general relevance than the above are Morris L. Berger, "The Settlement, the Immigrant, and the Public School," unpublished doctoral dissertation, Columbia University, 1956; Allen Freeman Davis, "Spearheads for Reform—The Social Settlements and the Progressive Movement," unpublished doctoral dissertation, University of Wisconsin, 1959; Marietta Johnson, *Thirty Years with an Idea,* n.d., deposited in Teachers College Library, Columbia University; Geraldine M. Joncich, "Science, Psychology and Education: An Interpretive Study of Edward L. Thorndike's Place in the Scientific Movement in Education," unpublished doctoral study, Teachers College, Columbia University, 1961; Anna M. Keppel, "Country Schools for Country Children: Backgrounds of the Reform Movement in Rural Elementary Education, 1890–1914," unpublished doctoral dissertation, University of Wisconsin, 1960; Mark Phillips, "*The Seven Arts* and Harold Rugg," unpublished master's essay, Columbia University, 1961; Frederick L. Redefer, "The Eight-Year Study—Eight Years Later," unpublished doctoral study, Teachers College, Columbia University, 1952; Malcolm Skilbeck, "Criticisms of Progressive Education, 1916–1930," unpublished master's essay, University of Illinois, 1958; Gertrude Almy Slichter, "European Backgrounds of American Reform," unpublished doctoral dissertation, University of Illinois, 1960; Sheila Tuchman, "The Progressive Education Association: The Pseudo-Progressive Revolt," 1959, deposited in Teachers College Library, Columbia University; and Howard R. Weisz, "Progressive Education and the First World War," unpublished master's essay, Columbia University, 1960.

A number of Stanwood Cobb's unpublished speeches and articles about the PEA are on deposit in the Teachers College Library, Columbia University. Some of these are quite valuable, although Cobb misspells names frequently, and in the later papers his memories of dates of early events are often inaccurate. Cobb, predictably, describes the PEA from his highly personal point of view.

Eugene Randolph Smith has prepared for Lawrence A. Cremin an unpublished autobiographical paper, "Educational Experimentation and Advances, 1894, As Observed or Taken Part In." This document is particularly interesting when compared with Cobb's writing, both for some factual differences and for Smith's attitude that the PEA's role was much less significant than that of some of the other educational organizations, such as the American Council on Education.

Serial Publications

A survey of the articles about progressive education in the general magazines is a sensitive indicator of the public's attitude toward the movement. The best single journal during this period to present the intelligent liberal's view of the movement is the *New Republic*. Particularly in the twenties and sporadically in the forties and early fifties, the *New Republic* contained perceptive articles on reforms in education. Among the best of these were Walter Lippmann's critical series on the testing fad that appeared in six consecutive issues: "The Mental Age of Americans," 32 (October 25, 1922), pp. 213–215; "The Mystery of the 'A' Men," 32 (November 1, 1922), pp. 246–248; "The Reliability of Intelligence Tests," 32 (November 8, 1922), pp. 275–277; "The Abuse of Tests," 32 (November 15, 1922), pp. 297–298; "Tests of Hereditary Intelligence," 32 (November 22, 1922), pp. 328–330; and "A Future for the Tests," 33 (November 29, 1922), pp. 9–11. Lewis W. Terman made a vicious reply to Lippmann, "The Great Confusion of the Impulse Imperious of Intelligence Testers, Psychoanalyzed and Exposed by Mr. Lippmann," 33 (December 27, 1922), pp. 116–120. Lippmann, however, had the last word in this round: "The Great Confusion," 33 (January 3, 1923), pp. 145–146.

Special issues of the *New Republic* on the high school, 36 (November 7, 1923) and the elementary school, 40 (November 12, 1924) were also thoughtful. A series on individual progressive schools, including Agnes DeLima, "The Dalton Plan," 37 (February 13, 1924), pp. 308–309, and Elizabeth Vincent, "The Lincoln School," 37 (February 20, 1924), pp. 330–333, were interesting. "The New Education: Ten Years After," which appeared in six consecutive issues in the summer of 1930, is probably the best contemporary statement available on the state of progressive education: Boyd H. Bode, "Apprenticeship or Freedom?" 63 (June 4, 1930), pp. 61–64; Joseph K. Hart, "Judging Our Progressive Schools," 63 (June 11, 1930), pp. 92–94; Francis Mitchell Froelicher, "A Program for Progressive Schools," 63 (June 18, 1930), pp. 123–125; Margaret Naumburg, "The Crux of Progressive Education," 63 (June 25, 1930), pp. 172–176; and John Dewey, "How Much Freedom in the New Schools?" 63 (July 9, 1930), pp. 204–206.

Among the particularly relevant later articles are Harold Laski, "A New Education for a New America," 87 (July 29, 1936), pp. 342–345; F. O. Matthiessen, "Harvard Wants to Join America," 113 (August 20, 1945), pp. 220–221; and "These Are the Facts About: The Crisis in Education," 115 (October 7, 1946), pp. 434–436.

Survey Graphic also included a number of articles on education, particularly during the period in which Beulah Amidon was a regular contributor. Among Miss Amidon's best articles is "Schools in a Changing World," 68 (June 1, 1932), pp. 228–231. A later special issue, "Schools: The Challenge of Democracy to Education," 27 (October, 1939), pp. 569–630, is a clear account of pedagogical opinion at the end of the thirties.

During the thirties other popular magazines also carried articles on educational reforms. Among the most revealing are Alice Beal Parsons, "The Despotism of Polly Ross," *Harpers*, 141 (November, 1930), pp. 665–675; Carl Joachim Friedrich, "This Progressive Education," *Atlantic Monthly* 154 (October, 1934), pp. 421–426; "Progressive's Progress," *Time* 32 (October 31, 1938), pp. 31–37; and Ann L. Crockett, "Lollipops vs. Learning," *Saturday Evening Post* 212 (March 16, 1940), pp. 29, 105–106.

The forties, particularly the late forties, was a period of widespread and intense criticism of the American educational system and its acceptance of progressivism. Typical of the mid-twentieth century muckraking articles are D. Gibson, "Pedagogues and Pedagese," *American Scholar* 22 (January, 1943), pp. 92–104; Gladys Denny Schultz, "Is This the School of Tomorrow?" *Better Homes and Gardens* 24 (September, 1945), pp. 15–18, 77 ff.; Richard Livingstone, "Some Tasks for Education," *Ladies' Home Journal* 64 (October, 1947), p. 11; Christian Gauss, "Aims of Education," *Ladies' Home Journal* 65 (January, 1948), pp. 42 ff.; F. T. Spaulding, "What Kind of High School Do You Want?" *Ladies' Home Journal* 65 (August, 1948), pp. 48 ff.; Agnes E. Meyer, "Are Our Public Schools Doing Their Jobs?" *Atlantic Monthly* 183 (February, 1949), pp. 32–36; and Albert Lynd, "Quackery in the Public Schools," *Atlantic Monthly* 185 (March, 1950), pp. 33–38.

Although much of the criticism of the educational system came from the popular press, the professional journals were not silent. Probably the most responsible periodical geared primarily to the interests of educators was *School and Society*, which, under the editorship of Isaac

L. Kandel and later William W. Brickman, included articles on a wide variety of educational topics. Among those most applicable to the PEA are Marvin L. Darsie, "The Philosophic Origins of Progressive Education," 30 (September 30, 1933), pp. 417–422; John S. Brubacher, "A Proposal for Judging What Is and What Is Not Progressive Education," 48 (October 22, 1938), pp. 509–519; Boyd H. Bode, "Is Progressive Education Obsolete?" 66 (November 29, 1947), pp. 414–416; and William W. Brickman, "The Secondary School," 72 (August 5, 1950), p. 90.

Some excellent early articles on the Eight-Year Study were "Committee on School and College Relations," *The School Review* 40 (April, 1932), pp. 241–245; Raymond Walters and Wilford M. Aikin, "Coordination of School and College Work," *School and Society* 35 (June 18, 1932), pp. 841–845; "Experimental College Entrance Units," *North Central Association Quarterly* 9 (January, 1935), pp. 345–363; and "The Schools Dominating the Colleges," *Bulletin of the Association of American Colleges* 21 (May, 1935), pp. 264–295. Later studies included Helmer G. Johnson, "Some Comments on the Eight-Year Study," *School and Society* 72 (November 25, 1950), pp. 337–339; and Paul B. Diederich, "The Eight-Year Study: More Comments," *School and Society* 73 (January 20, 1951), pp. 41–42.

Other articles appraising the educational scene have been scattered widely during the fifties and sixties. One of the best critiques of progressive education from the Marxian perspective is Joseph Nahem, "What is Progressive Education?" *The Worker*, September 30, 1951, p. 1. A criticism from an entirely different point of view is Geraldine Joncich, "Educational Research: Investigation or Vindication?" *Saturday Review* 45 (December 15, 1962), pp. 44–46. A revealing article concerning teachers' scholarship is Harold E. Mitzel and Lester Dubnick, "The Relative Scholastic Ability of Prospective Teachers," *Journal of Teacher Education* 12 (March, 1961), pp. 73–80. One of the most responsible defenses of progressive education is William VanTil, "Is Progressive Education Obsolete?" *Saturday Review* 45 (February 17, 1962), pp. 56–57, 82 ff. The most complete account of the death of the PEA was Frederick L. Redefer, "A Blow for Education," *Nation* 189 (October 8, 1955), pp. 303–304. Shorter accounts appeared in *Time* 66 (July 4, 1955), p. 34 and *Newsweek* 46 (August 1, 1955), p. 76.

Newspapers

The *New York Times* provides the most systematic coverage of the Progressive Education Association, although even it carries rather scanty reports. It is particularly valuable for its obituary articles for former leaders of the PEA, such as Harold Rugg's on May 18, 1960; Willard W. Beatty's on September 30, 1961; and Burton P. Fowler's on November 18, 1963. Its article on the demise of the PEA on June 21, 1955, is helpful. Articles in other papers, such as the *Washington Herald,* April 2, 1919; *Washington Star,* April 3, 1919; and *Baltimore Sun,* June 1, 1919, describing the founding of the PEA, are useful.

Annual Reports of Educational Organizations

The reports of the U.S. Office of Education (formerly Bureau of Education) provide an inestimably valuable source of statistical information about American education. The most helpful general reports are the *Biennial Surveys of Education in the United States* and the *Reports of the U.S. Commissioner,* which contain data about a wealth of topics. Individual research reports on a wide variety of subjects, such as the education of teachers, are also informative. Two of the best of these are J. C. Boykin and Robert King, *The Tangible Rewards of Teaching,* U.S. Bureau of Education Bulletin No. 16 (Washington, 1914), and Katherine M. Cook, *State Laws and Regulations Governing Teachers' Certificates,* Bureau of Educational Bulletin No. 22 (Washington, 1921). The reports on Life Adjustment in the 1950s were also published by the Office of Education.

The annual reports of the National Education Association, particularly after its enormous growth in the early 1920s, illustrate the diversity of interests in American education. Some of the commission reports are among the most perceptive educational documents of their time, and others are distressingly trite. The reports of the Committee of 17 on the Preparation of High School Teachers (1907), the Committee on the Economy of Time (1915–1919), the Commission on the Reorganization of Secondary Education (1918), and the Educational Policy Commission (1944) were widely read and influential. The volumes of Addresses and Proceedings of the NEA's annual meeting furnish the historian with a comprehensive account of contemporary educational problems.

The yearly output of the NEA is so great that it is sometimes difficult to see trends emerging, but the annual Yearbooks of the National Society for the Study of Education rectify this difficulty. These yearbooks are devoted to one or two topics annually, and throughout the years their editors have managed to select regularly issues of considerable importance. Thus the NSSE yearbooks are the single best guide to contemporary problems in education. The reports of the NEA's Committee on the Economy of Time were published as separate sections of the NSSE yearbooks from 1915 to 1919.

Contemporary Accounts on Education

Pre-World War I Reports The work of John Dewey dominates contemporary statements on education between 1890 and 1918. During that period he published *The School and Society* in 1899 (reprinted in Martin S. Dworkin, ed., *Dewey on Education* [New York, 1959]), *Schools of To-Morrow* (New York, 1915), and the most comprehensive discussion of his educational philosophy, *Democracy and Education* (New York, 1916). His daughter Evelyn collaborated with him on *Schools of To-Morrow,* and she brought out separately an idyll of the rural schoolteacher, *New Schools for Old* (New York, 1919). Other important works of Dewey on specific topics include *The Child and the Curriculum* (Chicago, 1902); *The Influence of Darwin on Philosophy* (New York, 1910); and *Vocational Education in the Light of the World War,* Bulletin No. 4, Convention of the Vocational Education Association of the Middle West (Chicago, 1918).

The most comprehensive study of American education during this period is the *Cyclopedia of Education* (New York, 1911, 1912, 1913), edited by Paul Monroe. Of particular interest for this study is Edwin A. Kirkpatrick's detailed article on the Child Study Movement (Vol. I, pp. 615–621). William James's two principal works for educators, *Principles of Psychology* (2 vols., New York, 1890) and *Talks to Teachers on Psychology* (New York, 1899), are of importance to any historian because of their considerable influence at the time of their publication.

The Gary schools were a source of much controversy during the second decade of the twentieth century. They were discussed in Abraham Flexner and Frank P. Bachman, *The Gary Schools* (New York, 1918) and Randolph Bourne, *The Gary Schools* (Cambridge, Massachusetts, 1916).

Scott Nearing, *The New Education* (New York, 1915) is the most inclusive account of educational reforms during the early twentieth century. Mabel Carney, *Country Life and the Country School* (Chicago, 1912) offers considerable information about new practices in rural schools.

More general statements about educational practices are found in Charles William Eliot, *Changes Needed in American Secondary Education* (New York, 1916) and Abraham Flexner, *A Modern School* (New

York, 1916). More specific prescriptions for improving education are John Franklin Bobbitt, *The Curriculum* (New York, 1918) and Frank Freeman, *Experimental Education* (Boston, 1916).

Education had a series of articles on new practices in education in 1905. Three of the most interesting were Frank O. Carpenter, "Industrial and Commercial Training in Public Schools," 26 (December, 1905), pp. 191–202; M. F. Andrew, "The Problem of Individualizing Instruction," 26 (November, 1905), pp. 129–136; and Frank Webster Smith, "Secondary Education in the Last Twenty-Five Years," 26 (September, 1905), pp. 1–13. William H. Kilpatrick, "The Project Method," *Teachers College Record* 19 (September, 1918), pp. 319–335 quickly became a classic in the literature of progressive education.

Education in the Twenties   The educational literature of the twenties emphasized children's creativity and means of releasing it. Typical examples of this interest are Stanwood Cobb, *The New Leaven* (New York, 1928); Ellsworth Collings, *The Project Curriculum* (New York, 1923); Agnes DeLima, *Our Enemy the Child* (New York, 1926); Gertrude Hartman, *Home and Community Life* (New York, 1924); Hughes Mearns, *Creative Youth* (New York, 1925); and Carleton Washburne, *New Schools in the Old World* (New York, 1926). Eugene Randolph Smith, *Education Moves Ahead* (Boston, 1924) has a somewhat less euphoric approach, as does Harold Rugg and Ann Shumaker, *The Child-Centered School* (Yonkers-on-Hudson, New York, 1928), which though essentially laudatory toward the new educational experiments is not blind to their faults. One volume, George Mirick, *Progressive Education* (New York, 1923), attempted to define the new movement.

Education in the Thirties and War Years   The thirties was a decade of major philosophical statements about progressive education, beginning with George S. Counts, *Dare the School Build a New Social Order?* (New York, 1932); William H. Kilpatrick, ed., *The Educational Frontier* (New York, 1933); and John Dewey, *Education and the Social Order* (New York, 1934). In 1938 two major critical statements appeared: Boyd H. Bode, *Progressive Education at the Crossroads* (New York, 1938) and John Dewey, *Experience and Education* (New York, 1938). Neither was inflammatory, and their theses were largely lost on their colleagues. Typical of the period were Stanwood Cobb, *New Horizons for the Child* (Washington, D.C., 1934); Carleton Washburne, *Adjusting the School to the Child* (Yonkers-on-Hudson, New

York, 1932); Mary Ross Hall, *Children Can See Life Whole* (New York, 1940); Thomas H. Briggs, *Pragmatism and Pedagogy* (New York, 1940); and Lester Dix, *A Charter for Progressive Education* (New York, 1939). Ernest Cobb attempted to curb his brother's enthusiasm in *One Foot on the Ground* (New York, 1932). Arguments from the leftist point of view were Howard Langford, *Education and the Social Conflict* (New York, 1936) and Zalmen Slesinger, *Education and the Class Struggle* (New York, 1937). Caroline Ware's excellent sociological study, *Greenwich Village: 1920–1930* (New York, 1935), included some interesting data on educational developments in that area.

Education in the Postwar Years   The period immediately following World War II was one of intense criticism of the schools and of the progressive education movement. In the plethora of criticism are Arthur Bestor, *The Restoration of Learning* (New York, 1955); Bernard Iddings Bell, *Crisis in Education* (New York, 1949); and Mortimer Smith, *And Madly Teach* (New York, 1949). Among the more thoughtful criticisms are Paul Woodring, *Let's Talk Sense About Our Schools* (New York, 1953), and Theodore M. Greene, *Liberal Education Reconsidered* (Cambridge, Massachusetts, 1953).

The two most significant policy statements about education during this period are the Harvard report, *General Education in a Free Society* (Cambridge, Massachusetts, 1946) and *Higher Education for American Democracy*, Report of the President's Commission on Higher Education (New York, 1947).

This period is also one of reminiscences. Margaret Naumburg had published her volume, *The Child and the World* (New York, 1928), much earlier. During these years three of her colleagues in progressive education experiments of the twenties produced their autobiographies: Caroline Pratt, *I Learn From Children* (New York, 1948); Lucy Sprague Mitchell, *Two Lives* (New York, 1953); and Harold Rugg, *The Teacher of Teachers* (New York, 1952).

Two of the most important recent books on education are Martin Mayer's fundamentally critical study, *The Schools* (New York, 1961), and James B. Conant's call for sweeping revisions in teacher education, *The Education of American Teachers* (New York, 1963). Although both discuss current problems, each has considerable importance for an understanding of the era in which these problems developed. Harold Rugg's *Imagination* (New York, 1963) is an example of a volume on current educational questions prepared by an established progressive educator.

American Educational History

By far the most comprehensive study of the progressive education movement is Lawrence A. Cremin, *The Transformation of the School* (New York, 1961). Other studies deal with facets of the progressive movement; among them Raymond E. Callahan, *Education and the Cult of Efficiency* (Chicago, 1962); Sol Cohen, *Progressives and Urban School Reform* (New York, 1964); John L. Childs, *American Pragmatism and Education* (New York, 1956); and Willis Rudy, *Schools in an Age of Mass Culture* (Englewood Cliffs, New Jersey, 1965).

General studies of teacher education and the rise of the teaching profession include Merle Borrowman, *The Liberal and Technical in Teacher Education* (New York, 1956); Charles A. Harper, *A Century of Public Teacher Education* (Washington, D.C., 1939); and Jesse Pangburn, *The Evolution of the American Teachers College* (New York, 1932).

Histories of educational developments in America include R. Freeman Butts and Lawrence A. Cremin, *A History of Education in American Culture* (New York, 1953); Merle Curti, *The Social Ideas of American Educators* (New York, 1953); Isaac L. Kandel, *American Education in the Twentieth Century* (Cambridge, Massachusetts, 1957); Frederick Rudolph, *The American College and University* (New York, 1962); Samuel Eliot Morison, *Three Centuries of Harvard* (Cambridge, Massachusetts, 1936); Charles A. Bennett, *History of Manual and Industrial Education, 1870–1917* (Peoria, Illinois, 1937); Edgar W. Knight, *Fifty Years of American Education* (New York, 1952); and Harold Rugg, *Foundations for American Education* (Yonkers-on-Hudson, New York, 1947).

Criticisms of progressive education from the Roman Catholic point of view include Joseph McGlade, *Progressive Educators and the Catholic Church* (Westminster, Maryland, 1953). Sr. Mary Ruth Sandifer has written on *American Lay Opinion of the Progressive School* (Washington, D.C., 1943). Reports on activities of educational foundations are found in Raymond B. Fosdick, *Adventure in Giving* (New York, 1962) and Edgar Wesley, *NEA, The First Hundred Years* (New York, 1957).

Histories of individual progressive experience of particular significance include Agnes DeLima, *The Little Red School House* (New York, 1942) and Carleton Washburne and Sidney P. Marland, Jr., *Winnetka, The History and Significance of an Educational Experiment* (Englewood Cliffs, New Jersey, 1963). A comparable study in higher education is Louis T. Benezet, *General Education in the Progressive College* (New York, 1943).

Periodical articles of particular note include Robert Beck, "Progressive Education and American Progressivism: Felix Adler, Margaret Naumburg, Caroline Pratt," *Teachers College Record* 60 (1958–1959), pp. 77–89, 129–137, 198–208; John Chenoweth Burnham, "Psychiatry, Psychology and the Progressive Movement," *American Quarterly* 12 (Winter, 1960), pp. 457–465; Louis M. Filler, "Main Currents in Progressivist American Education," *History of Education Journal* 8 (Winter, 1957), pp. 33–57; and Timothy Smith, "Progressivism in America," *Harvard Educational Review* 31 (Spring, 1961), pp. 168–193.

European New Education Movement

The relationship of the new education movement and the New Education Fellowship to the progressive education movement and the Progressive Education Association has never been systematically explored. Probably the best guide to the activities and interests of the NEF is the journal of the English section, *New Era*. Articles in it of particular interest include Laurin Zilliacus, "An Analysis of the New Education," 11 (December, 1930), pp. 170–174; William Boyd, "Social Progress Through Education," 14 (March–June, 1933), pp. 81–83, 97–99, 123–25, 145–47; C. D. L. Bereton, "The N. E. F. And English Education," 18 (September–October, 1937), pp. 258–261; and W. T. R. Rawson, "Authority and the New Education," 18 (December, 1937), pp. 295–298. The papers presented at several NEF Conferences were collected for publication, and although these reports are rather tedious reading today, they are valuable as indications of the NEF's interests. Among the collections are W. T. R. Rawson, ed., *Education in a Changing Commonwealth* (London, 1931); W. T. R. Rawson, ed., *A New World in the Making* (London, 1933); W. T. R. Rawson, ed., *The Freedom We Seek* (London, 1937); E. G. Malherbe, ed., *Educational Adaptations in a Changing Society* (Capetown and Johannesburg, 1937); A. E. Campbell, ed., *Modern Trends in Education* (Wellington, 1938); and K. S. Cunningham, ed., *Education for Complete Living* (Melbourne, 1938). William Boyd has prepared the most comprehensive summary of the NEF's policies in "The Basic Faith of the NEF," *Education and Philosophy*, Yearbook of Education, George Z. F. Bereday and J. A. Lauwerys, eds. (Yonkers-on-Hudson, New York, 1957), pp. 193–208. A general history of the NEF is William Boyd and Wyatt Rawson, *The Story of the New Education* (London, 1965).

Among the materials on the European new education movement

itself are Carleton Washburne, *Progressive Tendencies in European Education,* Bulletin No. 37, Department of the Interior (Washington, D.C., 1923); Carleton Washburne, *New Schools in the Old World* (New York, 1926); Michael J. Demiashkevich, *The Activity School, New Tendencies in Educational Method in Western Europe* (New York, 1926); Ernest Young, *The New Era in Education* (London, 1923); John Adams, *Modern Developments in Educational Practice* (New York, 1922); Frederick W. Roman, *The New Education in Europe* (New York, 1923); and Adolph Meyer, *Modern European Educators* (New York, 1934). A more recent study is Kalevi S. Kajava, "The Traditional European School and Some Recent Experiments in the New Education," unpublished doctoral dissertation, Columbia University, 1951.

A number of articles about educational developments in Europe appeared in *Progressive Education,* particularly during its first decade. Among the most interesting of these are Gertrude Hartman, "The Significance of the New Education," 1 (October–December, 1924), p. 123; Stanwood Cobb, "History of the New School Movement," 1 (October–December, 1924), pp. 124–128; and Augustus O. Thomas, "The World Movement in Education: Conception, Aims and Progress," 2 (April–June, 1925), pp. 85–87.

The adoption of the new education in the Soviet Union in the late 1920s was of great interest to a number of Americans. George Counts commented on it extensively: *A Ford Crosses Soviet Russia* (Boston, 1930); "Education in Soviet Russia," *Soviet Russia in the Second Decade,* Report of the American Trade Union Delegation to the Soviet Union (New York, 1928), pp. 268–303; "Education and the Five-Year Plan of Soviet Russia," *Education and Economics,* Yearbook of the National Society for the Study of Educational Sociology (New York, 1931), pp. 39–46; "The Educational Program of Soviet Russia," NEA *Addresses and Proceedings* (Minneapolis, 1928); and *The Soviet Challenge to America* (New York, 1931). John Dewey's clearest statement on Soviet education is "Impressions of Soviet Russia: New Schools for a New Era," *New Republic* (December 12, 1928), pp. 91–94. The best Soviet statement in English is A. P. Pinkevitch, *New Education in the Soviet Republic,* Nucia Perlmutter, trans. (New York, 1929).

American Social History

More excellent works are found in American social history than in all the other fields combined. Among the standard books for the twentieth century are Henry Steele Commager, *The American Mind* (New Haven, 1950); Nathan Glazer, *The Social Basis of American Communism* (New York, 1961); Oscar Handlin, *The Uprooted* (Boston, 1951); Richard Hofstadter, *The Age of Reform* (New York, 1955) and *Anti-Intellectualism in American Life* (New York, 1963); Robert Iversen, *The Communists and the Schools* (New York, 1959); Christopher Lasch, *The New Radicalism in America, 1889–1963* (New York, 1965); William Leuchtenburg, *The Perils of Prosperity* (Chicago, 1958); Henry F. May, *The End of American Innocence* (New York, 1959); Ralph Barton Perry, *The Thought and Character of William James* (2 vols., Boston, 1935); *Recent Social Trends*, Report of the President's Research Committee on Social Trends (New York, 1934). See particularly Charles H. Judd's chapter on "Education," pp. 325–381; Arthur M. Schlesinger, Jr., *The Crisis of the Old Order* (New York, 1956), and Rush Welter, *Popular Education and Democratic Thought in America* (New York, 1962).

Among the informal books on this period are Frederick Lewis Allen, *Only Yesterday* (New York, 1931) and *The Big Change* (New York, 1952); Malcolm Cowley, *Exile's Return* (New York, 1934); Leo Gurko, *The Angry Decade* (New York, 1947); and Frederick J. Hoffman, *The Twenties* (New York, 1955).

Any discussion of an organization such as the PEA requires some consideration of its role in the larger social scene. Aside from its historical role, its social role is an interesting one. Particularly in this study, the Association's role in the larger progressive education movement has been important. Although much of the literature on the sociology of social movements is interesting, it includes conflicting viewpoints. By Heberle's definition, the PEA, by its very organization, helped create a social movement. See Rudolph Heberle, *Social Movements: An Introduction to Political Sociology* (New York, 1957), especially pp. 5–12. See also Thomas H. Greer, *American Social Reform Movements* (New York, 1949); Neil J. Smelser, *Theory of Collective Behavior* (New York, 1963); and Jerome Davis, *Contemporary Social Movements* (New York, 1930). Although much older than the others, the Davis study with its schematic presentation of the development of a social movement is of the greatest value for this study.

Some of the particularly interesting recent articles dealing with this era are Lewis Feuer, "Travelers to the Soviet Union, 1917–1932," *American Quarterly* 14 (Summer, Part I, 1962), pp. 119–149; Richard Hofstadter, "The Child and the World," *Daedalus* 91 (Summer, 1962), pp. 501–526; Alfred Kazin, "The Bitter Thirties," *Atlantic* 197 (May,

1962), pp. 82–99; Arthur S. Link, "What Happened to the Progressive Movement in the 1920's," *American Historical Review* 64 (July, 1959), pp. 833–851; Henry F. May, "The Rebellion of the Intellectuals," *American Quarterly* 8 (Summer, 1956), pp. 114–126; Arthur Mann, "British Social Thought and American Reformers of the Progressive Era," *Mississippi Valley Historical Review* 40 (June, 1956), pp. 672–692; C. Vann Woodward, "The Populist Heritage and the Intellectual," *American Scholar* 39 (Winter, 1959–1960), pp. 55–72.

Index

Adams, James Truslow, 73, 112n
Adams, John, 36n, 184
Addams, Jane, 8, 12, 13, 153
Adler, Mortimer, 113n
Adolescents, Committee on, 91
Adult Education, Committee on, 92, 170
Agricultural Adjustment Act, 94
Aikin, Wilford M., 49, 49n, 67n, 76, 89, 90, 100, 110, 124, 133n, 135n, 139, 141, 169, 177
Albers, Edna, 138n, 169
Alberty, Harold, 103, 120
Alcoholic Consumption, Committee on, 170
All Youth Commission of the PEA, 168
Allen, Frederick Lewis, 58, 59, 185
Alexander, Thomas, 68
Alma College, 95n
Alschuler, Rose, 67n, 170
American Association of University Professors, 94, 95
American Association of University Women, 43, 94
American Civil Liberties Union, 95
American Committee on International Education, 92, 98, 170
American Council on Education, 92, 94, 175
American Education Fellowship, 21, 111
American Federation of Teachers, 79, 94, 115, 123
American Legion, 94
Amidon, Beulah, 68n, 176
Anderson, Archibald W., 117n, 118n, 119, 120n, 122n, 126, 143, 167, 173
Anderson, Florence, 100n, 173
Angell, James R., 95n
Antioch College, 20, 47
Arts in Education, Committee on, 170
Association for Supervision and Curriculum Development, 105, 142n, 163
August, Frank, 95n
Axtelle, George, 95n, 143n
Ayres, Gertrude Stevens (Mrs. Milan V.), 18, 20, 23n, 24–26, 33, 39, 58

Bachman, Frank P., 179
Bagley, William C., 101
Baker, Derwood, 170

Baker, Emily V., 122n
Baker, Frank E., 94, 104n, 132n, 166
Baldwin, Sara Emily, 171
Ball, Lester, 117, 120–122
Bamberger, Florence E., 80n
Barnard, Henry, 11n
Barnes, Fred, 116n
Barr, Stringfellow, 113n
Barzun, Jacques, 153n
Beale, Howard K., 86, 96, 112n
Beatty, Willard W., 68, 72, 90, 92, 129, 166, 169, 170, 171, 173, 178
Beaver Country Day School, 9n, 27, 37, 45n, 84
Beck, Robert H., 45n, 47n, 173, 183
Bell, Alexander Graham, 18
Bell, Bernard Iddings, 181
Benezet, Louis T., 47n, 183
Benjamin, Harold, 118n
Benne, Kenneth, 104n, 119, 122n, 124, 125n, 126, 167
Bennett, Charles A., 2n, 182
Bennington College, 47
Benson, O. N., 3n
Bereday, George Z. F., 183
Bereton, C. D. L., 183
Berger, Morris I., 3n, 174
Berkson, Isaac B., 126
Bestor, Arthur, 148, 181
Bigelow, Karl W., 92n
Blos, Peter, 169
Bobbitt, John Franklin, 180
Bode, Boyd H., 60n, 61, 70, 74n, 77, 86, 87, 90, 94, 104, 114, 115, 125, 126, 159, 165, 175, 177, 180
Bok, Edward, 152
Borgeson, Fritz, 93, 169
Borrowman, Merle, 182
Bourne, Randolph, 3n, 4, 12, 154, 179
Bovard, Berdine J., 23n, 173
Bowers, Chester A., 132n, 173
Bowman, John F., 117n
Boyd, William, 183
Boykin, J. C., 178
Brameld, Theodore, 22n, 105n, 110, 111, 117–125, 127, 131, 142n, 159, 173
Brickman, William W., 134, 177
Briggs, Thomas H., 181

Brim, Orville G., 77n, 78n, 103
Brooklyn College, 104, 109
Broome, Edwin C., 78n
Browder, Earl, 72, 74
Brown v. Board of Education, 154
Brubacher, John S., 177
Bruce, William F., 125n
Bruner, Jerome, 149
Brunner, Edmund DeS., 70, 93, 170
Buchanan, Scott, 113n
Bunker, Frank F., 33, 34
Burk, Frederick, 109
Burnham, John Chenoweth, 183
Burroughs, John, 89
Butts, R. Freeman, 182

Caldwell, Otis, 17, 54, 89n
Calkins, Fred, 114n
A Call to the Teachers of the Nation, 69
Callahan, Raymond E., 4n, 182
Campbell, A. E., 183
Camping, Committee on, 170
Cane, Florence, 88
Carnegie Corporation, 55, 70, 100, 140, 141
    Foundation for the Advancement of
        Teaching, 89
Carney, Mabel, 3n, 179
Carpenter, Frank D., 180
Carson College for Orphan Girls, 48n
Carswell, Marion, 132, 170
Cary, Miles, 143n
Carter, Letitia Hall, 173
Chamberlin, Dean, 133n, 169
Chevy Chase Country Day School, 9n, 18, 31, 45n
"Child-centeredness," 15, 47, 59, 107, 122, 145, 160
    child-centered school, 46, 60, 76
The Child-Centered School, 70
Child Development and Elementary
    Curriculum, Committee on, 170
Child Development Institute, 93
Child study, 148
Child Study Association, 23, 141
Childs, John L., 67n, 70, 75, 84, 110, 112n, 182
City and Country School, 9n, 145n
Civilian Conservation Corps, 95n, 151
Clapp, Elsie Ripley, 62, 66, 67n, 86, 93, 154, 159,166, 170
Clark, Harold T., 67n
Classon, R. H., 122n
Cobb, Ernest, 181
Cobb, Stanwood, 17–25, 30, 31, 32n, 38–41, 55–58, 61, 85, 97, 109, 142, 156n, 160, 166, 173, 174, 180, 184
Coe, George A., 73
Coffin, Rebecca J., 49n
Cohen, Sol, 182

College–school relations, *see* Relation
    of School and College, Commission on
Collings, Ellsworth, 180
Commager, Henry Steele, 185
Commission (or Committee) on . . .,
    see topic (for example: for Commis-
    sion on Human Relations, *see* Human
    Relations, Commission on)
Commonwealth College, 95n
Commonwealth Fund, 55
Community–school relations, Commit-
    tee on, 93, 170
Conant, James B., 157, 181
Conrad, Lawrence Henry, 91n, 169
Cook, Catherine M., 178
Cooke, Flora J., 48, 49n, 69, 78n, 89n
Cooke, Mr. and Mrs. George Paul, 24n
Coonley, Queene Ferry (Mrs. Avery),
    26, 39, 52, 53, 58, 67n, 85, 86
Coordination, Committee for, 168
Counts, George S., 14, 37n, 50, 57n,
    62–67, 67n, 68–70, 72, 74, 81, 82, 84,
    88, 105, 109, 112n, 115, 128–130,
    146, 159, 160, 171, 172, 180, 184
Cousinet, Roger, 37
Cowley, Malcolm, 58, 59, 185
Cremin, Lawrence A., 4n, 5n, 45n, 47n,
    57n, 118n, 148, 182
Crockett, Ann L., 102, 103, 176
Cultural Relations, Committee on, 92,
    170
Cunningham, K. S., 183
Curti, Merle, 7n, 68, 86, 112n, 182

Dalton Plan, 37, 66n
*Dare the School Build a New Social
    Order?* 64, 65
Darsie, Marvin L., 177
Darwin, Charles, 6
Darwinism, 5, 6
Davis, Allen Freeman, 174
Davis, Jerome, 95n, 158n, 185
DeBoer, John J., 22n, 104n, 115–117,
    118n, 119, 122n, 123–125, 127, 131,
    142n, 146, 147, 156, 159, 160, 167,
    173
DeCroly, Ovide, 36n, 37
DeLima, Agnes, 45n, 46n, 144, 175,
    180, 182
Demiaskevich, Michael J., 36n, 184
Dennis, Lawrence, 72
Dewey, Evelyn, 2n, 3n, 92n, 154, 161,
    179
Dewey, Jane, 6n
Dewey, John, 2n, 3n, 5, 6, 8, 12–16,
    23n, 27, 32, 35, 36, 37n, 41, 50, 51,
    59, 60n, 61, 65, 67n, 68, 70, 77–79,
    82n, 104, 107, 108, 112n, 114, 117n,
    126, 146, 156n, 159, 161, 179, 180,
    184
    disciples, 16

Diederich, Paul B., 135n, 177
Dix, Lester, 146, 167, 181
Donohue, Ellen, 95n
Dorey, J. Milnor, 41, 56, 166
DuBois, Rachel Davis, 93
DuBois, W. E. B., 117, 118
Dubnick, Lester, 123n, 177
Dutton, Wilbur Harvey, 7n, 174
Dworkin, Martin, S., 179

Eaton, Charles L. S., 68
Economic and Social Problems, Committee on, 64, 68
Education of Teachers for Progressive Schools, Committee on, 92, 170
Educational Freedom, Commission on, 76, 94, 168
The Educational Frontier, 70
Educational Reconstruction, Commission on, 139
Educational Records Bureau, 80
Education's Role in Reconstruction, Commission on, 123n, 169
Eight-Year Study, *see* Relation of School and College, Commission on
Elementary Curriculum, Committee on Child Development and, 170
Elementary Education, Committee on, 170
Eliot, Charles William, 23, 24, 24n, 41, 150, 179
Ensor, Beatrice, 42–44, 97, 98, 160
Erickson, Helen, 49n
Erskine, John, 113n
Erwin, Rachel, 67n
Ethical Culture Schools, 90
Evaluated Results of Progressive Education, Committee on, 170
Everett, Marcia A., 93, 171
Experimental Schools, Committee on, 93, 170

Fairhope School, 17
Federal Government in Education, Committee on the Role of, 170
Federal Support and Education, Committee on, 92, 170
Feuer, Lewis, 62n, 185
Filler, Louis M., 183
Field Services, Committee on Workshops and, 171
Fine, Benjamin, 142n
Flexner, Abraham, 3n, 8, 179
Fosdick, Raymond B., 55n, 58n, 182
Foster, Frances M., 86, 97, 166
Fowler, Burton P., 48, 49, 55, 56, 57n, 67n, 69, 76, 78n, 87, 89n, 166, 178
Frank, Lawrence, 139n, 170
Frank, Waldo, 59
Freeman, Frank, 180

French, John R. P., 75, 93, 170
Freud, Sigmund, 7
Freudian, 45
Friedrich, Carl Joachim, 176
Friends Select School, 48n
Froelicher, Francis M., 43, 52–54, 56, 60n, 61, 175
Froelicher, Hans, 9n, 173
Frontiers of Democracy, 110, 128, 130–132, 172; *see also The Social Frontier*

Gambs, John S., 68
Gans, Roma, 95n, 110, 122n, 125, 132
Gary, Indiana, Schools, 3, 4, 10, 153, 154, 161, 179
Gary Plan, 66n
Gaudig, Hugo, 36n
Gauss, Christian, 152n, 176
General Education Board, 54, 55, 70, 76, 90–92, 99, 100, 110, 140, 141
George, Anne, 17, 20
Germantown Friends School, 48n
Gibson, D., 176
Giles, H. H., 133n, 169
Glazer, Nathan, 185
Goodlad, John, 143
Gould, Arthur, 168
Greene, Theodore M., 181
Greer, Ellen W., 67n
Greer, Thomas H., 185
Grossman, Mordecai, 129, 130
Gruenberg, Sidonie Matsner, 173
Gurko, Leo, 62n, 185

Hall, Frederick B., 10
Hall, G. Stanley, 5, 7, 8, 21n, 32, 109
Hall, Mary Ross, 83n, 181
Hand, Harold, 95n
Handlin, Oscar, 185
Hanna, Paul R., 103, 169, 171
Harper, Charles A., 182
Harris, William T., 11n
Harrison, Margaret, 171
Hart, Joseph K., 60n, 61, 175
Hartman, Gertrude, 39n, 42, 43, 67n, 79, 86, 172, 180, 184
Hartmann, George, 129, 130
Harvey, Mrs. Porter, 92, 154
Haverford School, 48n
Health and Safety Education, Committee on, 170
Heaton, Kenneth, 171
Heberle, Rudolph, 185
Hegel, G. W. F., 6
Henderson, C. Hanford, 18n, 27
Hill, Patty Smith, 10, 34, 35, 49
Hines, Vynce, 143
History of Progressive Education, Committee on the, 170
Hocking, Richard, 9n, 173

Hocking, William Ernest, 9
Hoffman, Frederick J., 185
Hofstadter, Richard, 148, 151n, 157, 159, 185
Holmes, Henry W., 73
Home and School Relations, Committee on, 93, 170
Hook, Sidney, 70, 87
Horne, Herman H., 156n
Howe, F. J., 3n
Howe, James S., 25n, 26
Howe, Louis, 87
Hughes, Langston, 117, 118
Hullfish, H. Gordon, 70, 95, 103, 104n, 114n, 120, 122, 125–127, 142, 143n, 144n, 167, 168
Hulsizer, Alan, 67n, 92, 171
Human Relations, Commission on, 76, 90, 91, 93, 128, 138–140, 168
Hunt, Maurice, 143n
Hutchins, Robert, 113n
Hymes, James L. Jr., 130, 166

Illinois, University of, 104, 115, 126, 155
Indian Education, Commission on, 169
Indiana University, 104
Intercultural Education, Commission on, 93, 169
International Cooperation, Committee on, 171
International Relations, Committee on, 171
Irwin, Elisabeth A., 9, 44, 45, 162
Iversen, Robert W., 74n, 115n, 185

James, William, 5, 6, 179
Jefferson, Thomas, 81
Jewett, Robert, 143n, 173
Jewett, Victor, 95n
John Burroughs School, 89
John Dewey Society, 127–130, 143, 168
Johnson, Harriet, 44
Johnson, Helmer G., 135n, 177
Johnson, Marietta, 17–19, 27, 30, 33, 34, 39n, 42, 174
Joncich, Geraldine M., 7n, 174, 177
Jones, Howard E. A., 49n
Judd, Charles H., 63, 185

Kajava, Kalevi S., 36n, 184
Kallen, Horace M., 73
Kandel, Isaac L., 176, 182
Kazin, Alfred, 62n, 185
Keesler, Arthur, 132
Kefauver, Grayson, 123n, 139, 140, 169, 170
Kennedy, John F., 157
Keppel, Anna Marie, 3n, 174
Keppel, Francis, 109
Kerschensteiner, Georg, 36n 148, 159, 168, 173, 180
Kettering, Charles F., 9n

Kilpatrick, William Heard, 5n, 15, 32, 36, 67, 70, 74, 75n, 77, 78n, 84, 87, 88, 105, 110, 112n, 126, 129, 146, 148, 159, 168, 173, 180
King, Robert, 178
Kirkpatrick, Edwin A., 179
Knight, Edgar W., 182
Kotinsky, Ruth, 135, 136n, 166, 169
Keliher, Alice V., 62, 76, 77, 90–92, 103n, 128, 138, 139, 141, 169

Langdon, Grace, 114n
Langer, Walter C., 138n, 169
Langford, Howard, 73n, 74n, 181
Lasch, Christopher, 185
Laski, Harold, 78
Lauwerys, J. A., 183
Learned, William, 100
Leigh, Robert, 88, 112n, 155
Lenrow, Elbert, 170
Leuchtenburg, William, 61, 185
Lewenstein, Morris, 143
Libbey, May, 20
Life adjustment education, 122, 178
Lilienthal, David, 117
Lincoln School, 9n, 10, 17, 37, 45n, 46, 89, 149
Lindeman, Eduard C., 70, 77n, 117n, 118n
Link, Arthur S., 58n, 186
Lippmann, Walter, 31, 113n, 114n, 175
Liss, Edward, 171
Little Red School House, 45
Livingstone, Richard, 152n, 176
Lynd, Albert, 176
Locke, Alain, 126, 169
Long, Forrest, 115n
Lowell, A. Lawrence, 150

Macomber, F. G., 118n, 119n
McCarthy, Joseph, 160
McChesney, John, 95n
McCulloch, Frank W., 117n
McCutchen, S. P., 33n
McGlade, Joseph, 182
MacLennan, Hugh, 150
Malherbe, E. G., 183
Mann, Arthur, 186
Marcus, Lloyd C., 8n, 45n, 174
Marland, Sidney P. Jr., 9n, 10n, 182
Marshall Field Foundation, 140
Massachusetts State Loyalty Oath, 96
Matthiessen, F. O., 153n, 176
May, Henry F., 185, 186
May, Mark, 139n
Mayer, Martin, 109, 147, 181
Mead, A. R., 114n
Mearns, Hughes, 66, 78n, 180
Meek, Lois Hayden, 55, 57n, 63, 67n, 68, 70, 89, 93, 170
Meiklejohn, Alexander, 112n, 114n

Melby, Ernest, 118, 119n
Mental Hygiene in Education, Committee on, 171
Metcalf, Lawrence E., 142n, 143n, 167
Meyer, Adolph, 36n, 184
Meyer, Agnes E., 152n, 176
Meyers, Alonzo, 95n
Miller, Clyde R., 67n
Miller, Persis K., 34, 162
Mirick, George, 12n, 180
Misner, Paul J., 121n
Mitchell, Lucy Sprague, 9n, 44, 45n, 59, 181
Mitchell, Morris R., 67n
Mitchell, Wesley Clair, 59
Mitzel, Harold, 123n, 177
Monroe, Paul, 179
Montague, William Pepperell, 7n
Montessori, Maria, 18
Montgomery Country Day School, 48n
Moraine Park School, 9n, 20, 31, 34, 37, 45n
Morgan, Arthur E., 20, 24, 56, 166
Morison, Samuel Eliot, 150, 182
Morse, Lucia Burton, 43
Mort, Paul R., 92, 170
Museum–School Relations, Committee on, 171

Nahem, Joseph, 177
National Commission on Educational Reconstruction, 170
National Congress of Parents and Teachers, 95
National Council for Accreditation of Teacher Education, 105, 163
National Council on Religion in Higher Education, 95
National Education Association, 11, 77, 78, 89, 94, 141, 178
National Educational Planning, Commission on, 139, 170
National Society for the Study of Education, 77, 141, 178
National Youth Administration, 96, 151
Naumburg, Margaret, 15n, 44, 45, 59, 60n, 61, 62, 80, 176, 181
Nearing, Scott, 2n, 12, 152, 179
NEF, see New Education Fellowship
Neill, A. S., 36n
New Education Fellowship, 35–38, 42, 57n, 97, 98, 111, 132n, 140, 160, 172, 183
conferences, 43
"New psychology," 5, 6, 8
New York Society for the Experimental Study of Education, 44, 45
Newcomb, Theodore, 63
Newlon, Jesse H., 67n, 68, 70, 84
Noble-White, Edna, 171
Northwestern University, 104

NSSE, see National Society for the Study of Education
Nudd, Howard W., 88

Oak Lane Country Day School, 9n, 31, 45n, 48n
Oberholtzer, Kenneth E., 121n
Office of the Coordinator of Inter-American Affairs, 140
Ohio State University, 89, 92, 103, 104, 126, 155
Olsen, Edward G., 121n
Oppenheim, James, 59
Oppenheim, Nathan, 27
Organic School, see Fairhope School
Osborne, Ernest, 170, 171
O'Shea, Michael V., 25
Overstreet, Harry, 70, 87

Pankburn, Jesse, 182
Park School, 17, 27, 45n, 48n, 84
Parker, Beryl, 95n
Parker, Francis W., 11n, 21n, 79, 89, 108, 109
Parkhurst, Helen, 37
Parsons, Mrs. A. J., 19, 20, 23–25
Parsons, Alice Beal, 176
Patri, Angelo, 163
PEA, see Progressive Education Association
Perry, Arthur C., 76
Perry, Ralph Barton, 5n, 185
Pestalozzi, Johann, 27, 79
Phebe Anne Thorne School, 48n
Phi Delta Kappa, 95
Phillips, Mark, 174
Philosophy, Committee on, 104–108, 168, 172
Physical Educational, Commission on, 169
Pinkevitch, A. P., 36, 37n, 184
Poley, Irvin C., 77n
Pond, Frederick L., 117n
Post-War Child Care, Committee on, 171
Post-War Reconstruction, Commission on, 123n, 169
Pounds, Ralph, 143n
Pratt, Caroline, 9, 44, 45n, 60n, 61, 79, 88, 159, 181
Prescott, Daniel, 103n
Presler, Francis, 171
"Progressive," as label, 12, 13
Progressive education
  before and after World War I, 8–12
  common elements of, in schools, 50
  in U.S.S.R., 36, 63, 64, 74
Progressive Education, 39–41, 47, 65, 66, 72, 76, 77, 83–86, 94, 96, 112, 113, 116, 118, 128, 129, 131, 142, 143, 172

Progressive Education Association (PEA)
  additional principles of (1929), 51
  aims (1920), 28
  commissions and committees, 64, 68, 76, 89–94, 98, 100, 104–108, 110, 115, 123n, 128, 133–136, 138–140, 147, 152, 168–171
  conferences (1920's), 47, 48, 87, 88
  control of, 56–58, 104, 105, 125, 147
  doctrine (1920's), 46, 47
  financial status, 52–55, 99, 100, 139
  name change, 21, 111, 112, 114
  NEF, relations with, 36, 43, 97
  science of education, 49, 50
  Seven Principles, 28, 29, 62, 81, 103
Progressive Education in Rural Schools, Committee on, 92, 171
Public Education Association, 88, 143n
Pusey, Nathan M., 13n

Rackham Foundation, 140
Radio in Education, Committee on, 171
Raths, Louis, 103n
Raup, R. Bruce, 70, 77n
Rawson, W. T. R., 183
Reconstruction, commissions on, 123n, 139, 169
Redefer, Frederick L., 21n, 22n, 56, 57n, 66, 67n, 68, 72n, 73n, 87, 94, 95n, 97n, 99, 100, 102, 108–110, 122n, 133n, 134, 136n, 143n, 166, 170, 171, 173, 174, 177
Regionalism and Education, Committee on, 171
Relation of School and College, Commission on, 76, 89, 100, 110, 128, 133–135, 138, 139, 147, 152, 169
  Eight-Year Study, 90, 110, 128, 133–135, 136n, 150
Research in Secondary Education, Committee on Utilization of, 171
Resources and Education, Commission on, 169
Rice, Joseph Mayer, 12
Rockefeller Foundation, 55
Rogers, Virgil, 104n, 109, 131, 132, 170
Role of the Federal Government in Education, Committee on, 170
Roman, Frederick W., 35n, 184
Roosevelt, Eleanor, 87
Roosevelt, Franklin D., 82, 94
Rosecrance, F. S., 120n
Rosenblatt, Louise, 91n, 138, 139, 169
Rotzel, Grace, 122n
Rudolph, Frederick, 182
Rudy, Willis, 182
Rugg, Harold, 42, 43, 45n, 46n, 55, 56, 57n, 59, 65, 67n, 69, 70, 82, 84, 89, 92, 97, 98, 105, 108, 110, 117n, 121, 122n, 126, 127, 130–132, 159, 170, 171, 178, 180–182

Rural Schools, Committee on Progressive Education in, 92, 171
Ryan, W. Carson, Jr., 40, 43, 62, 63, 92, 98, 117n, 120n, 129, 135, 166, 169, 170

Sandifer, Sr. Mary Ruth, 182
Sarah Lawrence College, 46
Sassman, Erwin, 93, 171
Schilpp, P. A., 5n, 6n, 7n
Schlesinger, Arthur M., Jr., 185
School and Community Relations, Committee on, 93
Schultz, Gladys Denny, 176
Schultz, J. S., 122n
Schweppe, Emma, 92, 170
Sears, Paul B., 103n
Secondary School Curriculum, Commission on the, 76, 90, 91, 115, 128, 135, 136, 138, 139, 169
Secondary Education, Committee on Utilization of Research in, 171
Seeds, Corinne, 122n
Seeds, Nellie, 67, 159
Shady Hill School, 9, 45n, 48n, 138
Shane, Harold G., 104, 111n, 116n, 117, 120–122, 141n, 142, 159, 173
Shigley-Kent School, 95n
Shoemaker, F. I., 143n
Shott, Walter, 122n
Shumaker, Ann, 45n, 46n, 56n, 65, 67n, 70, 72n, 86, 99, 127, 166 172, 180
Sipple, E. M., 77
Sizer, Theodore, 13n
Skilbeck, Malcolm, 66n, 174
Slutz, Frank D., 33, 34, 40
Slesinger, Zalmen, 73n, 74n, 181
Slichter, Gertrude Almy, 174
Small, Albion, 63
Smelser, Neil J., 185
Smith, B. Othanel, 110, 121n, 167
Smith, Eugene Randolph, 17, 19, 20, 26, 27, 30, 49, 56, 84, 133n, 134, 166, 169, 173, 175, 180
Smith, Frank Webster, 180
Smith, Herbert W., 91
Smith, Mortimer, 181
Smith, T. V., 119
Smith, Timothy, 183
Smith, Winifred, 67
Snyder, Morton, 40, 41, 56, 166
Social and Economic Problems, Committee on, 171
The Social Frontier, 72, 79, 119, 128–130, 133, 141n, 172; *see also Frontiers of Democracy*
Social Problems, Committee on Economic and, 64, 68
Society for Experimental Education, 80
Sorokin, Pitirim A., 113n, 114n
Southern High School, 48n
Spaulding, F. T., 152n, 176

Speer, Robert K., 118n, 119n
Spock, Benjamin, 91n
Stern, Bernhard J., 91n, 138n, 169
Stevenson, Adlai E., 157
Stone, Virginia E., 49n
Streitz, Ruth, 103, 114n, 171
Summerhill, 36n
Summer Institutes, Committee on, 92
Sunnyside Nursery School, 48n

Taylor, Harold, 118n
Taylor, Katharine Whiteside, 90, 91n, 138, 169
Taylor, Toni, 131, 132, 166
Teacher Education, Committee on, 171
Teacher Placement, Committee on, 171
Teachers College, Columbia University, 11, 33, 104
Tenenbaum, Samuel, 5n, 14n, 15n
Tennessee Valley Authority, 20
Terman, Lewis W., 31, 147, 175
Thayer, Vivian T., 67n, 69, 70, 76, 81, 90, 92, 114, 120, 128, 135–139, 141, 169, 170
Thirty Schools Project, 133; *see also* Relation of School and College, Commission on
Thomas, August O., 184
Thomas, Norman, 87
Thorndike, Edward L., 5–8, 26 125, 147
Tibbetts, Vinal, 104n, 109, 110, 115n, 116, 118n, 129, 132, 153, 166
Tower Hill School, 48, 89
Trade School for Girls, 48n
Training of Teachers for Progressive Schools, Committee on the, 92
Tuchman, Sheila, 174
Tugwell, Rexford G., 68n
Tyler, Ralph, 133n, 134, 147, 169

Utilization of Research in Secondary Education, Committee on, 171

Van Doren, Mark, 113n
VanTil, William, 177
Vincent, Elizabeth, 175
Vocational education, 2, 3, 59, 148

Walden School, 9n, 45, 45n, 46, 59
Wallace, Henry, 13, 146, 156
Walters, Raymond, 177
Ware, Caroline, 162, 181
Warren, Constance, 67n
Washburne, Carleton, 9n, 10, 36n, 37, 43, 48, 69, 70, 78n, 86, 104, 108, 110, 117, 120, 122n, 125, 126, 159, 166, 180, 182, 184
Washington Montessori School, 17
Watson, Goodwin, 68, 70, 76, 77, 95, 173
Weisz, Howard R., 174
Welles, James B., 67
Wells, H. G., 27
Welter, Rush, 185
Wesley, Edgar, 82n, 182
Whitland, Nayan, 19
Wiener, Philip P., 5n
William Penn Charter School, 48n
Williams, Mrs. Laura, 20, 23–25, 67n
Winnetka plan, 66n, 109
Wirt, William, 4, 10n, 161
Witty, Paul, 103n, 170
Woelfel, Norman, 129, 130
Woodring, Paul, 181
Woodward, C. Vann, 186
Workshops and Field Services, Committee on, 171
Wunsch, W. Robert, 138n, 169

Young, Ernest, 35n, 184

Zachry, Caroline B., 91, 135–138, 170
Zachry, Greer, 137n, 173
Zechiel, A. N., 133n
Zilberfarb, Johanson I., 74
Zilliacus, Laurin, 183
Zirbes, Laura, 67n, 77n, 92, 103, 170